PRAISE FOR *ON ANIMALS*

"A close read of her new book suggests that beneath the surface variety of subjects and locales in her writing, there's an underlying unity: heedless, headlong enthusiasm. . . . She is a moth drawn to moths who are drawn to the flame. . . . Ms. Orlean has a rare knack for finding these people, and an even rarer one for starting them talking. . . . Do not underestimate her curiosity, or the sharpness of her eyes."

—Jeremy McCarter, *The Wall Street Journal*

"Spectacular . . . One is likely to imagine Susan Orlean's eyes sparkling as she composed the essays in *On Animals*. . . . Orlean strikes a perfect balance between hilarious and informative. . . . Orlean has a gift for the indelible detail. . . . Readers fond of seemingly effortless writing about animals will savor this book."

—*Minneapolis Star Tribune*

"She relies on her powers of observation, conveyed with unflappable curiosity. . . . Orlean is committed to investigating the dizzying multiplicity of roles animals serve—employee, best friend, harbinger of climate change—and the places where those functions intersect."

—Margaret Wappler, *Los Angeles Times*

"A broad meditation on how the connections we make, or fail to make, with animals mark us profoundly along our human journey . . . Orlean's tone is conversational and self-questioning."

—*USA Today* (4 out of 4 stars)

"Fabulously fun . . . Orlean is such a virtuoso of unexpected joys and delights that she can make even the story of a lost dog read like a thriller. . . . Orlean's high-octane enthusiasm never wanes. . . . Readers will find themselves completely diverted by *On Animals*' irresistible menagerie."

—*BookPage* (starred review)

"Delightful . . . Another winner featuring the author's trademark blend of meticulous research and scintillating writing."

—*Kirkus Reviews* (starred review)

"Entertaining and informative . . . Orlean's prose dazzles. . . . Animal lovers will find much to savor."

—*Publishers Weekly*

"Vibrant . . . A revelry for readers wild for animals . . . Orlean's deep pleasure in learning startling facts, her often wry tales about her personal life, her omnivorous attention to detail, and her juggler's skill with words yield vivid, provocative, amusing, and wondrous stories."

—*Booklist*

On Animals

Susan Orlean

AVID READER PRESS

New York London Toronto Sydney New Delhi

AVID READER PRESS
An Imprint of Simon & Schuster, Inc.
1230 Avenue of the Americas
New York, NY 10020

First Avid Reader Press trade paperback edition June 2022

AVID READER PRESS and colophon are trademarks of Simon & Schuster, Inc.

For information about special discounts for bulk purchases, please contact Simon & Schuster Special Sales at 1-866-506-1949 or business@simonandschuster.com.

The Simon & Schuster Speakers Bureau can bring authors to your live event. For more information or to book an event, contact the Simon & Schuster Speakers Bureau at 1-866-248-3049 or visit our website at www.simonspeakers.com.

These pieces originally appeared in slightly modified form in *The New Yorker*, *Smithsonian*, the *Atlantic*, and as an Amazon Original. For more detail, see page 239.

Interior design by Carly Loman

Manufactured in the United States of America

1   3   5   7   9   10   8   6   4   2

Library of Congress Cataloging-in-Publication Data has been applied for.

ISBN 978-1-9821-8153-6
ISBN 978-1-9821-8154-3 (pbk)
ISBN 978-1-9821-8155-0 (ebook)

*For John and Austin,
and for Ivy and Buck and Leo and Cooper and Molly and
Duffy and Laura and Beauty and Helen and Tweed
and Mabel and Sparky and . . .*

Animals first entered the imagination as messengers and promises.
　　　　　　　—John Berger, *Why Look at Animals?*

CONTENTS

Animalish

E ven before the cats, before the dogs, before the chickens, before the
turkeys, before the ducks and the guinea fowl and the betta fish and
the Black Angus cattle, I was always a little animalish. I don't just mean
as a child, since all children love animals and come by being animalish
quite naturally. I don't just mean as a young girl—that golden moment
when I, like millions of young girls throughout human history, fell into
an adolescent swoon over horses and, to a lesser degree, puppies. I mean
that somehow or other, in whatever kind of life I happened to be leading,
animals have always been my style. They have been a part of my life even
when I didn't have any animals, and when I did have them, they always
seemed to elbow their way onto center stage.

Has it been a simple matter of mathematics? That is, have there been
more creatures in my orbit than in other people's? Or do I merely notice
them more and draw them a little closer than someone else might? There
has certainly been an element of serendipity. I seem to have a higher-

than-average tendency to find animals in my path. In 1986, when I was relocating to Manhattan, I resigned myself to what I assumed would be a life with very little animal adjacency except for the occasional dog or two. The day I moved into my new apartment, I unpacked a few boxes and then decided to go outside for some air. As I stepped onto the sidewalk, I collided with a man who was walking a pet rabbit on a silver leash. I spun to a stop, flabbergasted. The man didn't register my surprise; he was too busy trying to manage the rabbit, which was huge, coffee-colored, and ornery. Each time the man took a step, the rabbit braced against the leash, stretching it taut, and only then, with a cold look in its eye, would it give a flabby, half-hearted hop.

"Please, Rover, *please*," the rabbit's owner called out, in an aching, exasperated voice. "Now, that's a good Rover. Come on, boy! Hop!"

>-<

I grew up wanting animals desperately. When I was young—four or five, or thereabouts—we had a cat, but she lived outside and came by the house only to collect her meals, a visit so brisk and purposeful that it made her seem less like our pet and more like a representative of some off-site cat charity who was dropping by to pick up contributions. Wanting a dog started early for me, but my mother was afraid of dogs, and she threatened to stand on a chair squealing and flapping her skirt if we ever brought one home. Consequently, we remained dogless, and I suffered. At regular intervals, I offered—or, more precisely, begged—to walk the neighbors' dogs, but we lived in the suburbs, and most dogs had roomy yards and weren't in need of walking. On Sundays, I read the pet section in the classifieds as if it were a love letter, circling ads and showing them to my parents. My father would say, "Ask your mother." My mother would shudder and say, "What would I do with a dog?"

At last, though, my brother and sister and I wore her down. We devised a marketing strategy. We had come across an ad for Black & White Scotch that featured a pair of adorable dogs—an ink-black Scotty, handsome and sharp-looking, and a West Highland white terrier with a merry face and the cleanest, brightest fur in the world. Since my mother's dread of dogs included fear that a dog would spread a haze of permanent dirtiness throughout our house, we thought the dazzle of the Westie's whiteness might do the trick. And it did. We ended up with a Westie puppy in a matter of days.

➤◄

I loved our Westie, but to be honest, I had set my heart on a German shepherd, since I'd imprinted early on *The Adventures of Rin Tin Tin*, and like most of the world I wanted a dog just like the star of the show. But I was thrilled to have a dog of any sort. Around that same time, I also got a mouse as a gift from a classmate, a boy with a permanently runny nose and pockets overflowing with twigs and rocks and leaves. How I convinced my mother to allow me to keep the gift mouse, I'll never know. The little creature was a beautiful butterscotch color, with soft white feet and ruby-red eyes. I named her Sparky and pretended that she was some kind of championship show mouse, and I made a bunch of fake ribbons and trophies for her and I told people she had won them at mouse shows.

You might think that with my champion mouse and my clean white Westie, I would have been satisfied, but I still felt I had animal work to do; I didn't have a pony yet, for instance. I began campaigning for one, unsuccessfully. In the meantime, one afternoon, I took Sparky over to my classmate's house so she could have a playdate with his mouse. The next thing I knew, Sparky built a nest in her cage and populated it with five baby mice, which were small enough to waltz right out of the cage without even brushing the bars. When my mother saw one of Sparky's babies skittering across the kitchen floor and disappearing under the dishwasher, she really did jump on a chair squealing and flapping her skirt. I had crossed the line. There would be no more animals added to my collection while I was still living at home.

As soon as I got to college, I decided I wanted a boyfriend and a dog.

I knew having a dog while in college was crazy. I had a wild schedule and a rented apartment, and no idea of where I would be after I graduated—life conditions that don't bode well for pet ownership. But now that I was away from home and away from our family dog, I missed having a pet. Plus, it seemed like all of my friends in Ann Arbor had dogs. As for the kind of dog I wanted, my tastes had changed. Rather than a German shepherd, I wanted an Irish setter. I didn't know any Irish setters personally, but I used to moon over another liquor ad—I think it was for Irish whiskey—featuring a man and woman in Kelly-green trench coats, walking a pair of leggy red-haired dogs. I was a not-so-leggy red-haired person, and the dogs, with their elegant, anxious faces and hair that matched mine, seemed like the perfect companions for me.

I started perusing the classifieds again. Sometimes there were Irish setter puppies for sale, but they cost too much for me to even consider. Then, one September day, I put on a pair of jeans I hadn't worn since I'd come back from Europe, where I'd gone on a summer school program. The pocket felt stiff. I reached in and pulled out a wad of paper and unfolded it. The wad was $300 worth of traveler's checks that I'd forgotten I had. By all rights I should have spent the money on books and rent and tuition, but finding it like that, by accident, made it feel like a windfall—as if an unseen and benevolent force had just tossed three hundred gold coins into my upturned palm. I took it as a sign and called one of the Irish setter breeders in the newspaper and bought a four-month-old puppy that I named Molly.

➤◄

My parents were dismayed. "What are you going to do with a dog?" my mother wailed. I told her I knew the responsibilities of owning a dog, and then pointed out that she should at least appreciate the fact that I had gotten a dog rather than a pig. I wasn't kidding. Someone had recently shown up on campus with a tiny Vietnamese potbellied pig, and I had seen it running around, wearing the same kind of bandanna all the campus dogs wore around their necks. The day I brought Molly home, I had noticed this little pig rooting around the bushes near the undergraduate library, its yellow bandanna splattered with mud. For a fleeting moment, I thought to myself, *Wow, wouldn't it be kind of cool to have a pig? No*, I thought in the next moment, *don't even think about it*. Unfortunately, positioning my dog acquisition as mature compared to the pig option did not reassure my mother. After a long silence she just sighed and said something along the lines of "Well, for heaven's sake, Susie. You and your *animals*."

>—<

Now and again, I have been asked—and have asked myself—the obvious question: Why animals? There's no simple answer. I'm curious about animals. They amuse me. They keep me company. They're nice to look at. Some of them provide me with breakfast food. I think I have the same response to animals that I would if Martians landed on Earth: I would like to get to know them and befriend them, all the while knowing we were not quite of the same ilk. They seem to have something in common with us, and yet they're alien, unknowable, familiar but mysterious.

Molly was twelve when I moved to Manhattan. I worried that the transition would be hard for her, since she had never lived in an apartment or ridden an elevator. I also worried that it would be hard to find an apartment that allowed dogs. Finding dog-friendly rentals had been the bane of my years since I had left Ann Arbor, where, like all university towns, centuries of slovenly, apartment-trashing students made dogs seem like responsible renters, and no landlord seemed to mind them very much. After graduating, I had moved out west, where the deer and the antelope play, and I'd expected dogs to be as ubiquitous and welcome as they had been in Ann Arbor. To my surprise, most landlords turned me away. I was also looking for work as a paralegal, which was the only thing I thought my BA in English qualified me to do, and it was around that time that I learned the hard fact that most employers, especially law firms, did not encourage workers to bring their pets to the office. I was getting an education at last; I was animalish, but the rest of the world might not be.

I assumed Manhattan would be even worse when it came to finding a place to live that allowed dogs. Back then, I was married to a man who had just finished law school, and we moved to New York so he could join a Midtown firm. We decided we would look for apartments without mentioning that we had a dog. Instead, we would try to charm the landlord, who would be so impressed by us that he would take the eleventh-hour mention of our quiet, elderly dog in stride.

We found a great two-bedroom on the Upper West Side, and sat down with the landlord to introduce ourselves and make our pitch. He was a blustery, red-faced Irishman whose thick glasses made his eyes look like blue pinpoints. We told him how much we loved the apartment. He seemed to approve of us, and after a few moments he pulled a pen and a blank rental agreement out of a drawer.

"Let's see, now," he said, turning to my husband. "What do you do for a living?"

"I'm a lawyer," he said, a little proudly. In our plan, we would emphasize this fact. Being a lawyer sounded so stable, so tenant-worthy, that we imagined if someone with those impeccable credentials just happened to own a dog, well, that would be a trifling thing.

The landlord put down the pen and slid the rental agreement back in the drawer, slamming it shut. He crossed his arms and leaned back. "Sorry," he said. "No lawyers. I don't rent to lawyers."

I felt faint. "But we have a dog!" I blurted out, nonsensically. "A twelve-year-old dog!"

"That's nice," the landlord said. "Dogs are fine. It's just lawyers that aren't okay."

After a frantic search, we finally managed to find an apartment that allowed both dogs and lawyers, and we settled in. I had come to Manhattan thinking it would be lonely for Molly. But almost everyone in our building had a dog—at least one dog, that is. Some had more than one. A woman who lived in a studio apartment on the ground floor had four huge gray Weimaraners. Their combined body mass must have taken up at least three-quarters of her apartment. My upstairs neighbor had a Great Dane, which he assured me was a perfect apartment dog because it liked to laze around most of the day. The cats in Manhattan were hard to count because they lived invisible lives, but I saw enough empty Friskies cans in the building's recycling bins to know there had to be dozens living there. And then the dog parks—so many of them, and so full, so much of the time! Our apartment was wonderfully close to the Met, but I was more taken with the fact that it was close to the Central Park Zoo. Before moving to Manhattan, I had pictured the city empty of all creatures save for the churning mass of humans. I do not know where I got this idea. The irony was that I have probably never been around so many animals in my life.

>—◄

My animal encounters in New York were many and, in some instances, mysterious. One day, out of the blue, a canary showed up in my apartment (I still don't know how or why). I found a cheap parking lot where I could store my car and discovered, after the fact, that it was right next door to a riding academy. Of all the millions of parking lots in New York City! It was just the sort of thing that made me feel like I was destined to be around animals, or they around me, whether by design or by accident. I loved that each time I went to get my car, I breathed in great whiffs of horse and hay. This was not what I thought living in Manhattan would smell like. Once in a while, a riderless horse got loose from its stall and came bursting out of the barn and into my parking lot, weaving in and around the parked cars, wild-eyed and agitated. The parking lot attendant, a tiny, wizened man, chased the horses back to the stable with a big broom. Every few weeks, a blacksmith showed up to work on the academy horses. He parked his van on the sidewalk and set up his forge and tools and proceeded to shoe horses all day as cabs and cars rumbled by. The blacksmith had evidently gotten tired of being asked questions by the people walking past—there are so many questions that come to mind when you happen upon a person shoeing horses on a Manhattan sidewalk, after all—so he wrote out a big list of answers to the usual questions ("1. NO. IT DOES NOT HURT THEM. 2. ONCE EVERY SIX WEEKS. 3. IRON NAILS.") and hung it on his truck. If anyone dared to speak to him, he gestured toward the sign and refused to glance up.

><

My dear dog Molly died during my first year in the city. I was so broken up by it that I thought I might never get another dog. It was peculiar to suddenly be in the city without one, because I had gotten so used to spending a few hours every day in the park with her, and felt she was my passport into the distinct and somewhat private nation of Manhattan dog owners, who spoke their own language and had rituals to which she had given me access. Now, dogless, I felt like I was in exile, hurrying past the big dog runs in Riverside Park where we had spent so much time.

I got divorced around then, too, so I was very single, alone for the first time in almost twenty years. Sometimes my mind wandered to dark, dark questions. What if I fell in love with someone but he hated dogs? What if he had no interest in someday owning a goat or a donkey? What if he liked dogs, but only poufy little rag dolls? What if he was—god forbid—allergic? *No*, I'd scold myself, *don't even think like that*.

But I met someone I really liked who mentioned, on our first date, that he had lost custody of his dog in his divorce and was miserable about it. I took this as a good sign. Also, not only did he know what Scottish Highland cattle were, but he said he hoped someday to have one, not because he was a rancher (he was actually in finance) but because he thought they were beautiful. Could I really be this lucky? We sailed along in the early stages of our relationship. Then our first Valentine's Day loomed. I figured on flowers. He told me he had gotten us tickets to see *The Lion King* on Broadway. Sweet, I thought. The tickets, John explained, were for a later date. On Valentine's Day itself, he said he'd just like to come visit me. Then he added that he had invited his best friend, Rick Lyon, to come over, too.

I found this odd, but with new boyfriends you just never know. I put on a cute skirt and dangly earrings and tidied my apartment. When John arrived, he looked me up and down and suggested that I change into something more casual. I was already a little peeved about Rick Lyon joining us—where was the romance in that, I wondered. Being told to dress down rubbed me all wrong. I stomped into my bedroom and came out in black pants and a turtleneck. "Nice, but I'd go even more casual," John said, after appraising me. I was furious. I retreated to my bedroom and changed into a dirty sweatshirt and jeans. When I came back into the living room, John was rolling up my rugs.

"What are you doing?" I asked sourly.

"I forgot to mention that Rick is bringing his daughter," John said, rolling another rug. "I'm just worried about your rugs. You know how babies are—and she's a real animal."

Did I mention that I was peeved? I was now seething. The only thing that kept me calm was telling myself that this was likely to be our last Valentine's Day together. Plus, I made it clear that I expected John to put the rugs back after our guests left.

At last, my doorbell rang. "I'll get it," John said, pointing me to a chair. "Just, uh, wait."

I stared at the ceiling. I heard the door open and close. When I looked back a moment later, a lion was sitting in my foyer. Not Rick Lyon. A *lion*, an African lion, tawny and panting, with soft, round ears and paws as big as baseball mitts, stretched out on my rugless floor. The lion's owner and three off-duty police officers stood behind the lion, holding his leash. The lion glanced around the apartment and then fixed his golden eyes on me. John took a video of me at this moment, and the look on my face is a lot like what you see on people in those Publishers

Clearing House ads who have just been told they've won $20 million. I found out later that John had met the lion's owner in a chance encounter. After John told him how much I loved animals, the man offered to bring the lion for a visit. He watched me gasping and sputtering with the kind of amused satisfaction you might feel if you had the ability to shock and delight someone that way.

The lion ate two raw chickens that we served to him in a salad bowl and then he allowed me to stroke his back, which radiated a coiled, heated energy I'd never felt before or since.

"Happy Valentine's Day," John said.

>—<

I think my relationship with John was sealed more by our acquiring a puppy together than by our marriage ceremony, which took place the following year. Our new dog, like Molly, had red fur, but he was a Welsh springer spaniel, with a spray of freckles on his nose and white patches highlighting his deep chestnut fur. Cooper was just as happy in the city as Molly had been, but then he struck the jackpot, because John and I decided to move to the country. The move was not exactly a whim. Living in a rural place with lots of animals had always been something I wanted to try, and before marrying John, I made sure he felt the same way. John had sold his company and was working on a book, which he was able to do from anywhere, and then our son was born, and the next move seemed obvious.

Imagine a person who loves pastries, and has always had only limited access to pastries, suddenly moving to Paris. That is what moving to the country felt like to me. There were animals *everywhere*. Wild, domestic, half-wild; with fur, with feathers, with fins; precious or affordable, or, quite often, free. Everyone had dogs, and everyone had cats—a few in the house and another uncounted population in the barn. Most of my neighbors had horses. Sheep abounded. My son's preschool was in the middle of a goat pasture. The goats belonged to the preschool teacher's father. Sometimes, in the middle of teaching the kids how to count, the teacher would notice that one of the goats had climbed the fence and was nibbling on the playground, so she had to run outside and shoo the goat back into the pasture and then run back inside to continue the lesson.

Now, with enough land for lots of animals, where would I begin? It was almost overwhelming to be in the company of so many creatures. It made me feel like I needed a niche. I had always assumed that I'd get a horse the minute I had room for one, but I was intimidated by the amount of work I knew a horse would be. I decided I should start smaller. Goats seemed like a good size, and they seemed easier to manage than horses. Besides, there were so many goats to choose among. Every day, when I dropped my son off at school, I lingered for a minute debating the goat question, because the teacher's father always had some goats for sale. I had a hatchback. Right after dropping Austin off, I could buy the goat, put it in the back of the car, stop at the feed store on the way home—wait, no. Impossible. I needed fencing, and I needed to buy *Goatkeeping for Dummies* first. Feeling confused, I headed home, goatless.

➤◄

Some years ago, when I was traveling in Nova Scotia, I spent the night at an extraordinary bed-and-breakfast. It wasn't just the gorgeous Victorian farmhouse, the matelassé bedspreads, or the freshly churned butter at breakfast. It was the perfectly curated collection of animals on the property. There were ten or twelve different species, all of them exceptional. Instead of merely having sheep, the owners had exotic black sheep with horns as curly as Slinkys. They didn't have chickens; they had Javan peacocks and Chinese ringneck pheasants. The horses were Normandy Cobs and Walkaloosas. The place was enchanted, and all the animals seemed to have been lifted out of a fairy tale.

I often thought about that Nova Scotia farm and began to wonder whether my paralysis in the face of so much animal abundance was the result of a conceptual failure. In other words, I wondered if I needed to have a theme. It seemed so random to have a goat, a duck, and perhaps a barn cat. Where was my organizing principle? The Nova Scotia farmers had been riffing on exoticness. I didn't dare go that route, since I wasn't experienced enough to take on livestock I could barely identify.

I picked up my red-haired son at school one day and drove home to be greeted by my red-haired dog. How had I missed the fact that I already had a theme? The farm of color-coordinated creatures! It made no sense at all, except in my fugue state it seemed logical to me. I told my husband that evening. He approved in part because he was already researching Scottish Highland cattle, which are usually russet red.

I was still shy about getting horses, but around this time I became inflamed with a desire to have chickens. As much as I had a general feeling of affection for all animals, I had never really been a bird person, so this poultry urge felt like it had come out of the blue. As it turned out, it came out of the blue to me at approximately the same moment it was coming out of the blue to thousands of people around the country. The desire for homesteading—even within city limits—had seized the nation. Chickens were the ideal starter farm animals, a perfect, easy accompaniment to other homesteading activities like making one's own yogurt and knitting.

Chickens are not just an ideal starter animal: They are also something of a gateway animal, leading very quickly to more chickens and often to ducks and turkeys and guinea fowl. Once you have invested in a coop and some fencing, it's hard not to slide into thinking you have plenty of room for a few more of something. Once I got chickens, I found myself acquiring at a healthy clip. One day, I went to CVS to buy shampoo and came home with four guinea fowl thanks to a "For Sale" sign I passed as I was driving home.

The guinea fowl were not red (they were black-and-white). This was a critical deviation from my Red Animals plan, but by the time I got them I had realized there was something a little insane about that plan anyway.

Or maybe I had just gotten so comfortable with my new life among the animals that I no longer felt the need to have a theme. Our other animals came into the picture by a variety of means. The turkeys were a gift from a friend. (Once people know you like animals, you do get those kinds of gifts.) We got cats—some on purpose, to rout the mice in the basement, and some by accident, when they showed up on our doorstep and refused to leave. I ended up with ducks because my neighbor asked me to babysit his flock over the winter and then seemed to forget I had them. The donkey—a species I have always loved and find irresistible—is for the moment just a donkey IOU, given to me by John as a birthday gift. I used to always hope I'd get jewelry on my birthday. I have changed. John got his cattle—ten Black Angus for now, but he still daydreams about Scottish Highlanders.

We don't have as many animals as some of the people I know up here. A farm nearby, for instance, has two thousand goats. But for nonfarmers, we have a pretty full house. Much of the time it bears a resemblance to a three-ring circus.

Recently, I got two new chickens. I had been visiting a friend and she gave them to me as a sort of luncheon favor on my way out the door. Chickens don't make friends easily, so I kept the two new birds separate from the rest of my flock, divided by a wire fence. There was some initial squawking and pecking through the divider and then they started to ignore each other. After a week of this peaceful coexistence, I assumed they were ready to live together. I opened the divider between the pens. Within approximately one second, the old chickens, led by my hen Mabel, set upon the new ones in a rage, and they would have killed them if I hadn't intervened. Two of my cats had sat outside the pen and watched the chicken fight with barely concealed glee. Then they noticed that a stray cat that had recently been hanging out in our yard had wandered over to watch the chicken fight, too. The three cats, disagreeing about which of them was entitled to see this fabulous dust-up in the chicken coop, froze in rigid fury and began yowling at each other as if they were plugged into amplifiers. This went on for an eternity. Meanwhile, Prince Charles and Camilla, two of my guinea fowl, showed up. I was surprised to see them, because I had kicked them out of the chicken coop earlier in the week when they were bullying the chickens. They honked and flapped in an irritated way, picking up right where they left off. Our dog came running out to see what the commotion was and became hysterical with excitement at the sight of the fighting chickens and the swaggering guinea fowl. The dog lunged for Prince Charles, who flew over the fence and into the chicken coop, where he immediately started pecking Mabel. Camilla, who is rather meek, stood by and then began pecking a spider to death for her lunch. By then, Gary, the more belligerent of my cats, grew tired of yowling at the stray cat and wandered into the bushes for a moment, killed a rabbit, and then gave herself a bath. In the middle of this pastoral tableau, John arrived with the day's mail, which included a package of thirty thousand baby predator wasps that will be released in the cow pasture, where they are supposed to eat the flies that have been pestering the cattle. I suddenly felt I needed a break from the peacefulness of my animalish life, so I went inside to play Scrabble online.

➤◄

The art critic and philosopher John Berger once said that we like to look at animals because they remind us of the past and particularly of the agrarian life we used to lead that included the regular presence of animals. I agree, but I also think we look at animals because they're funny and companionable and interesting. Some of my animals have jobs. My chickens lay eggs. My dog scares the FedEx man. The cats, by their arrogant disregard of duty, serve to remind me that I have to schedule Terminix to come and chase the mice out of the basement. All of these creatures serve a purpose, even if that purpose is to have no real purpose other than to give a warm, wonderful, unpredictable texture to my life every day. I wouldn't have it any other way.

I've wanted to write about animals as long as I've wanted to have animals. The first book I ever produced was a manuscript written in pencil on a scratch pad, bound with staples, called *Herbert the Near-Sighted Pigeon*. It was the story of a myopic pigeon who has relationship troubles on account of not being able to recognize his friends. Once he is properly diagnosed and fitted with glasses, he repairs his friendships and feels better about himself. I wrote the book when I was five years old—I'm not sure I was quite that young, but that's the family legend, anyway. After *Herbert*, I wrote a million horse stories, mostly as an attempt to conjure a horse into my life. When I began writing professionally, I always had a soft spot for stories about animals. These always turned out to be stories about people, as seen through their relationships with animals, as much as they were about animals. Writing the animal part of these stories was challenging. People can be figured out, but animals are enigmatic, so the best we can do is try to understand them through the lens of people living with them or using them or raising them or wanting them.

The closest I ever came to writing about an animal exclusively, removed from the context of the people around it, was a profile I did of a show dog named Biff. I decided to write the story because I wondered what life was like for the canine equivalent of a supermodel. As much as I was interested in Biff's entourage—his owners, his handler, his groomer—I wanted to try to get to know *him*, not as a reflection of the people around him but as an individual living being. To do this, I felt I needed time alone with him. This request is often a point of friction when you're writing a story about a celebrity. The writer wants one-on-one time, but the celebrity's posse is wary, wanting to provide a mediating buffer to protect the celebrity from too-close scrutiny. In this case, though, I insisted. I wanted to get to know Biff independently, I explained to his owners, to get a sense of who he was when he was on his own. Finally, grudgingly, they agreed. They suggested I hang out with him while he was at his handler's house. The day of the meeting arrived, and I drove out to Long Island, where his handler lived. She led me out to her garage, where she had a special dog treadmill called a Jog-Master.

She clipped Biff into place on the machine, turned it on, gave me a skeptical parting look, and said, with an arch tone, "I'll leave you two alone." I settled into a chair and pulled out my notebook. Biff trotted along on the Jog-Master, panting lightly and mostly ignoring me. A few minutes passed. I closed my notebook and put it back in my bag, after making one note in it: *Dogs don't talk.*

>—◄

I've written about domesticated animals and wild animals, and while I enjoy writing about both, I've found myself more intrigued by domesticated animals—and perhaps most interested in animals that straddle these worlds. My most recently published story in this book is about rabbits, a species to which I had never given much thought, and what I found most fascinating was the fact that rabbits fit in just about every animal category. They're wild as well as domesticated; they're pets as well as meat; they're beloved as well as being considered pests. One of the oldest stories in this collection is about Keiko, a wild orca who was captured as a baby and sold to a Mexican aquarium. Some years later, he was tapped to play a whale in the movie *Free Willy*, which is about a whale living in an aquarium who is set free by a boy who befriends him. After appearing in *Free Willy*, Keiko was returned to his aquarium, but audiences rose up in protest, demanding that he should be freed, just like the whale in the movie. The trouble is, Keiko had been in captivity for so long that he had neither the skills nor the desire to live on his own, and the machinations to try to convince him to return to the wild were extraordinary.

The animal world is our world. Even the wildest places have human fingerprints on them, so wildness is hard to find in its pure form. When I was writing about a man in South Africa who works with lions, I was shocked to learn how little of Africa is unrestricted wilderness—almost all of the "wild" spaces are managed in one fashion or another, and in South Africa, in particular, everything is fenced, and all animal populations are metered. On that same note, I was flabbergasted that there are more tigers in captivity than in the wild. Although we may think of the animal world as something separate from us, like a moon orbiting around the earth, it's more of a weave, with some animals farther away from the cross-threads of the human world and others closer. But we are certainly cohabitants of one place, and the separation is shrinking rather than expanding. A bear strolled down a street in a Los Angeles suburb recently—a noteworthy but not uncommon event. I see coyotes and deer here all the time. Animals in zoos around the world came down with COVID-19 just like humans did.

I think I'll always have animals and I think I'll always write about them. Their unknowability challenges me. Our affection for them intrigues me. I resist the urge to anthropomorphize them, but I do think they know something we don't about living elementally. I'm happy to be in their company.

The It Bird

If I had never seen Janet Bonney reenact the mouth-to-beak resuscitation of her hen Number Seven, who had been frozen solid in a snowstorm, then was thawed and nursed back to life—the hen was hand-fed and massaged and encouraged to watch doctor shows on TV—I might never have become a chicken person. But a few years ago, I happened to watch a documentary called *The Natural History of the Chicken*, which opens with the story of Bonney and Number Seven, and for the first time the thought of owning chickens entered my mind. I had watched the film with no preexisting chicken condition. But seeing Number Seven's resurrection, followed by beauty shots of exotic hens and segments about small backyard flocks, I suddenly found myself wanting chickens, and wanting them with an urgency that exceeded even my mad adolescent desire to have a pony. At first, I thought this chicken fixation was a phase that I alone was going through, but it turns out that right now, across the country and beyond, there is a surging passion for raising the birds. Chickens seem to be a perfect convergence of the economic, environmental, gastronomic, and emotional matters of the moment, plus, in the past few years, they have undergone an image rehabilitation so astonishing that it should be studied by marketing consultants. Now that

I actually have chickens—seven, at last count, but that number, because of predators, is disturbingly variable—I am the object of more pure envy than I have ever experienced in my life.

On a Venn diagram plotting the interest in chicken ownership and circumstances related to age, gender, acreage, appetite, and aesthetic tolerance, I would land in that pitch-dark center where all the sets overlap: I am the target chicken audience. Even now, well into my chicken stewardship, this is a big surprise to me. I am an animal fancier, but fur-bearing has always been my type. I never wanted a bird. When I left Manhattan a few years ago and moved a hundred miles north to a house with plenty of land and animal-friendly zoning, the first creature I planned on getting was a horse, which I later downgraded to a donkey. I did fleetingly consider a duck, because I had seen some at my neighbor's house and thought they were darling. But we didn't have a pond, and the idea of getting ducks and then having their water source be a plastic kiddie pool from Toys "R" Us seemed to undermine the rusticity of the experience.

By the time I saw *The Natural History of the Chicken*, something had been stirring in the poultry world for a while. In 1982, Martha Stewart published her first book, *Entertaining*, which showcased her flock of rare-breed chickens and their pretty pastel-colored eggs. The photographs of Stewart with the flock were a revelation. For the previous forty years or so, chicken farming had been viewed as a lowly profession, stuck in a peculiar netherworld between the high-stakes cattle business and the matter-of-fact farming of crops. Factory-raised chickens seemed to be the worst of both. When crowded in their miserable quarters, factory chickens seemed almost more plant than animal, but still messy and smelly and sentient. No glamour attached itself to chickens.

Stewart's book went on to sell hundreds of thousands of copies. Readers might have been more interested in how to cook her Curried Walnut Chicken than in how to raise and care for a living chicken, but they couldn't have helped noting Stewart's endorsement of chicken-keeping.

Within the next few years, Stewart launched her magazine, which often featured her chickens in supermodel-style head shots that made them look ennobled and fabulous. She also introduced a beautiful paint collection, which was based on egg colors from her flock. All in all, she began making chickens seem less like livestock and more like useful and companionable creatures that were lovely and interesting. She advocated for them all the time. "All of my chickens had names, all of them," she said recently. "I knew all of them. I worried about them. I was really unhappy when anything happened to them. For instance, I was unhappy when my Egyptian Fayoumi hen froze to death." She sighed and then added, "It was awful. I'll never get another Egyptian Fayoumi again."

➤•◄

Not long ago, I was in the waiting room of my veterinarian's office with one of my chickens, who was ailing. A red-faced man with a gimpy poodle was sitting next to me. I had my chicken in a cat carrier. When the man leaned over to peek at my carrier, I could tell by the look on his face that he had expected to see a mewling kitten. He did a double take, plopped back in his chair, and said, "Chickens are the new hot pet, I guess."

Well, yes and no. Until the 1950s, it was common to keep a few chickens around. They were cheap and simple to raise. Unlike cows or sheep, they were tolerant of most weather, could subsist on table scraps and bugs, took up little space, required the simplest of housing, and fertilized the garden while they scratched through it. Gathering eggs was so easy that children were often assigned to do it; by contrast, getting milk or meat or wool was a major undertaking requiring a trained adult. A chicken was a good investment. A hundred years ago, a baby chick cost about fifteen cents and a laying hen cost a few dollars. A hen in her prime, which lasts two or three years, could produce an egg every day or two in the laying season, and once she stopped laying, she could be cooked.

Buying eggs year-round at a supermarket is a relatively recent development. People used to only eat eggs when their chickens were laying. Commercial incubators, allowing for large-scale chicken enterprise, weren't invented until the late 1800s, and they weren't used widely for decades after that. Even when they became common, egg production was slow. Until the 1930s, when the Department of Agriculture launched its National Poultry Improvement Plan and the subsequent development of factory farms, eggs were still available only seasonally, like shad roe, and many people kept their own chickens so they could have a reliable source.

Part of what is unusual about chickens is that they have always been considered "women's livestock"; women and chickens seemed to have a natural harmony. The covers of early chicken magazines, such as *Everybody's Poultry Magazine*, *Poultry Success*, and *Farm Journal and Farmer's Wife*, featured illustrations of women and children on sunny farms with hens and chicks at their feet. A book published in 1919, *A Little Journey Among Anconas*, which extolls the Ancona chicken breed, is highlighted by a photograph of a young woman in a crisp summer dress, gazing adoringly at a black chicken that is perched on her right hand. Small and manageable, chickens were just a walking, squawking extension of a kitchen garden, the plot of herbs and vegetables that women were expected to cultivate for their cooking needs. Farm women often sold extra eggs to make some money of their own. The 1893 book *What Can a Woman Do* guided women to the professions of journalism, dentistry, poetry, and hen-keeping. (Beekeeping and gardening are the only other agricultural jobs on the list.) The author, Martha Louise Rayne, wrote, or rather, declared, that there is "MONEY IN EGGS," and recounts the story of two "tempest-tossed and homeless women" who set up a poultry farm together and enjoy great success. (The story comes to a bad end, though, when one of the chicken women decides to marry a male biped, forsaking her hens and her poultry partner.) Rayne recommended that even married women keep chickens, because, she explained, it can be done without interfering with other domestic duties.

The usual barnyard chicken in the early nineteenth century had a red comb and glossy red or brown feathers. These were sleek and solid creatures, somewhat unremarkable in appearance. Then, in the 1840s, chicken enthusiasts introduced a breed of Chinese chicken to North America and Great Britain. The fattest and fluffiest of these birds were bred to produce an ornamental variety called a Cochin that resembled a walking powder puff. The Cochin set the world agog. A frenzy of Cochin breeding and showing and trading began, resulting in a speculative bubble nearly on the scale of Dutch tulip mania or Victorian orchidelirium. Prices for Cochins reached absurd levels. In one instance, a pair of Cochins were valued at $700, which was about 10,000 percent more than the price of an ordinary pair of chickens. Everyone from Queen Victoria to members of Congress wanted one of these extraordinary chickens, especially because the Cochins were reported to have great intelligence and the ability to produce eggs that weighed more than a pound apiece. Interestingly, even though chickens had been so completely associated with women, "hen fever," as the mania for Cochins was called, affected men more than women. *The Century Magazine* reported on it in 1898, explaining that a "hen-man," besotted by chickens, might lose all interest in life except for his birds. He "may have been an ardent admirer of Shakespeare . . . but now he reads to himself *Farm Poultry* or *The Care of Hens*."

Eventually, crooks and swindlers and even P. T. Barnum infiltrated the trade. (In some cases, chicken dealers glued feathers onto ordinary chickens so they could pass them off as Cochins.) Soon, though, it became clear that the imagined profits in rare-chicken trading were entirely imaginary. Chicken trendsetters like Prince Albert began to tire of the hobby. Then the chickens, collected in overly large numbers into too-small houses, began to die. Hen fever cooled. Men resumed their reading of Shakespeare, and chickens returned to their previous status as sturdy, steady farmworkers.

Still, chickens remained such a fixture in most households that, even as Americans moved from the country to urban areas, they took their chickens with them. Very few cities specifically outlawed chickens until many decades later. You couldn't bring the family cow along when you moved to town, since you couldn't possibly accommodate it, but anyone with a little patch of grass could still support a chicken or two.

Inexpensive supermarket eggs became readily available in the 1950s, around the same time that Americans became enchanted with the notion of a hygienic, suburbanized life. Can you picture ambitious young couples in the fifties wanting chickens pecking around the split-level colonial and the flagstone patio and the swing set? What felt modern, what *defined* modern, was to leave the farm behind, to shed any association with that life. Many philosophers, including John Berger, maintain that what we consider modernity began at the moment when we no longer relied on animals for utility—we didn't ride them or raise them or milk them—and they were absent from daily life except as ornaments.

Thus, the keeping of chickens was shrugged off as old-fashioned. Then eggs themselves became suspect. In 1964, Konrad Bloch and Feodor Lynen were awarded a Nobel Prize for their research on cholesterol, conjuring terrifying images of hardened arteries and vascular lesions. In the wake of their research, an assault on eggs, with their cholesterol-rich yolks, began. In an effort to counteract it, the American Egg Board launched its Incredible Edible Egg campaign in 1976, but the cumulative effect of the bad news meant that casual chicken-keeping in this country seemed doomed.

>-◄

When I first decided that I had to have chickens, I had trouble figuring out how to go about it. Living in the country, I saw plenty of chickens on working farms. I occasionally stopped and asked the owners if they would be willing to sell me a couple of hens, but no one was interested in parting with any, since a mature hen who is a good egg layer is too valuable to give up. In the spring, my local feed store set up a tower of little cages filled with peeping chicks, still cottony and clumsy, but you were required by law to buy at least a six-pack of them, and the prospect of heat lamps and high chick mortality rates made me uneasy. More worrisome was the fact that unless you are a professional chicken sexer (a critical job in the poultry industry) it is impossible to tell the sex of a baby chick, so your six chicks might turn out to be six roosters. That might be fine if you like deluxe feathers, but not much use if you're hoping for eggs.

To be clear, my chicken thing was not, initially, an egg thing. Having never had a really fresh egg, I didn't find much fault with what I got at ShopRite. Anyway, for years I hardly ate any eggs, keeping my cholesterol in mind. But, as it happens, by the time I started thinking about getting chickens, eggs had been exonerated. A widely reviewed 2001 study by researchers at Kansas State University established that eating an egg or two a day is fine because the human body doesn't absorb a substantial amount of the cholesterol in egg yolks. (Egg whites, of course, are completely innocent.) High-protein diets such as the Atkins, trending at the time, promoted omelets as an almost perfect meal. By 2007, the American Egg Board felt confident enough in the rehabilitation of egg-eating that it relaunched the Incredible Edible Egg campaign. In this new iteration, the campaign included a number of pro-egg health professionals who were known as Egg Ambassadors.

Around this same time, the concept of the hundred-mile diet—that is, eating food that is not only organic but is grown or raised within a hundred miles of your home—had gained traction. The term "locavore" entered the vernacular. What could be more local than your backyard? It was a fine thing to grow your own lettuce and tomatoes and make salad or a side, but raising chickens was even better, since it meant that you could cook a main dish with ingredients kept right outside your door. For the squeamish, eggs had the added appeal of being a protein source that didn't involve killing anything. If you were trying to design a product that satisfied the social preoccupations of the moment, you couldn't have done better than to come up with a hen.

When I first thought about getting chickens, I hadn't realized that there was a poultry movement underway. I was chicken uninitiated. I had yet to come across the dozens of online chicken groups and websites such as Chickens 101, Housechicken, Cotton-Pickin Chickens, Yard-poultry, and My Pet Chicken; I was not one of the forty thousand members of the BackYardChickens.com forums, and I was not one of the fifteen thousand people who log on each month to watch the writer Terry Golson's "HenCam," which webcasts live from her backyard coop near Boston, and I had not bought Christine Heinrichs's 2007 book, *How to Raise Chickens*, a plainspoken guide for people who might not ever have seen a live chicken, which keeps selling more and more copies.

I did notice that every time I mentioned to my friends that I wanted chickens, they all exclaimed that they wanted them, too. It was a species-specific response: when I added that my husband wanted Scottish Highland cattle, those same people were taken aback and inevitably said, "That's weird. How come?" My friends looked upon my urge for chicken-keeping as mild and understandable, rather than evidence that we'd tipped over the edge of sanity and were throwing ourselves recklessly, *Green Acres* style, into livestock. Chickens seemed to go hand in glove with the postfeminist reclamation of other farmwife domestic arts—knitting, canning, quilting. Keeping chickens was a do-it-yourself hobby at a moment when doing things for yourself was newly appreciated as a declaration of self-sufficiency, a celebration of handwork, and a pushback from a numbing and disconnected big-box life.

I started shopping for a chicken coop, but everything I found had a design that was half doghouse, half toolshed, and gigantic, made for at least twenty hens, whereas I pictured myself with a modest flock of four. I knew my limits. I pictured myself with my humble array of hens, housed in some sort of groovy little chicken structure that didn't look like a miniature Swiss ski hut in a failed housing development. One night, on the Internet, I was searching phrases such as "cool-looking chicken coops" and "modern design chicken house" and came across the Eglu. A squat plastic dome that came in bright colors, the Eglu, compact and cute, was meant for just four hens. Better still, you could order it *complete with* hens—not six chicks of indeterminate gender, like I might get at the local Agway, but as few as two hens, guaranteed to be females, on the brink of maturity (what chicken people call "point-of-lay"). And they would be delivered to my local post office. I had found my coop—and my chickens.

Recently, I spoke to Johannes Paul, one of the founders of Omlet, the British company that makes the Eglu. Paul was not initially a chicken person. He and the other three Omlet founders were industrial-design students at the Royal College of Art, in London, who in 2004 were facing the paralyzing prospect of their thesis project. They were supposed to reconsider an ordinary object, and Paul's mother, who had chickens, suggested they try designing a better chicken house. Commercially available coops, like homemade ones, were almost always built of wood, which is hard to clean, hard to keep dry, and hard to seal well for insulation. "Plastic really is fantastic," Paul said to me. "Using the kind of rotational molding that we do for the Eglu means it has inherent insulation, and it's seamless, and it can be made in saturated colors." For the first time, a chicken house could look and feel modern. In fact, when the Eglu was first launched, a lot of people thought it was a new product from Apple.

Their professors loved it, and friends and families were so enthusiastic that the students decided to try out the Eglu in the real world. They priced it at the equivalent of about $600 and launched it online in Europe, without any advertising. They sold a thousand Eglus in the first year, and sales have tripled every year since. Most people ordered the Eglu complete with the optional chickens. According to Paul, most of their customers were first-time chicken owners. Initially, Omlet was reluctant to sell the Eglu in the United States, because the cost of shipping was so high, and because the company felt that Americans were at least a

decade behind Europeans in having an interest in organic, local food—
that is, we were not yet a nation of chicken keepers. But there were so
many inquiries that, in 2006, Omlet decided to introduce it here.

Since then, TreeHugger.com, which monitors ecological trends, has
gone from describing urban chicken-raising as a "weird eco-habit" to
declaring it a "movement across North America." There have been successful legal challenges to anti-chicken-keeping laws in dozens of cities, including Cleveland; Missoula; Ann Arbor; Madison; and South
Portland, Maine, and guides have been published for anyone wanting
to challenge anti-chicken ordinances in their town. A petition in 2009
urged the Obamas to add a chicken flock to the White House garden.
("Sasha and Malia will love them," one petitioner wrote. "Tad Lincoln
kept a turkey he named Jack in the White House. Bring back this happy
practice!") *Backyard Poultry*, a magazine that began publishing a few
years ago, is now distributing a whopping hundred thousand copies. The
publisher, Dave Belanger, says that stores are now eager to carry it, while
in the past, "I don't think you could have gotten a chicken magazine on a
newsstand." Many pet stores are now carrying chicken feed alongside the
racks of Fancy Feast and rawhide rolls. I recently came across the ultimate
evidence of contemporary chicken ownership: instructions, on the blog
IKEAhackers, for building a chicken coop out of furniture from IKEA.

The optional chickens available for the Eglu are supplied in the United
States by McMurray Hatchery, an Iowa company that is the largest rare-
breed poultry hatchery in the world. The McMurray catalogue offers 110
breeds. The company was founded in 1917 by Murray McMurray, an
Iowa banker who sold chickens as a hobby. During the Depression, his
bank failed, but his chicken business took off—a correlation that sounds
a lot like the present day—and thus Banker McMurray became Hen-
Man McMurray. In 2009, McMurray Hatchery, which caters to people
with backyard flocks rather than commercial poultry enterprises, sold 1.7
million chickens, ranging from day-old chicks, which cost $2.00 each, to
point-of-lay hens, which cost $12.95. For the past two years, the hatch-

ery has been operating at capacity, and even so, it has sold out of all of its birds even before they were ready to ship. The only other year in recent memory in which it sold out was 1999. Bud Wood, the company president, attributes that 1999 run on chickens to fear about the millennium. "When times are tough," he said, "people want chickens."

>-<

I ordered a chartreuse Eglu complete with four red hens. The Eglu came via UPS. A few days later, the hens were delivered to my local post office. "You have a package here," the postal clerk said when she called, "and it's clucking." I rushed into town and picked up the package. It was heavier than I had expected, smaller than I had pictured, as noisy as I had been warned. At home, I opened the box and decanted the hens into the wire pen that attaches to the Eglu. They were young Rhode Island Red hybrids called Gingernut Rangers, with bright brown eyes and rich red feathers speckled with white. Their combs were small and pink and their knobby legs were bright yellow. Within six weeks or so, their combs would redden, and their legs would pale—signs that they were about to start laying.

The knock on chickens has always been that they're stupid. Even some chicken fanciers hold this opinion. I recently read an online comment from someone who announced cheerily that her chickens were "extremely entertaining due to the fact that they are dumb as stumps!" But my hens didn't seem stupid. They explored the pen with that stop-action motion that makes chickens look like cartoon characters, but with a brisk alertness and sharp curiosity. Right away, I figured out that "pecking order" isn't just a figure of speech. They adhered to a strict social system, with each hen taking her turn at the feeder and corrective nips doled out to any chicken that stepped out of line.

When a few weeks had passed and the birds were settled in, I let them out of their pen during the day to range around. If I was outside, they stayed near me, chuckling and purring as they pecked at bugs and grass.

We have more than fifty acres where they could have roamed free, but of course they exhibited the contrarian impulse of all pets and decided that their favorite place to spend the afternoon was napping next to my front door or roosting in the planter box in the courtyard. Anyway, I was smitten. I found watching them soothing. I don't like housework, but to my surprise, I enjoyed all my chicken-related labors—I loved feeding and watering them and hosing out their Eglu. I especially loved going to the feed store and buying bales of hay for their nests and fifty-pound sacks of feed. Among other things, it made me feel that I had legitimized myself as a local rather than a naive carpetbagging city person. When one of my hens laid an egg for the first time, I was as proud as if I had been attending my daughter's bat mitzvah.

There have been difficult moments, too. A few months after my hens arrived, my neighbor's indolent old mutts loped onto our property, clawed open the Eglu, and killed two of my birds. I was sick about it, but I soon restocked with four young chickens that I found through an online chicken group. Then I lost two of those. They were picked off in broad daylight, probably by a hawk or an owl or a coyote or a raccoon or a fox—everyone in the woods loves chicken, and chickens, which don't fly well, don't run fast, and don't fight hard, are sitting ducks. After that catastrophe, I built a big fenced-in yard with netting over the top, and put the Eglu in it, and stopped letting the hens wander around loose. I had never thought of them as prey before. In the bucolic scenes I'd imagined of chickens strolling across my lawn, all the lip-smacking predators had been cropped out of the picture.

➤◄

At one point, when I was down to just two chickens, I noticed that one hen wasn't standing up properly. She also stopped laying eggs and lost a lot of weight. If I were a real farmer, I would have culled her—that is, killed her—and been done with it. But I'm not a real farmer, so I began hauling her back and forth to the vet. He couldn't diagnose the problem, but he gave her an injection of steroids and a prescription for antibiotics. She didn't get better. She was so unsteady that she couldn't even reach her food unless I held her up to the feeder. My vet apologized that he couldn't figure out the problem, and explained that his knowledge of birds was limited (unless a student plans to specialize in birds, veterinary school curriculums require only one semester of avian medicine). I tracked down an avian expert in Boston, who wasn't sure what to make of my bird's ailment, either. My research led me to suspect something called Marek's disease, a contagious kind of chicken cancer that attacks the bird's nervous system and can kill a whole flock if it spreads. The sick bird had been my friendliest, calmest hen, the one that most enjoyed being held and stroked. Until she got sick, she laid big brown eggs like clockwork. Her name was Beauty, but the patient name on the vial of her antibiotics said "Chicken Orlean," which even in my funk I found hilarious.

After a month of hand-feeding her, dripping antibiotics down her beak, and getting no diagnosis beyond my hunch that she might have Marek's disease, I finally realized that Chicken Orlean was miserable and there was nothing more I could do for her. I eat chicken all the time, so I have no right to morally oppose the killing of a chicken, but I couldn't kill my own pet, so I took her back to the vet. After the vet injected her with a fatal dose of pentobarbital, I went out into the waiting room and sobbed. The room was empty except for a husky woman holding a fat tan pug. The woman crossed the room and put an arm around me and said, "Oh, honey, I'm sorry. Was it your dog?"

"No," I sobbed, my face in my hands, "it was my chicken."

➤◄

Now I have seven chickens. I would say that I have seven hens, except that one—sweet, demure, shy Laura—recently proved my point about the challenges of chicken-sexing, as she sprouted big red wattles and started crowing at dawn. So the correct accounting is that I have six hens and an unanticipated rooster. Meanwhile, the chicken movement seems to be expanding exponentially. I do detect a little overripening on the edges. I've noticed some late-stage trend phenomena such as chicken diapers, for people who want to keep their chickens as house pets, and there will undoubtedly be chicken coops that go beyond the crisp functionality of the Eglu, perhaps incorporating flourishes that push into the decadent.

People central to the chicken world are wondering what might supplant chickens, if and when the passion for chickens runs its course. Dave Belanger, of *Backyard Poultry*, thinks it will be goats. McMurray Hatchery's CEO Bud Wood thinks the next trend will be for ducks. But chickens seem to me to have staying power. They have already survived hen bubbles and cholesterol scares and the enormous social change that chased them out of the backyard. They should be able to survive diapers and jeweled coops and an uptick in ducks. The chicken, that thing with feathers, always sunny and useful, will endure.

Show Dog

If I were a bitch, I'd be in love with Biff Truesdale. Biff is perfect. He's friendly, good-looking, rich, famous, and in excellent physical condition. He almost never drools. He's not afraid of commitment. He wants children—actually, he already has children and wants a lot more. He works hard and is a consummate professional, but he also knows how to have fun.

What Biff likes most is food and sex. This makes him sound boorish, but he is not—he's just elemental. Food he likes even better than sex. His favorite things to eat are cookies, mints, and hotel soap, but he will eat just about anything. Richard Krieger, a friend of Biff's who occasionally drives him to appointments, said not long ago, "When we're driving on I-95, we'll usually pull over at McDonald's. Even if Biff is napping, he always wakes up when we're getting close. I get him a few plain hamburgers with buns—no ketchup, no mustard, and no pickles. He loves hamburgers. I don't get him his own french fries, but if I get myself fries, I always flip a few for him into the back."

If you're ever around Biff while you're eating something he wants to taste—cold roast beef, a Wheatables cracker, chocolate, pasta, aspirin, whatever—he will stare at you across the pleated bridge of his nose and let his eyes sag and his lips tremble and allow a little bead of drool to

33

percolate at the edge of his mouth until you feel so crummy that you give him a taste. This routine puts the people who know him in a quandary, because Biff needs to keep an eye on his weight. Usually, he is as skinny as Kate Moss, but he can put on three pounds in an instant. The holidays can be tough. He takes time off at Christmas and spends it at home, in Attleboro, Massachusetts, where there's a lot of food around and no pressure and no schedule and it's easy to eat all day.

Any extra weight goes to his neck. Luckily, Biff likes working out. He runs for fifteen or twenty minutes twice a day, either outside or on his Jog-Master. When he's feeling heavy, he runs longer, and skips snacks, until he's back down to his ideal weight of seventy-five pounds.

Biff is a boxer. He is a show dog. He performs under the name Champion Hi-Tech's Arbitrage. Looking good is not mere vanity; it's business. A show dog's career is short, and judges are unforgiving. Each breed is judged by an exacting standard for appearance and temperament, and then there's the incalculable element of charisma in the ring. When a show dog is fat or lazy or sullen, he doesn't win. When he doesn't win, he doesn't enjoy the ancillary benefits of being a winner, such as appearing as the celebrity spokesmodel on packages of Pedigree Mealtime with Lamb and Rice, which Biff will be doing soon, or picking the best-looking bitches and charging them $600 or so for his sexual favors, which Biff does three or four times a month. Another ancillary benefit of being a winner is that almost every single weekend of the year, as he travels to shows around the country, he gets to hear people applaud for him and yell his name and tell him what a good boy he is, which is something he seems to enjoy at least as much as eating a bar of soap.

>—◄

Pretty soon, Biff won't have to be so vigilant about his diet. After he appears at the Westminster Kennel Club's show this week, he will retire from active show life and work full-time as a stud. It's a good moment for him to retire. Last year, he won more shows than any other boxer, and also more than any other dog in the purebred category known as working dogs, which also includes such breeds as Alaskan malamutes, Bernese mountain dogs, Doberman pinschers, Great Danes, Newfoundlands, Portuguese water dogs, Rottweilers, Saint Bernards, Siberian huskies, and standard schnauzers. Boxers were named for their habit of standing on their hind legs and punching with their front paws when they fight. They were originally bred to be chaperones—their job was to look forbidding while being pleasant to spend time with. Except for show dogs like Biff, most boxers lead a life of relative leisure. Last year at Westminster, Biff was named Best Boxer and Best Working Dog, and he was a serious contender for Best in Show, the highest honor any show dog can hope for. He is favored to win his breed and group again this year and has a serious shot once again for Best in Show, although the odds are against him, because this year's judge is known as a poodle person.

Biff is four years old. He's in his prime. He could stay on the show circuit for a few more years, but by stepping aside now he is making room for his sons Trent and Rex, who are just getting into the business, plus he's leaving while he's still on top. He'll spend less time on airplanes, which is the one part of show life he doesn't like, and more time with his owners, William and Tina Truesdale, who might be persuaded to waive his snacking restrictions.

Biff has a short, tight coat of fox-colored fur, white feet and ankles, and a patch of white on his chest roughly the shape of Maine. His muscles are plainly sketched under his skin, but he isn't bulgy. His face is turned up and pushed in. He has a dark mask, spongy lips, a wishbone-shaped white blaze, and the earnest and slightly careworn expression of a small-town mayor. Someone once told me that he thought Biff looked a little like Bill Clinton. Biff's face is his fortune. There are plenty of people who like boxers with bigger bones and a stockier body—boxers who look less like marathon runners and more like weight lifters—but almost everyone agrees that Biff has a nearly perfect head.

35

"Biff's head is his father's," William Truesdale, a veterinarian, explained to me one day. We were in the Truesdales' living room in Attleboro, which overlooks acres of hilly fenced-in fields. Their house is a big, sunny ranch with a stylish pastel kitchen and boxerabilia on every wall. The Truesdales don't have children, but at any given moment they share their quarters with at least a half-dozen dogs. If you watch a lot of dog-food commercials, you may have seen William—he's the young, handsome, dark-haired veterinarian declaring his enthusiasm for Pedigree Mealtime while his boxers gallop around behind him.

"Biff has a masculine but elegant head," William went on. "It's not too wet around the muzzle. It's just about ideal. Of course, his forte is right here." He pointed to Biff's withers and explained that Biff's shoulder-humerus articulation was optimally angled, bracketing his superb brisket and forelegs, or something like that. While William was talking, Biff climbed onto the couch and sat on top of Brian, his companion, who was hiding under a pillow. Brian is a toy Prince Charles spaniel who is about the size of a teapot and has the composure of a hummingbird. As a young competitor, Brian once bit a judge—a mistake Tina Truesdale says he made because at the time he was going through a little mental problem about being touched. Brian, whose show name is Champion Cragmor's Hi-Tech Man, will soon go back on the circuit, but now he mostly serves as Biff's regular escort. When Biff sat on him, he started to quiver. Biff batted at him with his front paw. Brian gave him an adoring look.

"Biff's body is from his mother," Tina was saying. "She had a lot of substance."

"To be honest, she was even a little extreme for a bitch," William said. "She was rather buxom. I would call her zaftig."

"Biff's father needed that, though," Tina said. "His name was Tailo, and he was fabulous. Tailo had a very beautiful head, but he was a bit fine, I think. A bit slender."

"Even a little feminine," William said, with feeling. "Actually, he would have been a really awesome bitch."

The first time I met Biff, he sniffed my pants, stood up on his hind legs and stared into my face, and then trotted off to the kitchen, where some-one was cooking macaroni. We were in Westbury, Long Island, where Biff lives with Kimberly Pastella, a twenty-nine-year-old professional dog handler, when he's working. Last year, Kim and Biff went to at least one show every weekend. If they drove, they took Kim's van. If they flew, she went coach and he went cargo. They always shared a hotel room.

While Kim was telling me about their work schedule, I could hear Biff rummaging around in the kitchen. "Biffers!" Kim called out. Biff trotted back into the room with a phony look of surprise on his face. His tail was ticking back and forth. It is cropped so that it is about the size and shape of a half-smoked stogie. Kim explained that there was a bitch in her downstairs bedroom who had been sent from Pennsylvania to be bred to one of Kim's other stud clients, and that Biff could smell her and was a little out of sorts. "Let's go," she said to him. "Biff, let's go jog." We went into the garage, where a treadmill was set up with Biff's collar suspended from a metal arm. Biff hopped on the treadmill and held his head out so that Kim could buckle his collar. As soon as Kim leaned to-ward the power switch, he started to jog. His nails clicked a light tattoo on the rubber belt.

Except for a son of his named Biffle, who rubs him the wrong way, Biff gets along with everybody. Matt Stander, one of the founders of *Dog News*, said, "Biff is just very, very personable. He has a je ne sais quoi that's really special. He gives of himself all the time." One afternoon, the Truesdales were telling me about the psychology that went into making Biff who he is. "Boxers are real communicators," William was saying. "We had to really take that into consideration in his upbringing. He seems tough, but there's a fragile ego in there. The profound reaction and hurt when you would raise your voice at him was really something."

"I *made* him," Tina said. "I made Biff who he is. He had an overbearing personality when he was small, but I consider that a prerequisite for a great performer. He had such an *attitude*! He was like this miniature *man*!" She shimmied her shoulders back and forth and thrust out her chin. Tina is a chic, dainty woman with wide-set eyes and the neck of a ballerina. She grew up on a farm in Costa Rica, where dogs were considered just another form of livestock. In 1987, William got her a Rottweiler for a watchdog, and a boxer, because he always loved boxers, and Tina decided to dabble in showing them. Now she makes monogrammed Christmas stockings for each animal in their house, and she watches the tape of Biff winning at Westminster approximately once a week. "Right from the beginning, I made Biff think he was the most fabulous dog in the world," Tina said.

"He doesn't take after me very much," William said. "I'm more of a golden retriever."

"Oh, Biff has my nature," Tina said. "I'm very strong-willed. I'm brassy. And Biff is an egotistical, self-centered, selfish person. He thinks he's very important and special, and he doesn't like to share."

➤◄

Biff is priceless. If you beg the Truesdales to name a figure, they might say that Biff is worth around $100,000, but they will also point out that a Japanese dog fancier recently handed Tina a blank check for Biff. (She immediately threw it away.) That check notwithstanding, campaigning a show dog is a money-losing proposition for the owner. A good handler gets $300 or $400 a day, plus travel expenses, to show a dog, and any dog aiming for the top will have to be on the road at least a hundred days a year. A dog photographer charges hundreds of dollars for a portrait, and a portrait is something that every serious owner commissions, and then runs as a full-page ad in several dog show magazines. Advertising a show dog is standard procedure if you want your dog or your presence on the show circuit to get well known. There are also such ongoing show dog expenses as entry fees, hair care products, food, health care, and toys.

Biff's stud fee is $600. Once he retires from showing, he can be bred several times a month. Breeding him would have been a good way for him to make money in the past, except that whenever the Truesdales were enthusiastic about a mating, they bartered Biff's service for the pick of the litter. As a result, they now have more Biff puppies than Biff earnings. "We're doing this for posterity," Tina says. "We're doing it for the good of all boxers. You simply can't think about the cost."

On a recent Sunday, I went to watch Biff work at one of the last shows he would attend before his retirement. The show was sponsored by the Lehigh Valley Kennel Club and was held in a big, windy field house on the campus of Lehigh University, in Bethlehem, Pennsylvania. The parking lot was filled with motor homes pasted with life-size decals of dogs. On my way to the field house, I passed someone walking an Afghan hound wearing a snood, and someone else wiping down a saluki with a *Flintstones* beach towel. Biff was napping in his crate—a fancy-looking brass box with bright silver hardware. Luggage tags from Delta, United, and American Airlines dangled from the door. Dogs in crates can look woebegone, but Biff actually likes spending time in his. When he was growing up, the Truesdales decided they would never reprimand him, because of his delicate ego. Whenever he got rambunctious, Tina wouldn't scold him—she would just invite him to sit in his crate and have a time-out.

On this particular day, Biff was in the crate with a bowl of water and a gourmet Oinkeroll, which is a pigskin chew toy. The boxer judging was already over. There had been thirty-three in the competition, and Biff had won Best in Breed. Now he had to wait for several hours while the rest of the working breeds had their competitions. Later, the breed winners would square off for Best in Working Group. Then, around dinnertime, the winner of the working group and the winners of the other groups—sporting dogs, hounds, terriers, toys, nonsporting dogs, and herding dogs—would compete for Best in Show. Biff was stretched out in the crate with his head resting on his forelegs so that his lips draped over his ankles like a café curtain. He looked bored. Next to his crate, several wire fox terriers were standing on tables getting their faces shampooed, and beyond them a Chihuahua in a pink crate was gnawing on its door latch. Two men in white shirts and dark pants walked by eating hot dogs. One of them was gesturing and complaining to the other, "I thought I had good dachshunds! I thought I had *great* dachshunds!"

Biff sighed and closed his eyes.

While he was napping, I pawed through his suitcase. In it was dog food; towels; an electric nail grinder; a whisker trimmer; a wool jacket in a lively southwestern pattern; an apron; some antibiotics; baby oil; coconut-oil coat polish; boxer chalk powder; a copy of *Dog News*; an issue of *ShowSight* magazine featuring an article titled "Frozen Semen: Boon or Bane?" and a two-page ad for Biff, with a full-page, full-color photograph of him posed with Kim in front of a human-size toy soldier; a spray bottle of fur cleanser; another Oinkeroll; a rope ball; and something called a Booda Bone. The apron was for Kim. The baby oil was to make Biff's nose and feet glossy when he went into the ring. Boxer chalk powder—as distinct from, say, West Highland white terrier chalk powder—is formulated to cling to short, sleek boxer hair, in order to whiten their white markings.

Unlike some of the other dogs, Biff did not need to travel with a blow dryer, curlers, nail polish, or detangling combs, but unlike some less sought-after dogs, he did need a schedule. He was registered for a show in Chicago the next day, and had an appointment at a clinic in Connecticut the following week to make a semen deposit, which had been purchased by a breeder in Australia. Also, he had a date that same week with a bitch named Diana who was about to go into heat. Biff has to book his stud work after shows, so that it doesn't interfere with his performance in the ring. Tina Truesdale told me that this was typical of all athletes, but everyone who knows Biff is quick to comment on how professional he is as a stud. Richard Krieger, who was going to be driving Biff to his clinic appointment in Connecticut, once told me that some studs like to goof around and take forever, but Biff is very businesslike. "Bing, bang, boom," Krieger said. "He's in, he's out."

"No wasting of time," said Richard's wife, Nancy. "Bing, bang, boom, he gets the job done."

After a few minutes, Kim showed up and asked Biff if he needed to go outside. Then a handler who is a friend of Kim's came by. He was wearing a black-and-white houndstooth suit and was brandishing a large comb and a can of hair spray. While they were talking, I leafed through the show catalogue and read some of the dogs' names to Biff, just for fun—names like Aleph Godol's Umbra Von Carousel and Champion Spanktown Little Lu Lu and Ranchlake's Energizer O'Motown and Champion Beaverbrook Buster V Broadhead. Biff decided that he did want to go out, so Kim opened the crate. He stepped out and stretched and yawned like a cat, and then suddenly he stood up and punched me in the chest. An announcement calling for all toys to report to their ring came over the loudspeaker. Kim's friend waved the can of hair spray in the direction of a little white poodle shivering on a table a few yards away and exclaimed, "Oh, no! I lost track of time! Kim, I have to go! I have to spray up my miniature!"

>-<

Typically, dog contestants in a show competition begin by circling the ring together. Then each contestant poses individually for the judge, trying to look perfect as the judge lifts its lips for a dental exam, rocks its hindquarters, and strokes its back and thighs. The judge at Lehigh was a chesty, mustached man with watery eyes and a grave expression. He directed the group with looping hand signals that made him appear to be roping cattle. The Rottweiler was very handsome, and so was the giant schnauzer. I started to worry. Biff had a distracted look on his face, as if he'd forgotten something back at the house. Finally, it was Biff's turn to be examined. He snapped to attention and pranced to the center of the ring. The judge ran his hands over him and then gestured for him to circle the ring. Several people near me began clapping. A flashbulb flared. Biff held his position for a moment, finding his best angle, and then he and Kim bounded across the ring, Biff's feet moving so fast that they blurred into an oily sparkle, even though he really didn't have far to go. Kim gave him a cookie when he finished the performance, and another cookie when the judge wagged his finger at him, indicating that Biff had won again.

>-<

You can't help wondering whether Biff will experience the depressing letdown that retired competitors often face. At least he has a lot of stud work to look forward to, although William Truesdale complained to me once that the Truesdales' standards for a mate are so high that "there just aren't that many right bitches out there." Nonetheless, he and Tina are optimistic that Biff will find enough suitable mates to become one of the most influential boxer sires of all time. "We'd like to be remembered as the boxer people of the nineties," Tina said. "Anyway, we can't wait to have him home."

"We're starting to show Biff's son Rex," William said. "He's been living in Mexico, and he's a Mexican boxer champion, and now he's ready to take on the American shows. He's very promising. He has a fabulous rear."

Just then, Biff, who had been on the couch, jumped down and began pacing. "Going somewhere, honey?" Tina asked him.

He wanted to go out, so Tina opened the back door, and Biff ran into the backyard. After a few minutes, he noticed a ball on the lawn. The ball was slippery and a little too big to fit in his mouth, but he kept scrambling and trying to grab it. In the meantime, the Truesdales and I sat, stayed for a moment, fetched ourselves turkey sandwiches, and then curled up on the couch. Half an hour passed, and Biff was still happily pursuing the ball. He probably has a very short memory, but he acted as if it were the most fun he'd ever had.

The Lady and the Tigers

On January 27, 1999, a tiger walked through the suburban township of Jackson, New Jersey. According to the Tiger Information Center, a tiger's natural requirements are "some form of dense vegetative cover, sufficient large ungulate prey, and access to water." By those measures, Jackson is really not a bad place to be a tiger. The town is halfway between Manhattan and Philadelphia, tucked in a corner of Ocean County, a green respite from the silvery sweep of electric towers and petroleum tanks to the north and the bricked-in cities and mills farther south. Only 43,000 people live in Jackson, but it is a huge town, more than a hundred square miles, all of it as flat as a tabletop and splattered with ponds and little lakes. A lot of Jackson is built up with subdivisions and Wawa food markets, but the rest is still primordial New Jersey pinelands of broom sedge and pitch pine and sheep laurel and white oaks, as dense a vegetative cover as you could find anywhere, making it especially tiger-friendly. The local ungulates may not be up to what a tiger would find in its more typical habitats, like Siberia or Madhya Pradesh: in Jackson there are only pet ponies, panhandling herds of white-tailed deer, and a milk cow or two, unless you include the nearby Six Flags

Wild Safari, which is stocked with zebras and giraffes and antelopes and gazelles. And there is plenty of water all around.

Nevertheless, the Jackson tiger wasn't long for this world. A local woman preparing sandwiches for lunch saw it through her kitchen window, announced the sighting to her husband, and then called the police. The tiger slipped into the woods. At around five that afternoon, a worker at an engineering firm, the Dawson Corporation, complained to his superiors that a tiger was loitering in the company parking lot. By seven, the tiger had circled the nearby houses, drawing attention. When he later returned to the Dawson property, the tiger had gained a following: the Jackson police, state wildlife officials, and an airplane with an infrared scope. He picked his way through a few more backyards and the scrubby fields near Interstate 195, and then, unfazed by tranquilizer darts fired at him by a veterinarian, headed in the general direction of a middle school. One witness there described the animal as an "orange blur."

At last, at around nine that night, the authorities gave up on capturing him alive, and the tiger was shot dead by a wildlife official. A pathologist determined that he was a young Bengal male, nine feet long and more than four hundred pounds. Nothing on the tiger indicated where he had come from. There had been no callers to the Jackson police reporting a missing tiger. Everyone in town knew that there were tigers in Jackson—that is, everyone knew that there were fifteen tigers at Six Flags Wild Safari. But not everyone knew that there were other tigers in Jackson. In fact, there were as many as two dozen of them, belonging to a woman named Joan Byron-Marasek. Thanks to her, Jackson, New Jersey, has more tigers per square mile than almost anywhere in the world.

Joan Byron-Marasek is famously and intentionally mysterious. She rarely leaves the compound where she lives with her tigers, her dogs, and her husband, Jan, except to go to court. On videotapes of her that were made by the New Jersey Department of Environmental Protection (DEP), she looks petite and unnaturally blond, with a snub nose and a small mouth and a startled expression. Evidently, she has no Social Security number, which makes her actual age difficult to establish. She is either an oldish-looking young person or a youngish-looking old person. She has testified that she was born in 1955 and was enrolled in New York University in 1968. When it was once pointed out that this would have made her a thirteen-year-old college freshman, she admitted that she wasn't very good with dates. She worked for a while as an actress and is rumored to have appeared on Broadway in Tom Stoppard's play *Jumpers*, in which she swung naked from a chandelier. A brochure she designed for her tiger preserve shows her wearing silver boots and holding a long whip and feeding one of her tigers, Jaipur, from a baby bottle. Among the qualifications she listed on an application for a wildlife permit, Byron-Marasek said that she had been an assistant tiger trainer and a trapeze artist with the Ringling Bros. and L. N. Fleckles circuses; that she had trained with Doc Henderson, the illustrious circus veterinarian; and that she had read many books about animals, including *The Manchurian Tiger*, *The World of the Tiger*, *Wild Beasts and Their Ways*, *My Wild Life*, *They Never Talk Back*, and *Thank You, I Prefer Lions*.

➤◄

The Maraseks moved to Jackson in 1976. They bought land in a featureless and barely populated part of town near Holmeson's Corner, where Monmouth Road and Millstone Road intersect. At that time, they had five tigers—Bombay, Chinta, Iman, Jaipur, and Maya. Jackson must have seemed to be a good place to raise tigers. There was not much near the Maraseks' property except for a church and a few houses. It was the kind of place where everyone left everyone to their own business. One neighbor, a Russian Orthodox priest, ran a Christmas-tree farm next to his house. Another lived in a bungalow with a rotting cabin cruiser on concrete blocks in the front yard.

For a long time, there were no restrictions in New Jersey on owning wildlife. But in 1971, after alarmingly frequent reports of monkey bites and tiger maulings, the state began to require exotic-animal owners to register with the state and apply for a permit. According to these new regulations, ownership of exotic animals was allowed only if it could be shown that the animals were being used for educational purposes, performance, or research. When she moved to Jackson, Byron-Marasek applied for and received the necessary New Jersey permit as well as an exhibitor's license from the United States Department of Agriculture, which supervises animal welfare nationally.

After settling in with her five tigers, Byron-Marasek got six more—Bengal, Hassan, Madras, Marco, Royal, and Kizmet. She got a few of them from an animal trainer named Dave McMillan. The rest were overstock she bought from Ringling Bros. The next batch of her tigers—Kirin, Kopan, Bali, Brunei, Brahma, and Burma—came about naturally, born in the backyard after Byron-Marasek allowed her male and female tigers to commingle. Over time, more cubs were born, and more tigers were obtained, and the tiger population of Holmeson's Corner steadily increased. Byron-Marasek named her operation the Tigers Only Preservation Society. She described its mission as an effort to conserve all tiger species, to return captive tigers to the wild, and "to resolve the human/tiger conflict and create a resolution."

"I eat, sleep, and breathe tigers," Byron-Marasek told a local reporter, back when she still spoke to the press. "I never take vacations. This is my love, my passion." A friend of hers told another reporter, "Joan walks among her tigers just like Tarzan. She told me, 'I have scratches all along the sides of my rib cage and both my arms have been cut open, but they're just playing.' Now, that's what I call love."

➤◄

You know how it is—you start with one tiger, then you get another and another, then a few are born and a few die, and you start to lose track of details like exactly how many tigers you have. As soon as reports of the loose tiger in town came in, the police asked everyone in Jackson who had tigers to make sure that all of them were accounted for. There were two entities with tigers. Six Flags Wild Safari had a permit for fifteen and could account for all fifteen. The Maraseks, on the other hand, weren't sure how many they had. A group of police and state wildlife officers spent more than nine hours poking around tumbledown fences, crates, and sheds in the backyard to try to get a tally. Byron-Marasek's permit was for twenty-three tigers, but the wildlife officers could find only seventeen.

Part of the disparity could be accounted for. Over the years, some of Byron-Marasek's tigers had died. A few succumbed to old age. Muji had an allergic reaction to an injection and passed away. Diamond had to be euthanized after Marco tore off one of his legs. Also, Marco killed Hassan in a fight on Christmas Eve of 1997. Two other tigers died after eating road-killed deer that Byron-Marasek believed had been contaminated with antifreeze. But that still meant a handful of tigers were missing.

The officers filmed the visit as they were doing the tiger count.

"Joan, I have to entertain the notion that there are five cats loose in town, not just one," an officer says on the videotape.

Byron-Marasek's lawyer, Valter Must, explains to the officers that there must have been some sloppy math when she filed for the most recent permit.

The officers shift impatiently and make a few notes.

"For instance, I don't always count my kids, but I know when they're all home," Must adds.

"You don't have twenty-three of them," one of the officers says.

"Exactly," Must says.

"You'd probably know if six of your kids were missing," the officer adds.

Must nods slowly and says, "I would agree."

On the tape, Byron-Marasek, who is agitated, insists that no matter how suspicious the discrepancy between her permit and the tiger count appears, the loose tiger was not hers. No, she does not know whom it might have belonged to, either, she says. She repeatedly warns the officers not to stick their fingers into any nooks or crannies, because, well, tigers.

The officers ask to see Byron-Marasek's paperwork and her permits. She tells them that she is embarrassed to take them into her house because it is a mess. The tiger quarters look cheerless and bare, with dirt floors and chain-link fences and blue plastic tarps flapping in the January wind, as forlorn as a bankrupt construction site. During the inspection, a ruckus starts up in one of the tiger pens. Byron-Marasek, who claims to be one of the world's foremost tiger authorities, runs to see what is going on. She reappears, wild-eyed and frantic, yelling, "Help me! Help! They're going to . . . they're going to kill each other!" The officers head toward the tiger fight, but then Byron-Marasek waves at them to stop and screams, "No, not everyone! Just Larry! Just Larry!" She means Larry Herrighty, the head of the state wildlife permit division, about whom she will later say, in an interview, "The tigers hate him."

>-◄

The day of the tiger count was the first time that the state had inspected the Maraseks' property in years. New Jersey pays some attention to animal welfare—for instance, it closed the Scotch Plains Zoo in 1997 because of substandard conditions—but it says it doesn't have the resources to regularly monitor all its wildlife permit holders. Nor does it always manage to investigate complaints. There had been a number of them about the Maraseks' tigers. In 1983, someone reported that the Maraseks played loud recordings of jungle drums over a public-address system between 4 and 6 a.m., inciting their tigers to roar. In this case, the State Office of Noise Control did respond, measuring the noise level outside the compound one night and then warning Byron-Marasek that there would be monitoring in the future to make sure she complied with noise ordinances, although it doesn't appear that anyone ever came back. Multiple complaints from neighbors about strange odors emanating from the property were never investigated.

Her permit was renewed annually, even as the number of animals increased and there was no evidence that her ownership of the tigers met any of the state requirements. Anyone with the type of permit Byron-Marasek had must file information about the animals' work schedule as proof that they are being used for educational or scientific purposes. After the incident with the loose tiger, the state discovered that it had no proof that her tigers had ever performed, or that anyone had ever attended an educational program at Tigers Only. The only one of Byron-Marasek's tigers with any sort of public profile was Jaipur, who weighed more than a thousand pounds, earning him a listing in the *Guinness World Records* as the largest Siberian tiger in captivity. Later, in court, Byron-Marasek described Marco as "a great exhibit cat"—she said this by way of explaining why she continued to dote on him, even though he had killed Diamond and Hassan—but, as far as anyone could tell, Marco had never been exhibited.

Now the state was paying overdue attention to the Tigers Only Preservation Society, and it wasn't happy with what it found. In court papers, DEP investigators noted, "The applicant's tiger facility was a ramshackle arrangement with yards (compounds), chutes, runs, and shift cages . . . some of which were covered by deteriorating plywood, stockade fencing and tarps, etc. . . . . The periphery fence (along the border of the property), intended to keep out troublemakers, was down in several places. There was standing water and mud in the compound. There was mud on the applicant's tigers." The investigators also noted that there were deer carcasses scattered around the property, rat burrows, and a lot of large, angry dogs in pens near the tigers. One wandering tiger in town suddenly seemed relatively inconsequential. The inspectors now were much more concerned about the fact that Byron-Marasek had at least seventeen tigers living in what they considered sorry conditions, and that the animals were being kept not for theatrical or educational purposes but as illegal pets. Byron-Marasek, for her part, was furious about the state's inspections. "The humiliation we were forced to suffer is beyond description," she said later, reading from a prepared statement at a press conference outside her compound. "Not only did they seriously endanger the lives of our tigers—they also intentionally attempted to cut off their food supply."

The one suspicion that the state couldn't confirm was that the loose tiger had belonged to Joan Byron-Marasek. DNA tests and an autopsy were inconclusive. But whose tiger was he? Maybe he had been a drug dealer's guard animal, or a pet that had gotten out of hand and was dropped off in Jackson in the hope that the Tiger Lady would take him in. There were the conspiracy theorists in town who believed that the tiger had belonged to Six Flags, and that his escape was covered up because the park is the biggest employer and the primary attraction in the area. In the end, however, the tiger was simply relegated to the annals of suburban oddities—a lost soul, doomed to an unhappy end, whose provenance will never be known.

>-◄

It is not hard to buy a tiger. At the time of the tiger's walk through Jackson, only eight states prohibited the ownership of wild animals. Three states had no restrictions whatsoever, and the rest had regulations that ranged from trivial to modest and were barely enforced. Exotic-animal auction houses and animal markets thrive in the Midwest and the Southeast, where wildlife laws are the most relaxed. Dealers have also proliferated on the Internet. One recent afternoon, I browsed a website called Hunts Exotics, where I could have placed an order for baby spider monkeys ($6,500 each, including delivery); an adult female two-toed sloth ($2,200); a northern cougar female with blue eyes, who was advertised as "tame on bottle"; a black-capped capuchin monkey, needing dental work ($1,500); a paca; a porcupine; or two baby tigers "with white genes" ($1,800 each). From there I linked to more tiger sites—Mainely Felids and Wildcat Hideaway and N.O.A.H. Feline Conservation Center—and to pages for prospective owners titled "I Want a Cougar!" and "Are

You Sure You Want a Monkey?" It is so easy to get a tiger, in fact, that wildlife experts estimate that there are at least fifteen thousand pet tigers in this country—more than seven times the number of registered Irish setters or Dalmatians.

One reason that tigers are readily available is that they breed easily in captivity. There are only about six thousand tigers left in the wild, and three tiger subspecies have become extinct in just the last sixty years. In zoos, though, tigers are abundant, plus they have babies all the time. The result is thousands of "surplus tigers." In the zoo economy, these are animals that are no longer worth keeping, because there are too many of them or because they're old—zoo visitors prefer baby animals to mature ones. Many zoos began breeding excessively during the seventies and eighties, when they realized that baby animals drew big crowds. In turn, the trade in exotic pets thrived because zoos sold their older, unwanted animals to dealers and game ranches and unaccredited zoos once they were no longer young and luring audiences. In 1999, the San Jose *Mercury News* reported that many of the best zoos in the country, including the San Diego Zoo and the Denver Zoological Gardens, regularly disposed of their surplus animals through dealers. Some zoo directors were so disturbed by the practice that they opted to euthanize their surplus animals rather than use dealers to dispense with them. According to the *Mercury News*, the director of the Detroit Zoo euthanized two healthy Siberian tigers he didn't have room for, because he didn't want to risk them ending up as mistreated pets or on hunting ranches. Sometimes dealers buy surplus animals just for butchering. An adult tiger, alive, costs as little as $200 or $300. A tiger pelt sells for $2,000, and body parts, which are commonly used in aphrodisiacs, can bring five times as much.

>-<

Between 1990 and 2000, Jackson's human population increased by almost a third. Cranberry bogs and chicken farms began yielding to condominiums and center-hall colonials. It was probably inevitable that something would come to limn the town's changing character, its passage from a rural place to something else entirely. It was becoming a bedroom community attached to nowhere in particular, with clots of crowdedness amid a sort of essential emptiness; a place exploding with new people and new roads that didn't connect to anything and fresh, clean sidewalks of concrete that still looked damp; the kind of place made possible by highways and telecommuting, and made necessary by the high cost of living in bigger cities, and made desirable, ironically, by the area's quickly vanishing rural character. A tiger in town had, in a roundabout way, made all of this clear.

In 1997, a model house was built on the open property immediately east of the Maraseks' compound. In the next two years thirty more houses went up there. The land had been dense, brambly woods. It was wiped clean before the construction started. The development was named, unironically, the Preserve. The new landscaping trees were barely tooth-picks, held in place with rubber collars and guy wires, and the houses looked as if they'd just been unwrapped and set out, like lawn orna-ments. They were airy and tall and had showy entrances and double-car garages and amenities like Jacuzzis and wet bars and recessed lighting. The average price for one was around $300,000. They were the kind of houses that betokened a certain amount of achievement—the promotion to company vice president, say. The purchasers were people who were disconcerted to note, as they stood outside playing catch with their kids or pampering their lawns, that on certain mornings dozens of buzzards lined up on their roofs, staring hungrily at the Maraseks' backyard.

"If someone had told me there were tigers here, I would have never bought the house," one neighbor, Kevin Wingler, said not long ago. Where Wingler's lawn ends, the Maraseks' property begins. Wingler is a car collector, and when we spoke, he was in his garage, tinkering with a classic red Corvette. He was irate when he learned that the Department of Sanitation had been bringing road-killed deer to Byron-Marasek for years, providing her with tiger food. It was probably those deer carcasses that interested the buzzards. "I love animals," Wingler said, wiping his hands on his jeans. "We get season passes every year for the Six Flags safari, and whenever I'm out I always pet all the cows and all the pigs, and I think tigers are majestic and beautiful and everything. But we broke our asses to buy this house, and it's just not right. I could have bought in any development! I even had a contract elsewhere, but the builder coaxed me into buying this house." He licked his finger and dabbed at a spot on the dashboard and laughed. "This is just so weird," he said. "You'd think this would be happening in Arkansas, or something."

I drove through the Preserve and then out to a road on the other side of the Maraseks' land. This was an old road, one of the few that had been there when the Maraseks moved in, and the houses were forty or fifty years old and weathered. The one near the corner belonged to the owner of a small trucking company. He told me that he had helped Joan Byron-Marasek clean up her facilities after the state inspection. "I knew she was here when I moved in fifteen years ago," he said. "Tigers nearby? I don't care. You hear a roar here and there. It's not a big concern of mine to hear a roar now and then. The stench in the summer was unbearable, though." He said he didn't think that the wandering tiger was one of hers, because her tigers were always dirty and the tiger that was shot looked clean and fit. He said that Byron-Marasek had come by his house a few years ago with a petition to try to stop the housing development. He didn't sign it. He sounded ambivalent nonetheless. "The new neighbors, they're not very neighborly," he said. "They're over there in their fancy houses. She's been here a lot longer than they have." Still, he didn't want to get involved. "Those are Joan's own private kitty cats," he said, lighting a cigarette. "That's her business. I've got my own life to worry about."

>--<

The tiger that had walked through Jackson for less than eight hours had been an inscrutable and unaccountable visitor, and, like many such visitors, he disturbed things. A meeting was held at city hall soon after he was shot. More than a hundred people showed up. A number of them came dressed in tiger costumes. They demanded to know why the roving tiger had been killed rather than captured, and what the fate of Byron-Marasek's tigers would be. Somehow the meeting devolved into a shouting match between people from the new Jackson, who insisted that Byron-Marasek's tigers be removed immediately, and the old guard, who suggested that anyone who knew the town—by implication, the only people who really deserved to be living there—was aware that there were tigers in Holmeson's Corner. If the tigers bothered the residents in the Preserve so much, why had they been stupid enough to move in?

Soon after the meeting, the state refused to renew Byron-Marasek's wildlife permit, citing inadequate animal husbandry, failure to show theatrical or educational grounds for possessing potentially dangerous wildlife, and grievously flawed record-keeping. The township then invoked its domestic animal ordinances, demanding that Byron-Marasek also get rid of some of her thirty-odd dogs or else apply for a formal kennel license. Shortly after this, the homeowners in the Preserve banded together and sued the Preserve's developer for consumer fraud, claiming that he had withheld information about the tigers in his off-site disclosure statement, which is required to notify prospective buyers of things nearby that might affect the resale value of a house like toxic-waste dumps and prisons. The neighborhood group also sued Byron-Marasek for creating a nuisance with both her tigers and her dogs.

Here was where the circus began. It was not the circus where Joan Byron-Marasek had once worked and where she had developed the recipe for "Joan's Circus Secret," which is the concoction that she feeds her tigers, but the legal circus, the amazing three-ring spectacle that went on in Jackson for several years. The state denied Byron-Marasek's request to renew her permit, so she could no longer legally keep her tigers. She requested an administrative review, but the permit denial was upheld. She appealed to a higher court. She was ordered to get rid of the animals while awaiting the results of her appeal of the permit case. She appealed that order. "Tigers are extremely fragile animals," she said at a press conference. "Tigers will die if removed by someone else. If they are allowed to take our tigers, this will be a tiger holocaust." Byron-Marasek won that argument, which allowed her to keep the tigers during her permit appeal, as long as she agreed to certain conditions, including taking measures to prevent the tigers from breeding. Nevertheless, during the next couple of years as the court case dragged on, two of her tigers gave birth to cubs, which she hid from state inspectors for several weeks. She declared that the state was trying to destroy her life's work. Through her Tigers Only website, she supplied form letters for her supporters to send to state officials and to the DEP that read:

Dear Senator:

I am a supporter of the Tigers Only Preservation Society and Ms. Joan Byron-Marasek in her fight to keep her beautiful tigers in their safe haven in Jackson, New Jersey. . . . We should all be delighted with the fact that these tigers live together in peaceful harmony with their environment and one another right here in New Jersey. If anything, the T.O.P.S. tigers should be revered as a State treasure, and as such, we citizens of New Jersey should all proudly and enthusiastically participate in this State-wide endeavor to keep the T.O.P.S. tigers in New Jersey.

If we are successful . . . future generations of constituents will be eternally grateful for your efforts in keeping these magnificent creatures living happily in our midst for all to enjoy.

In the meantime, legal proceedings stalled while Byron-Marasek changed attorneys five times. Her case moved up the legal chain until it reached the state's appellate court. There, in December 2001, the original verdict was finally and conclusively upheld. Byron-Marasek was denied, once and for all, the right to keep tigers in New Jersey.

The Byron-Marasek case reminded some people of the 1995 landmark lawsuit in Oregon against Vickie Kittles, who lived in a school bus with 115 dogs. Wherever Kittles stopped with her wretched menagerie, local officials gave her a tank of gas and instructions to get out of town. She ended up in Oregon, where she was finally arrested. There she faced a district attorney named Joshua Marquis. Marquis had made his name as an animal advocate by prosecuting the killer of Victor the Lobster, the twenty-five-pound mascot of Oregon's Seaside Aquarium. Victor had been abducted from his tank. When the thief was apprehended, he threw Victor to the ground, breaking his shell. No lobster veterinarian could be found quickly enough to help, and Victor died three days later from his injuries. Marquis was able to persuade a jury to convict the lobster abductor not only of theft but of criminal mischief as well. In the case of Kittles, Marquis decided to prosecute her on grounds of animal neglect. Kittles contended that she had the right to live with her dogs in any way she chose. Marquis argued that the dogs, which got no exercise and no veterinary care and were evidently suffering, did not choose to live in a school bus. Vickie Kittles was convicted, and her dogs were sent to foster homes around the country.

The Kittles case was the first prominent lawsuit in the nation against an "animal hoarder"—that is, a person who engages in the pathological collecting of animals. Tiger ladies are somewhat rare, but there are cat ladies and bird men all over the country, and often they end up in stories with headlines like "201 Cats Pulled from Home" and "Pets Saved from Horror Home" and "Cat Lover's Neighbors Tired of Feline Fiasco." A study published by the Hoarding of Animals Research Consortium says that more than two-thirds of hoarders are females, and most often they hoard cats, although they have been known to hoard dogs, birds, farm animals, and, in one case, beavers. The median number of animals that hoarders own is thirty-nine, but many have more than a hundred. Hoarders, according to the consortium, have a constellation of problems, including "concentrating and staying on track with any management plan."

On the other hand, animal hoarders seem to have boundless energy and focus when it comes to fighting in court to keep their pets. Even after Byron-Marasek lost her final appeal, she devised another way to frustrate the state's efforts to remove her tigers. The Department of Environmental Protection had found homes for the tigers at the Wild Animal Orphanage in San Antonio, Texas, and come up with a plan for moving them there via the orphanage's Humane Train. In early January 2002, Superior Court Judge Eugene Serpentelli held a hearing on the matter. The Tiger Lady came to court wearing a dark-green pantsuit and square-toed shoes and carrying a heavy black briefcase. She was edgy and preoccupied and waved off anyone who approached her except for a local radio host who had trumpeted her cause on his show and a slim young man who huddled with her during breaks. The young man was as circumspect as she was, politely declining to say whether he was a contributor to the Tigers Only Preservation Society or a fellow tiger owner or perhaps someone with his own beef with the DEP.

Throughout the hearing, Byron-Marasek dipped into her briefcase and pulled out sheets of paper and handwritten notes and pages down-loaded from the Internet, and passed them to her latest lawyer, whom she had retained the day before. Her argument was that the Wild Animal Orphanage was not a suitable alternative home for her tigers. The material documented infractions for which the orphanage had been cited by the USDA over the years. These included storing outdated bags of monkey chow in an un-air-conditioned shed and leaving the carcass of a tiger in a meat freezer until its eventual necropsy and disposal. None of the infractions were serious and none remained unresolved, but they raised enough questions about the fitness of Wild Animal Orphanage to delay the inevitable once again, and Judge Serpentelli adjourned to allow Byron-Marasek more time to present an alternate plan. "Throughout this period of time, I've made it clear that the court had no desire to inflict on Mrs. Marasek or the tigers any hardship," the judge announced. "But the tigers must be removed. I have no discretion on the question of whether they should be removed, just how."

Before the state acts, however, there is a good chance that the Tiger Lady will have taken matters into her own hands. Last fall, in an interview with the *Asbury Park Press*, she said that she was in the process of "buying land elsewhere"—she seemed to think it unwise to name the state—and suggested that she and her dogs and her tigers might be leaving New Jersey for good. Typically, people who have disputes with the authorities about their animal collections move from one jurisdiction to another as they run into legal difficulties. If they do eventually lose their animals, they almost always resurface somewhere else with new ones. According to researchers, recidivism among animal hoarders is close to 100 percent. In the not-too-distant future, in some other still-rural corner of America, people may begin to wonder what smells so strange when the wind blows from a certain direction, and whether they actually could have heard a roar in the middle of the night, and whether there could be any truth to the rumors that there was a lady with a bunch of tigers in town.

➤◄

I had visited Jackson countless times, and circled the Maraseks' property, and walked up and down the sidewalks in the Preserve, but I had never seen a single tiger. I had even driven up to the Maraseks' front gate once or twice and peered through it. I could see some woolly white dogs scuffling behind a wire fence, and I could see tarps and building materials scattered around the house, but no tigers, no flash of orange fur, nothing. I wanted to see one of the animals, to assure myself that they really existed.

One afternoon, I parked across from the Winglers' and walked past their garage, where Kevin was still monkeying around with his Corvette, and then across their backyard and past where their lawn ended, where the woods thickened and the ground was springy from the decades' worth of pine needles that have rained down, and I followed a tangy, slightly sour smell that I guessed was tiger, although I don't think I'd ever smelled tigers before. There was a chain-link fence up ahead. I stopped and waited. A minute passed and nothing happened. A minute more, and then a tiger walked past on the other side of the fence, its huge head lowered and its tail barely twitching, the black stripes of its coat crisscrossed with late-day light, its slow, heavy tread making no sound at all. It reached the end of the fence and paused, and turned back the other way, and then it was gone.

Riding High

The things they carry are Band-Aids, bullets, and cardboard cases of Meals Ready to Eat; also sand for making concrete, Stinger missiles, rucksacks, machine guns, body armor, blankets, boots, Kevlar helmets. In another setting—someplace other than a battlefield in Afghanistan, that is—the load lashed to a mule's sawbuck saddle would be entirely different. It would consist of hunting supplies, perhaps, or tents, or cookstoves, strung together by a single long piece of rope, looped and knotted and then cinched tight into an assemblage of odd shapes and volumes. A mule is entirely nonpartisan about the contents of its load. It will carry as much as three hundred pounds, seven hours a day, twenty days straight, without complaint, strolling along under the huge, heavy cargo as if it were a bag of balloons.

On the other hand, a mule knows its limits. It is characteristic of the breed to have an inviolable commitment to self-preservation, which is often misinterpreted as stubbornness. In truth, it is probably a form of genius. A horse will eat until it founders and dies. A mule, though, will eat only as much as it can hold, even if it happens upon an open bin of oats. A horse can be enticed to gallop over a cliff to its death. A mule will do no such thing. In 1942, the U.S. Army was researching ways to deliver mules to combat zones. Someone thought that teaching the animals to skydive would be a good way to accomplish this. As an experiment, twelve mules were fitted with parachutes and taken up in a cargo plane. The first six, caught by surprise, were pushed out the door and immediately fell to their deaths. The next six survived. This is because they figured out what was going on and absolutely refused to go near the door.

The mule's commitment to survival is interesting in a Darwinian context, because mules—the hybrid result of mating a male donkey with a female horse—have an uneven number of chromosomes and are sterile. Every mule, then, is sui generis. It can leave no legacy beyond itself. There can be no radiating gene pool to mark its visit to this world. It is as if each mule knows that it has one shot at being here on earth, and realizes that risky behavior, such as jumping out of an airplane at ten thousand feet, would interfere with that. Even the sheer persistence of the breed seems a stroke of genius. Since a horse and a donkey rarely mate on their own, they have to be encouraged to do so by an interested party. In other words, mules are essentially man-made. It has been a successful invention. In fact, mules are probably the most successful and most enduring of all man-made animal hybrids, with beefalo coming in a distant second.

Mules have been so easily replaced by machines, and are so outdated, that it would not have been surprising if they had disappeared altogether. Yet something has always intervened to save them. The recently renewed interest in old ways of farming, for instance, has called for mules. War in a place like Afghanistan demands mules, an animal with sure feet and an instinct for survival, to traverse mountain roads. So once again, against all odds, the mule has managed to find its way back into favor.

➤◄

The Marine Corps Mountain Warfare Training Center, in Bridgeport, California, is where American and foreign military personnel learn how to use pack animals in war. The center sits at the base of the Sierra Nevada, terrain that is said to be quite similar to Afghanistan's Hindu Kush. The shadows cast by the Sierras are so deep and chilly that there is often ice on the road in late summer. When I visited recently, snow had socked in the training center, so the mules, instructors, and students had decamped to a warmer, flatter army depot an hour south, in Hawthorne, Nevada. A group of marines from Camp Pendleton, California, who were preparing to deploy to Afghanistan this fall, had just begun the two-week animal-packing course. First they had watched PowerPoint presentations on mule anatomy, personality, and maintenance. The day I arrived, they were practicing tying the half hitch and the box hitch for securing loads to the animals' saddles, and working on what Tony Parkhurst, a training specialist who runs the program, likes to call the human-mule interface.

A few of the marines, holding long coils of rope, were standing near a big sorrel mule named Edgar, who had a long, soft nose and mild eyes but the reputation of being a kicker.

"Private, ever work with a mule?" Parkhurst asked one of the young men.

"Negative, sir. I'm from the suburbs, sir."

"You, Private?" Parkhurst asked the next marine. "Ever work with a mule? A donkey? A llama? A goat?"

"Negative, sir. I'm a surfer."

It turned out that none of the marines had ever been near a mule before. None of them, except one, even had a casual acquaintance with a horse. This is typical of the troops that take the animal-packing course. There was a time when a young man without mule experience would have been the exception rather than the rule. As recently as 1930, there were more than five million mules in the United States, and mules were active in the military until December 1956, when the last two army mules, 583R and 9YLL, otherwise known as Trotter and Hambone, were deactivated.

Among the first mules in the United States were a herd belonging to George Washington. They were sired by an Andalusian donkey named Royal Gift, which Washington had received from the king of Spain.

Washington believed that a good mule was essential to successful agriculture. In his estimation, mules were preferable to donkeys, which were too ornery, and to horses, which were too fragile. Washington was so devoted to mules that he set out to breed "a race [of mules] of extraordinary goodness." He always used a female horse and a male donkey for his mules. (If you breed in the reverse—a male horse and a female donkey—the offspring is called a hinny. It is widely believed that hinnies inherit the worst of both parents, so they are far less popular than mules.)

Washington's enthusiasm for mules was contagious, and soon farmers were breeding mules by the thousands in the United States. For the next 150 years, mules did every sort of farm job. They pulled plows, dragged carriages, hauled loads, carried riders. A mule was a solid investment, happy to labor for a decade or two in exchange, as William Faulkner once wrote, "for the privilege of kicking you once."

Before the military was mechanized, mounted troops rode horses and used mules for moving supplies and equipment. Mules were prized almost more than horses were because they ate less, broke down less often, and could carry more. In 1855, the army undertook a brief, ill-fated experiment at a post in Texas, using camels to do the jobs usually assigned to mules. The camels proved superior to mules in terms of strength, but otherwise, they were a disaster. They were vicious, tended to cough up foul-smelling chunks of food, and made horrible groans and roars that terrified the horses. In *Shavetails and Bell Sharps*, a comprehensive history of military mules, Emmett Essin wrote that mules were valued because of their steadiness and efficiency. Only rarely do they require some special attention. For instance, light-colored mules were sometimes dyed dark brown so that they would be less easily spotted by the enemy. And on occasion, unusually noisy mules had to be surgically "de-brayed." Mules are what military people call a "force multiplier," that is, they double or triple what troops without mules can do. Thousands of mules served as force multipliers in the Civil War and in both World Wars, as well as in conflicts in the Philippines, Burma, and Greece.

The 1950s marked a low point for mules. Quite simply, mechanization did them in. Trucks, jeeps, and helicopters replaced mules in the military, while tractors replaced them on the farm. Horses, which had also been made obsolete by machinery, were able to transition from being kept for utility to being a hobby. By 1950 the number of horses in the United States had dropped almost 75 percent from the early part of the century. But racing and riding horses found an audience, and the horse population started to grow again. Mules—not fast, not glamorous—were another matter. By 1950, just two million mules existed in the United States.

Ed Ceaser, a robust, round-faced former master sergeant in the army who had completed multiple tours for the U.S. Foreign Service in Asia, arrived in Sumner County, Tennessee, in the early 1980s. At the time, the mule business was in the doldrums. This was to his advantage, since his company, American Export Group, needed to buy a lot of mules, to satisfy a purchase order from the U.S. Army. Ceaser contacted Hub Reese Jr., a member of one of the biggest mule-trading families in Tennessee. (Hub's grandfather Rufus Sr. started the business in the 1920s in Nashville.) After a quick negotiation, Ceaser arranged to buy 1,200 mules from Reese. The animals would be shipped from Tennessee to the army base at Fort Campbell, Kentucky. Then they would be flown to Islamabad, Pakistan, and trucked to Peshawar. From there, they would be taken to the border with Afghanistan and handed over to mujahideen forces who were fighting the Soviet invasion of Afghanistan. The mujahideen would use the mules to transport supplies and equipment. Most important, the mules would carry the cumbersome anti-aircraft missiles that were effective against the Soviet Air Force up the Hindu Kush along the narrow, cragged mountain trails.

Every mule person in Tennessee seems to have a story about the Afghanistan mule shipments. Reese didn't have 1,200 mules on hand, so he needed to round them up, and everyone in the area either sold Reese a few of their mules or helped persuade someone they knew to part with one. It was tough sledding, because even by the standards of a depressed mule market, the amount Ceaser was offering was measly. Lack of profits notwithstanding, a lot of the mule people in Sumner County enjoyed the attention the big transaction brought Reese. He was said to be an old-fashioned mule man, the sort of irrepressible guy who could talk you into buying a mule whether or not you had any intention of owning one. He was well loved but soon mourned: not long after fulfilling his contract to provide 1,200 mules to American Export Group, Reese developed lung cancer, smoked his way through chemotherapy, and died. Many people in the area became good friends with the jovial Ceaser, who has also since died. As chummy as Ceaser was, no one really knew what, exactly, his American Export Group did, but it was generally assumed to be a front for the CIA.

The only specification regarding the mules in Ceaser's contract was that the animals had to be healthy and a minimum of fourteen hands high—fifty-six inches—at the withers. That was a lot of mule for the money, so Reese saw to it that they were measured with a stainless-steel ruler that happened to be sunk a few inches into the ground. "Ed told us the mules had to be fourteen hands," George Coles, a Tennessee veterinarian who examined the mules and flew overseas with the first load, told me recently. "But he didn't tell us how we were supposed to measure them, now, did he?"

The first load consisted of 114 mules and one spotted horse, which was to be a gift for the Pakistani general who met the plane in Islamabad. The animals left Tennessee in October of 1987. As Coles recalls, they were first trucked to Fort Campbell, then were to be loaded onto a Boeing 747 that had been gutted and filled with sawdust to accommodate them. When Coles arrived at the base, he discovered that the nine stable hands who were supposed to care for the animals on the flight had gotten drunk on rum-and-Cokes the night before and were passed out in the sawdust. When Coles first saw them, they were so inert that he thought they were dead. The mules, on the other hand, were anything but inert:

They were absolutely kick-the-doors-down wild. "Let me tell you, these were not trained mules," Coles said. "No, they most definitely were not." He said that the intractability of the mules was no surprise to him. He knew that some people had used Reese's deal as an opportunity to sell off their most unmanageable animals. At last, the stable hands shook themselves awake, the mules were loaded, and the plane took off. It stopped to refuel in Belgium. When customs officials stepped into the plane and got a look at the mules, the sawdust, and the disheveled men, they skipped the inspection and waved them on.

This was at a delicate moment for Pakistan with regard to Afghanistan. President Zia-ul-Haq of Pakistan was being pressured by the opposition and by the press to get out of the Afghanistan fray. The Pakistanis were not thrilled about this incoming load of animals because they were destined for Afghanistan. Eventually they agreed to allow the flight to land in Islamabad, but, Coles says, they insisted that the plane be a civilian aircraft rather than a military one, and that it land at night and be gone by daybreak, to avoid being conspicuous. It was a moonlit scramble to get the animals off the plane in Islamabad and onto the trucks. The Pakistanis grew even more unhappy about hosting the subsequent shipments of mules. They allowed only the briefest amount of time on the ground and refused to allow the stable hands to muck out the plane in Islamabad, insisting that the mules' manure be flown back to the United States.

Coles, who has had a veterinary practice in Sumner County since 1975, is rumpled and good-natured, with a thatch of gray hair and an ambling way with a tale. When I stopped in to see him at his clinic, he had just finished surgery on a kitten, and was in the midst of planning a mule ride into the Tennessee hills with some friends, paying particular attention to which of the riders would be bringing the moonshine. He told me about getting off the plane in Islamabad and bumping along the bad roads to Peshawar and back again, and then heading home to Tennessee to help Reese prepare the next load. He said that he had always wondered what became of the mules. He shrugged and said, "You never know. They were too valuable to eat, though." There were nine more shipments from Tennessee to Islamabad. The last one was in 1990.

The plan for the mules was at least partly logical. The mujahideen needed pack animals to carry supplies and ordnance into the mountains, and the Soviets had placed a high priority on destroying the existing mujahideen caravans. The Tennessee mules were twice the size and the strength of the little gray donkeys that are common throughout Afghanistan. What hadn't been factored in was the mules' unruliness—they really were not Tennessee's finest—or the fact that the mules were unaccustomed to Afghanistan's altitude, food, water, and indigenous equine diseases. When Walid Majroh, a mujahideen commander, came to collect the mules, he was appalled. "I was amazed by their size," he told me not long ago. "They were very big, very muscular animals. But just having a mule isn't enough. You need them to be trained, and you need a handler. And you need them to be adapted to the environment. These mules? We couldn't even put a harness on them. We couldn't get them to walk. And we couldn't get them to stand still." After some time, a handful of the animals were calmed down and inducted into service, but Majroh assumes that most of them died within a few months, wiped out by local diseases. As for the rest, he isn't certain. "We sent them back to Peshawar," Majroh said, "and then, who knows?" To this day, he finds the mule shipments one of life's great mysteries. "I sometimes wonder if it was a Reagan stimulus package for Tennessee," he said.

>-<

All in all, the Soviet invasion of Afghanistan was good for the Tennessee mule economy, subtracting enough mules from the population to boost the value of the remaining supply. Then came more good news. The Amish population in the United States was exploding, growing more than 80 percent between 1992 and 2008. Many Amish are farmers. The simple, unautomated lifestyle espoused by their religion does not include such assets as a John Deere 5000 Series tractor with a four-cylinder PowerTech engine, but does warmly embrace mules. Hub Reese Jr.'s cousin Dickie Reese owns Reese Brothers Mule Company with his brother Rufus. Their auctions used to be packed to the rafters with chesty, tobacco-chewing farmers in Carhartt overalls. Then the crowds thinned out to a few nostalgic locals. Soon, though, the auctions began attracting groups of Amish from communities in Pennsylvania, Missouri, and West Virginia, solemn and studious in their wide black hats, looking for six- or eight-mule teams. By the mid-nineties, Amish farmers were buying almost 80 percent of the work mules at the Reese Brothers' auctions. Their preference for large, heavy-boned animals made its mark: breeders began chasing after the biggest male donkeys and mating them with Percheron and Belgian draft mares to produce huge mules for the Amish market.

I went to the Reese Brothers' November auction in 2009 and sat in the auctioneer's booth with Dickie Reese and J. B. Driver, the auctioneer. The auction is held three times a year, in a creaky old stockyard in Dickson, Tennessee, a few miles off the interstate, behind a sprawling Travel-Centers of America truck stop. I stopped in the parking lot before going inside and watched two young women easing their mules between rows of horse trailers and vendors selling harnesses, saddle pads, and mule-themed T-shirts. The young women's mules were copper-colored, sleek, and decked out in hobnailed Western saddles, and they loped through the parking lot with a smooth, lazy gait.

Knee-replacement surgery seems to have given another boost to the mule business. Reese guessed that more than half the mules he sells these days are used as riding animals. Most of them are purchased by middle-aged pleasure riders, many of them women, many with one or two re-tooled knees, who have discovered that mules provide a smoother ride than horses and are thus easier on the knees. Plus, mules are simpler to care for than horses, which makes them even better for a late-in-life rider. A nice, well-trained riding mule costs about $2,500, which can be amortized over the twenty-five or so years of its usable life. It's a better investment than a horse, which may have only fifteen good years and probably costs more to begin with. Also, mule people have long maintained that mules are better than horses because they're smarter. This opinion might have begun as folklore, but a 2008 study of mule cognition at the University of Sussex found that mules do understand things better than either horses or donkeys and are better at following instructions. The riding-mule hobby has been growing steadily in recent times. A mule could only have dreamed of competing in a horse show in the past, but now it is not unusual for mules to be shown alongside horses, even in the refined world of dressage.

There were some four hundred mules at the November auction I attended. It was a healthy offering that included a few dozen yearlings, still wide-eyed and whiskery; a score of experienced teams, with high-gloss rumps and bunchy muscles; and dozens of riding mules, their ears waggling as they trotted around the stockyard ring. One guy was selling a mule that he had bought on the Internet only to discover that it didn't suit his purposes. "If you want a garden mule, a good, honest mule, this is your mule," he said as part of his sales pitch. "He's just too small for me." He added that he already had ninety-two mules and that he "played with them and plowed with them." He admitted that he really, truly had enough mules but that he couldn't resist a good-looking one, which is how he ended up buying this one on the Internet. "I'll tell you what it is when you start collecting mules," he said, smiling, as he stroked the pendulous lower lip of the too-small mule. "It's a goddamn disease."

Dickie Reese told me that recently the average price of a mule at the auctions had dropped. The recession had sucked away some of the discretionary income spent on mule-keeping, and some people at the auction were there to get rid of animals they no longer could afford to keep—although, as Reese said more than once, having a couple of mules was still a lot cheaper than having a bass boat. Some mule people grumbled about the closing of equine slaughterhouses in the United States because it had depressed the price of mules. The last equine slaughterhouse in the country, which was in DeKalb, Illinois, ceased operation in 2007. When the slaughterhouses were still operating, an average-size mule, weighing nine hundred pounds, was worth at least thirty-nine cents a pound as meat. The meat was exported to Europe and Japan, where it was in high demand. Opponents of horse and mule slaughter say that the closing of the market will encourage more responsible breeding, now that an unwanted animal has no market value, and that it may also discourage horse thieves, who could always count on selling a stolen horse to a slaughterhouse. Those who complain about the closing note that now there is no floor on prices, and more animals will be abandoned or neglected if owners can't afford to keep them. Instead of sending them to a slaughterhouse, they might just turn them loose to fend for themselves, which never goes well. Reese told me that if people bring their mules to the auctions and don't get a bidder, they sometimes take off and leave their mules behind—they can't countenance the cost of hauling them back home, let alone continue feeding them. Reese always dreads walking around the barn when the auction ends, knowing he is likely to find an abandoned mule or two. He tries to get people to take in the animals, but he doesn't always succeed.

As the auction started, I wandered around the stalls, reveling in the soft sounds of snuffling and chewing and the occasional thump of a hoof as it hit the wood floor, and then I made my way over to the main ring. A pair of brawny black mules, fretting and pacing, had just been bought by an Amish father and son sitting in the front row of the grandstand, the gavel smacking down at $2,650. Next in the ring was a chestnut mule with a bristling blond mane and the sleepy, watchful gaze of a bank guard. In the stands, the crowd was stirring. No one bid: Rufus Reese, who is square-built and ruddy-faced, grabbed the microphone from the auctioneer. "Take a look at her, boys!" he boomed. "She's a nice mule. Her name is Muley." The crowd quieted. "This is a broke mule," Reese went on. "If you don't like your mother-in-law, don't put her on this mule, because she'll love this mule and she'll move in with you." Laughter. A hand went up, then another, and another; the price teetered around

$625 and then settled there, and the auctioneer slammed his gavel and shouted, "Sold!"

≻—≺

The animal-packing course at the Marine Corps Mountain Warfare Training Center was launched in 1983, as an experiment. It had been three decades since Trotter and Hambone, the last army mules, had retired, and four decades since the army's pack-animal field manual had been written, but many people still believed that mules had a place in the military. However misbegotten the Tennessee shipments to Afghanistan had turned out to be, it was undeniable that pack animals were essential in certain kinds of terrain. The packing course taught troops how to load, handle, and take care of the animals, and also how to go about buying or renting good mules or donkeys from local breeders, which was determined to be preferable to bringing them from home. The course was offered alongside other specialty programs at the center, such as wilderness medicine and mountain-scout sniper training. It had been mandated to be offered only for five years, but it was so popular that it continued beyond its original expiration date, and the Department of Defense recently established it as a formal offering through the Training and Education Command. Animal packing was largely a hypothetical exercise until 2001, when the United States began Operation Enduring Freedom in Afghanistan. Animals were involved from the start. Special Forces soldiers on horseback helped capture the city of Mazar-i-Sharif in late 2001. Other American troops made their way into the mountains leading mule trains.

Tony Parkhurst, who has been running the packing course on and off since 1988, expanded the stable to its present size of twenty-nine mules, five donkeys, and eleven horses. He keeps all three types of equines on hand so that troops are familiar with the variations in their build and disposition and are prepared for whatever pack animals they might encounter when they're deployed. The mules—imperturbable, alert, stalwart—are Parkhurst's preferred classroom tools. The training course runs nine times a year and can accommodate forty-eight students in a session. It is fully booked with marines, army troops, and NATO soldiers throughout the year. In 2004, an updated field manual, FM 3-05.213, *Special Forces Use of Pack Animals*, was issued, after a lag of forty years. The U.S. military was back in the mule business.

The afternoon that I visited the training center, the troops from Camp Pendleton were practicing balancing their loads, using stacks of milk cartons, cardboard boxes, and empty tubes from AT4 anti-tank rockets, which are forty inches long and weigh fifteen pounds fully armed, and are an awkward shape to settle against square boxes. The next day, they planned to hike into the mountains with the mules, set up camp, wake at midnight, practice loading the mules in the dark, and then attempt to recover Recon Randy, a 180-pound rubber dummy who would stand in for a dead body. During the class, the mules—Edgar the kicker, Arlo, Kate, Bill, and Karen—endured the tugging and hitching with a weary patience. Parkhurst buys his mules from Warren Johnson, an outfitter in Montana, who seasons and steadies them before selling them. "Some mules are still snortier than others," Parkhurst told me, "but from Johnson I get a product that's pretty user-friendly." Parkhurst said that his favorite part of the job is watching the troops get used to the animals. "They transform from '*Oh, God, he's gonna stomp on me*' to hugging on them and loving them and wanting to take them home." After a moment, he added, "Anyway, when people are shooting at you, anything you can attach to emotionally means something."

When I got home, I spoke by phone to a number of military people stationed in Afghanistan who were using pack animals regularly. They use donkeys, mostly, because even though there are mules in Afghanistan, donkeys are still more common. One of the people I spoke to was a captain working with a provincial reconstruction team in the Panjshir Valley. He said that there was authorization for his unit to rent pack animals when they were "essential to mission accomplishment." He told me,

"The category on the requisition sheet is *Animals for Missions*." Then he interrupted himself and said, "No, the exact terminology is *Live Animals for Training Aids and Cargo and Personnel Transport*." The captain was impressed by the animals' endless composure—how they just keep going, carrying whatever needs to be carried, trudging up and over the ragged ridges, then turning around and walking back, to be loaded and sent on their way again.

Little Wing

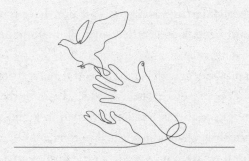

On a bright, breezy Saturday not long ago, Sedona Murphy gave her homing pigeons away. Earlier that morning, the birds had flown around the neighborhood, looping over the shaggy old trees and the peaked rooftops of South Boston before returning to their home, a gray shed in Sedona's backyard. The birds then toddled obligingly into a wooden case. These were racing birds, accustomed to being crated and carried, so the close quarters were nothing new, but they had no way of knowing that this was the last time they would ever fly free.

Sedona was giving the pigeons away because her family was moving, and the pigeons would not assent to the move. No matter how much nicer the yard would be at the Murphys' new house in Southborough, a suburb west of Boston, the pigeons would always consider home to be the narrow wooden house on East Fifth Street that the Murphys were leaving behind. If the birds moved to Southborough and ever managed to get out of their coop, they would race back to East Fifth Street, believing they were heading home. Once in a while, pigeons that have to be moved—that is, pigeons whose owners are moving—can be trained to feel bonded to a different coop, but it is difficult to do. Birds raised by hand and housed in a coop have no aptitude for living in the wild, so they can't just be released and left on their own. Homing pigeons that have to be moved must be caged for the rest of their lives—they become what pigeon people call "prisoners." In the best of circumstances, prisoners can be kept in a large aviary, so that they have room to fly even though they can't be let loose. In the worst of circumstances, they never fly much again.

Sedona got into the car with her mother, Maggie, and her twin brother, Patrick. She put the pigeons in their wooden case in the back seat, where they sat, muttering to themselves like old men in a bingo hall. Maggie pulled out of the driveway and navigated to the highway. We ticked past several exits, until we were minutes from the headquarters of the South Shore Pigeon Flyers, one of the two dozen or so clubs in Massachusetts for homing-pigeon fanciers, where we would be leaving the birds.

Sedona was quiet on the ride. She is thirteen years old, a lean, leggy girl, with the luxuriant golden hair of a princess but a grave, precise manner. Her posture is elegant. Her diction is occasionally exactly that of a person her age—earlier in the day she had announced, with amazement, that Grand Tetons means "big boobs"—but more often she expresses herself in a way that is sophisticated beyond her years. She is what a lot of people refer to as an "old soul." Once when I was visiting her, she had a friend over and was showing her one of the pigeons. The bird was squirming and pecking at her hand. Sedona's friend squealed and said she thought the bird was icky. Sedona gave her an impatient look, then turned the bird on its back and addressed it firmly, saying, "Hey! You're being a dominant, dominant bird!"

South Shore Pigeon Flyers is housed in a slumping barn behind the home of the club's president, Damian Levangie. When we pulled in, Levangie was standing on a small terrace off the second floor of the barn, his head tilted up. Maggie called out a greeting. "I can't come down," Levangie called down to her. "I'm waiting for birds." Earlier that morning, thousands of pigeons from the Boston area had been released near the Berkshire Mountains for a two-hundred-mile race, and Levangie's flock was likely to be reaching home any minute. He would need to lure them across an electronic finish line so that their leg bands would trigger the timer used in official scoring.

"We have Sedona's birds," Maggie said to him.

"Just leave them," Levangie said distractedly. Spotting a flash of wing in the sky, he swiveled around and began shaking a can full of grain to attract his birds' attention, so they wouldn't dawdle in the air too long before landing and would score the best time possible. Maggie and Sedona waited for a bit, but Levangie wasn't budging. Finally, Sedona placed the case of pigeons near the barn, and then climbed into the car. By the time we got back to the Murphys' house, a friend of the family's, Jim Reynolds, was dismantling Sedona's pigeon coop, restoring it to its original incarnation as a garden shed. Sedona stood at a distance, observing. "It looks empty," she said. Her tone was pinched and sad. "It looks pigeonless." Maggie watched the demolition with her. Out came the perches, the bird bath, the fifty-pound sacks of pigeon feed; off came the Lucite door the birds hopped through after they'd been flying around and were ready to come home.

>-◄

This is both the marvelous and the problematic thing about racing pigeons: they have a fixed, profound, and nearly incontrovertible sense of home. Americans move, on average, every five years. Pigeons almost never move. As a result, the hobby of raising homing pigeons has a curious permanence, a fixedness in space. It's as if you had pasted your stamp collection on your bedroom walls and then, when it came time to move, you couldn't get it unglued. Some pigeon racers, facing the problem of relocation, end up deciding they just can't move. The Murphys' new house didn't have an aviary, so Maggie felt the best solution was to persuade Sedona to give the pigeons to people in her racing club who did.

I became interested in racing pigeons not long before I met Sedona, and I spent some time with Matt Moceri, who flies his birds with the

Gloucester Racing Club, north of Boston. Matt, who is fifty-six, is slight and dark-haired, with a foghorn voice and a cheery manner. He has been raising birds since 1982, and always maintains a flock of at least sixty birds. Matt has lived in the same house in Gloucester for almost his entire life. He would love to leave the cold, wet winters there for somewhere pleasant, like Tampa, Florida. He began to feel this most acutely five years ago, when he learned that he had cancer. "My wife wants to get a place in Florida before I croak," he said to me recently. "But I can't do it with the birds. They belong to this house."

➤◄

In the Kentucky Derby, if all the horses were trucked together to a remote spot and set loose, then galloped back to their respective barns, where they crossed a finish line, and their times were then compared and ranked by a race secretary (factoring in the difference in the distances to the various barns), you would have the equivalent of a pigeon race. It is the inverse of a group spectator sport. Birds in a race are together only when they are first released. The release is done by a driver who transports all the competitors—thousands of them, in the big races—to the starting point of the race. It is rare that any of the bird owners accompany them, because the birds fly as fast as sixty miles per hour, and if the owners went with them to the start of the race, they might miss being home to watch them return. There is no gathering of owners at the end of the race, either: everyone wants to see their own flock come back to their own coop. "You hang out in the yard by yourself, waiting," a pigeon racer recently explained to me. "You put on some music or the baseball game, have a cocktail, and just watch the friendly skies."

Homing pigeons find their way on instinct, but they need practice. Pigeon racers get up early, because practice sessions—known as "training tosses"—are usually done at dawn, before it's too hot for flying. Most people drive their birds farther and farther away each day, several days a week, to build their stamina and to strengthen their attachment to home.

The American Racing Pigeon Union oversees two racing seasons each year. There is one in the spring, for birds more than a year old, and one in the fall, for younger birds. The races are held regionally each week. They range in distance from one hundred to six hundred miles. Some races have cash awards for winners. In some cases, the awards are as much as several thousand dollars. One series of races in South Africa has a purse of a million dollars. But most of the time, you race pigeons just for the thrill of it, and you get nothing but glory.

There are scores of pigeon breeds. All of them are variations on the rock dove, the street bird you see strolling sidewalks in cities. Fancy pigeons—this includes pigmy pouters, Oriental frills, and short-faced tumblers—are raised for show and for performance. Homing pigeons are raised exclusively to race home. Their ability to find their way—and their choice to do so—has been remarked upon since before the Roman Empire. The Egyptians and Turks trained pigeons to carry messages. Dynastic China used pigeons to carry mail. It is rumored that Count Rothschild used the early news of Napoleon's defeat at Waterloo, delivered to him by pigeon, to manipulate investments. In the nineteenth century, Paul Julius Reuter founded his news service as a string of pigeon posts. London stock-market quotations were regularly conveyed from London to Antwerp by bird. Pigeons have been used by the German, French, Dutch, English, Belgian, and American armies to carry microfilm and messages. Some military birds have conducted surveillance. "If you should ever wake up in the morning and see perched on your windowsill an uncanny little bird pointing a miniature camera at you, you might be sure that he was a United States feathered photographer," Marion Cothren wrote in her book *Pigeon Heroes* in 1944. "Not to be outdone by Germany, Russia and Japan, our Pigeon Service trained . . . these birds to carry two-inch aluminum cameras attached to their breasts . . . These clever camera-birds were used to photograph troops or ammunition dumps." During the Second World War, a pigeon was cited for bravery by the U.S. Army. During a storm, the bird, known as U.S. 1169, carried a distress message from a foundering Coast Guard vessel and alerted rescuers. Between 1943 and 1949, the Dickin Medal—a British award for animal bravery—was bestowed on thirty-two pigeons, nearly twice the number given to hero dogs.

➤◄

Pigeon racing, as a competitive sport, was developed in Belgium in the early nineteenth century, when messenger birds were bred to have greater endurance and speed. By the 1880s, races of five hundred to a thousand miles were held regularly in Europe and the United States. There have been changes in the sport since then. Electronic finish lines were introduced ten years ago. Before that, racers had to grab their birds as they entered the coop, remove their leg bands, and register the leg bands with a manual timer. Now the birds simply fly into their coop and an electronic eye records their arrival. There is also software designed for owners of pigeon-racing teams ("Pigeon Loft Organizer . . . a quick and easy way for you to manage all your pigeon data . . . records, pedigrees, race results"). Modern husbandry practices stimulate stronger feather growth. Some pigeon feed on the market contains magnetic particles, which is peddled as an aid in navigation. There are newly developed techniques to increase speed. One is a system called "widowhood," in which mating pairs are kept apart, to increase their longing for each other—and, accordingly, to increase their haste to get home. But, fundamentally, the sport has remained unchanged for more than a hundred years. It is simply a contest to see whose birds are fastest coming back to their coop.

No one is exactly sure how the birds accomplish this feat. Scientists have been studying homing pigeons for decades to try to figure it out. Avian experts at Cornell have been conducting experiments on homing pigeons' homing instincts since 1967. One popular theory, called inertial routing, suggests that the birds register the physical experience of the journey from their coop to the starting line and then retrace it, but it doesn't entirely account for their ability. Nor can the other theories. It had long been believed that pigeons navigated by sight, until researchers fitted pigeons with opaque contact lenses, and they were still able to find their way home. Another notion was that they used the sun as a compass, disproved by the fact that pigeons can find their way home on overcast days. Scientists have wondered if they navigated by smell or sound or infrasound or telepathy or magnetic sensitivity. Many now believe that pigeons use a combination of all of these to steer themselves. The explanation that pigeon fanciers often use is that if pigeons like where they live, they use all their animal intuition—which is beyond our capacity to measure—to find their way back to it. Sedona believes that magnetism is partly responsible, but she mostly subscribes to this more emotional idea, the irresistible lure of home. "I believe it's the love of the loft," she told me. "They return to where they feel is their home."

Occasionally, pigeons get lost. The reasons are many. They might be blown sideways by a stiff wind and be unable to correct themselves. Also, cell phone transmissions are suspected of disrupting their sense of direction. In 1998, twelve hundred birds competing in a race from Virginia to Pennsylvania went off course; more than half of them were never seen again. No one knows why they went astray, but many people wondered if it was cell interference. As a special treat at a St. Peter's Fiesta in Massachusetts a few years later, someone released a hundred white pigeons. It was assumed they would head home immediately, but weeks after the fiesta ended, the birds were still fluttering around the area, lost and disoriented. One of Sedona's favorite pigeons, Soleil, went missing after a training toss. He still hasn't returned. Sedona says she thinks she's seen him a few times since then, wandering the streets of downtown Boston. Her birds are so attached to her that they will come when she calls, like pet dogs, but Soleil seems to have found a new home.

Most of the time, though, homing pigeons can be counted on. Last fall, I went with Matt Moceri on a training toss. He was working with several dozen of his own birds and a number that belonged to some of his pigeon-racing friends. The start of the toss would be a parking lot in

Greenfield, Massachusetts, which is about a hundred miles away from his house. We left Gloucester in the dark and arrived in Greenfield just a few minutes after sunrise, early enough that the birds would do most of their flying before the day warmed up. An emu ranch bordered the parking lot, and as we pulled in, we could see the emus peering at us suspiciously through the fence.

There were about a thousand pigeons in the back of Matt's pickup, their cages stacked tightly. As soon as Matt opened the cages, the pigeons poured out of the truck like a gush of gray water, and then they whooshed into the sky and disappeared into the morning. I couldn't believe they would find their way home or even want to, now that they were loose in the wide world. Even if they did choose to come home, I figured we would have to wait for several hours in Gloucester before we would catch a glimpse of any of them. But by the time we got back to Matt's house and walked into his yard, his birds were already lined up on the roof of their coop. They had flown a hundred miles at breakneck speed, but they were unruffled, burbling and cooing, shuffling and bowing, as if they were performing the finale of a magic trick.

➤◄

You can buy a racing pigeon for $100, or you can spend $30,000 or more for birds from champion racing stock. In general, though, the costs involved in pigeon racing are reasonable. Pigeon feed is about twenty-five cents a pound. Basic gear costs a few hundred dollars. Club membership and racing fees are about $250 a year. The biggest expenses are an electronic timer, which can run close to $1,000, and veterinary bills, if your birds get sick.

Sedona got her first pigeons a couple of years ago. They were a gift from a friend of Maggie's named Bill Hussey, who calls his hundred-bird racing team Hussey-N-Da Lofts. Sedona had always been crazy about animals. At the time, the Murphys already had an Australian shepherd, a cat, and a gecko. Sedona loved them, but she was fascinated by birds.

When she was small, she would lie on the grass in the park near home and study wild pigeons for hours.

To help Sedona train her pigeons, Maggie had to wake at 5 a.m., wait for a babysitter to come and watch Sedona and her brother, then drive the birds as much as an hour away, release them, get back in the car, and make her way to police headquarters, where she is a detective, and start her workday. Maggie is divorced from the children's father. Sedona doesn't talk about him much, but one afternoon she said to me, "My father had a parrot once, but he had to give it away. I think he was allergic to it, and it didn't like women." Several years ago, the Murphys' neighbors, Jim and Mary Reynolds, offered to walk the Murphys' dog during the day. The Reynoldses have no children. Walking the Murphys' dog led them to more involvement with Sedona and Patrick, and over time the Reynoldses have become like grandparents to them, babysitting while Maggie is at work and helping with projects around the house. The attachment is powerful. When Maggie told the Reynoldses that they were moving to Southborough, the Reynoldses decided that even though they'd been in South Boston for decades, it might be time for them to move, too, to stay close to the Murphys.

Bill Hussey gave Sedona two baby birds—the footloose Soleil and the more domesticated Stella Luna. When Sedona joined South Shore Pigeon Flyers, some club members gave her a few more. Her birds mated and soon she had a flock of eighteen. At first, the pigeons lived in an old rabbit cage in the house, which caused the dog, the cat, and the gecko to be somewhat discomfited. After it became impossible to walk through the kitchen without crunching on pigeon feed underfoot, Maggie bought a garden shed to use as a coop. Jim Reynolds erected it at the far end of the long, narrow backyard. When he was a kid, some of Jim's friends had homing pigeons, so he knew how to care for them and was able to help Sedona set up her coop. Patrick liked the birds and spent a little time with them, but he is more of a dog-and-cat guy; it was Sedona who fell in love. She thought the pigeons were beautiful—"I know people think they're plain or even homely," she said, "but I think they're little works of art"—and she loved seeing them in competition. She raced her young birds in the one- and two-hundred-mile races. She lost a few to hawks that picked them off during races, and a few more to a virus that spread through the birds in the club.

She knew she was competing against grown-ups who had large flocks of pedigreed racing champions, but Sedona was proud of her birds. One day when I was visiting, she presented the birds to me as if they were in a beauty contest, lifting and turning them every which way so that I could see their features. All the while, she carried on a commentary about each one's qualities with the meticulousness of an auctioneer touting yearling colts at Keeneland. "This one's texture is really excellent. . . . This one's coloration is called a white grizzle, a beautiful bird. . . . Now, this one here has a proud chest. . . . This one, Patches, is too fat. We have to get her on a diet. . . . This one, Lightning, has very good genetics."

➤◄

By the time I met Sedona, Maggie had already made the decision to move. A hopscotch of packing boxes stretched from the front to the back door, and real estate pamphlets lay in a heap on the kitchen table. It hadn't been an easy decision. The house had been in Maggie's family since the early 1900s. But the neighborhood had changed, Maggie explained to me. Everyone she knew was moving away, and the new neighbors were the fussy type who scolded her kids for horsing around near their yards or for playing tag in the street. She made an offer on a handsome old house in the suburb of Southborough that had almost an acre of land. It would give them tons of space, especially compared with South Boston, where the houses crowd in on one another.

Sedona likes to play softball and soccer, and is an accomplished ballerina, but she loves pigeon racing more than anything else she does. Having to give up her birds was a blow. Training them, working with them, and taking care of them was more compelling to her than figuring out how to hit a line drive or perform a jeté. She knew that soon, she would no longer see her pigeons floating over the top of the house and zooming back to the coop, so she doted on them, dreamily speculating about which birds might have made a mark in the races. To be sure, her racing successes had been modest. Her best finish was her bird S.J., who came in forty-ninth in a race of three hundred birds. But, for that moment, the prospects still seemed limitless.

One hot afternoon near the end of summer, we sat out near the coop talking about the move. Sedona acknowledged that the new house was roomy and nice. Then she abruptly changed the subject and said she wanted to give the birds a bath to show me how affectionate they were with her. The coop was tiny—the two of us just fit in, squeezing through the door—but it was clean and pleasant, filled with the odd, almost noiseless sound of the birds, a sort of cadenced vibration, like an unplugged electric guitar being strummed. Sedona picked up a dappled tan pigeon and hugged it close. "You know," she said, "you can actually become a millionaire from your birds."

There persists in Sedona's mind the possibility that she will get her birds back someday—the possibility that she and her mother will build a huge aviary at the new house, and even though the birds would be prisoners, never free to fly outside, they would live there happily. Recently, she has also said she might look into raising show pigeons instead of racing pigeons once she moved. She thinks show pigeons are gorgeous, and she had seen one riding on the back of a dog at a circus and was very impressed. Moreover, they are fat and placid, and they fly in circles if they fly at all, rather than always yearning to race home.

➤•◄

Pigeon devotees have included Mike Tyson, Walt Disney, Picasso (who named one of his daughters Paloma, which is Spanish for "dove"), Marlon Brando (as Terry Malloy in *On the Waterfront*), Roy Rogers, and King George V. Pigeon racing is multinational. In Belgium, its popularity is said to be on par with that of cycling and soccer. It is thriving in England (where not long ago one exceptional racing pigeon sold for nearly $200,000). Elsewhere in Europe, videotapes about pigeon-racing stars like Marcel Sangers, "the Wonderboy of Holland," are marketed with breathless tag lines like "Racing in the hotbed of Zutphen against some of the sport's giants, Marcel has achieved what many can only dream about." The sport is fashionable in the Middle East, and the Taiwanese have gone mad for it. Prize money in Taiwan's biggest races can reach $3 million, and gambling on them is commonplace. So is pigeon-related crime, which has included stringing gigantic nets across the route of a race and holding the trapped birds for ransom, and sneaking birds onto airplanes to hurry them to the finish line. Sharing affection for pigeons seems to fill people with an all-embracing global emotion. "Whatever language and whatever country you're in," the president of the American Racing Pigeon Union, Frank Greenhall, told me, "you sit down with a pigeon man and you speak one language—pigeon."

The American Racing Pigeon Union has ten thousand members and oversees eight hundred clubs around the country. Another several hundred clubs are affiliated with the International Federation of American Homing Pigeon Fanciers. Still, the numbers aren't what they once were. For instance, there are about half as many members in Boston-area clubs as there were twenty years ago. Where have all the pigeon flyers gone? Some complain that they wearied of the never-ending care that a sport involving living things requires, compared with a pastime like golf. It has also become more difficult lately to keep pigeons—concerns about disease and about whether the sport violates animal rights have prompted some cities to start regulating coops. Chicago has made it unlawful to keep pigeons at all. The resurgence of hawks, especially in urban areas, has made some people quit in frustration after their well-trained racing teams got eaten. But recently, newcomers from China and Vietnam have begun joining the sport in the United States, bolstering numbers, and people who love pigeons see other signs to be hopeful. Last summer, I

went to Fall River, Massachusetts, to attend the annual auction and picnic at the racing club there. Frank Greenhall was addressing the crowd.
"People keep saying the sport is dying, but the sport is bigger than ever
before," he said. His voice was barely audible over the din. A few dozen
kids were shouting at one another in the SpongeBob SquarePants bounce
house, and a group of men were loudly discussing the virtues of the birds
being auctioned, and the people jostling in line for barbecue were chat-
tering. "For instance," Greenhall continued, "we are close to having the
Boy Scouts recognize pigeon racing as a merit badge. And we have nine
school systems using pigeons to teach math and science." He looked
around the picnic, nodding with satisfaction, and added, "We even have
some prisons that have started pigeon racing!"

As a pigeon flyer, Sedona is atypical. Fans of the sport are mostly male
and largely middle-aged or older. The pigeon clubs are clubby. The motto
of the Greater Boston Homing Pigeon Concourse—the governing body
of the pigeon clubs in the Boston area—is "Camaraderie Through Competition." On the nights before races, members gather at their clubhouses
to wait for the truck to collect their birds, and also to play cribbage,
watch sports on TV, have a few drinks, tell dirty jokes. Maggie preferred
to take Sedona and her birds to the South Shore Pigeon Flyers headquarters early to avoid some of the ribaldry. They chat for a short time, drop
off the birds, and head right home.

There are only a handful of female pigeon flyers, but what really set
Sedona apart is her age. She was well known in the Boston pigeon-racing
world because there are so few kids in the sport. I once asked her if that
distinction was kind of cool. She thought about it for a moment. "The
other people in the club were not exactly fun," she said, slowly. "But
they were, um, interesting." The pigeon people I met found their failure
to interest their own children in the sport exasperating. They said their
children thought pigeons were too much work; they complained that
their kids were only into computers, that their sons were only interested
in girls. Some people I met had first taken up pigeon racing as children

and then abandoned it and had returned to it later in life. I thought this would have reassured them that their kids would eventually find their way to the sport. But many of them had an uneasiness, a foreboding that, regardless of the good news about the Boy Scouts and math classes and prisons, pigeon racing is on the wane. That worry seemed to be also an expression of their ambivalence about a pastime that is unusually confining. The morning of the Greenfield training toss, I waited for Matt in the parking lot of a Wal-Mart, along with five other pigeon racers. It was 5:45 in the morning. I asked one of the racers how he was, and he said, "Honestly, I'm tired. I mean, honestly . . . I'm driving out here and I'm asking myself, I'm getting up at five a.m. for some bird?"

Matt is the race secretary of the Greater Boston Concourse, and yet he confided to me that he thinks he is starting to talk himself out of being a pigeon racer. Even so, he seems exhilarated each time his birds lift into the air and then miraculously reappear at home, in spite of the fact that he has set his birds free and watched them return hundreds and hundreds of times. That morning in the parking lot, he was eager to take the birds out to Greenfield and let them fly. "Hey, let's get these birds and get going!" he hollered at me. "We're four minutes late already!"

>-<

The day we were in Greenfield, some of Matt's other birds were competing in a race. The release was in Ilion, New York, about two hundred miles from Boston—224.592 miles from Matt's coop, to be exact, for purposes of calculating their time and speed. After setting the birds loose in Greenfield, Matt wanted to rush back home so he could see the birds in the Ilion race come home. He was feeling optimistic, even though he was not having the best season of his career. "Since I've been sick, I haven't done so well, so everyone likes me," he said, slapping the steering wheel. "When my birds were doing really well, there was lots of envy. With pigeon guys, there are always lots of feuds." His cell phone rang. He grabbed it. "Birds went up at seven forty-five," he said into the phone. "Okay, good luck." Within a minute, the phone rang again. He responded with the same message. During the rest of the drive back to Gloucester, his phone rang every few moments, all calls from other racers wanting to know how things were looking after the release.

Matt was in a philosophical mood. Before he got cancer, he did construction and remodeling work. Now he devotes his time to tending his birds and puttering around the house and speculating about the future. His wife, Joan, often drives to the training tosses, because he tires easily. She probably has more pigeon action in her life than she counted on. When Matt underwent chemotherapy, he was too sick to clean the coop and feed the birds for a year, so Joan did it all herself and eventually developed a lung condition that is usually caused by exposure to bird dander. Their vacations are limited to times when they can find someone to bird-sit, which isn't often. "And whenever we do go on vacation, I spend some time doing pigeons," Matt said. "I leave Joan at the pool and go find some pigeon guys. I have to."

The day was hot and still. When we got back to Gloucester, we sat in Matt's yard, listening to the cicadas click and the leaves on an enormous maple tree beside his house rustle and sigh. I mentioned what a beautiful tree it was. "Well, it is," Matt said, squinting up at the tree. "It's just that it blocks my view of the birds when they're heading in." He had a cordless phone next to him, which rang every few minutes. "Hello, Louie. . . . No, I don't have any birds yet. . . . Okay, good luck." He checked his watch, checked the sky, checked his watch again. The phone rang again. "No, John, I don't have any yet." Another ring. He turned the ringer off, saying he didn't want to know whose birds were back, because that meant they had beaten his birds. His own team was unusually late. "I'm disgusted," he said. "I don't want to talk to anybody."

I asked Matt if he knew Sedona. He remembered meeting her briefly, at a pigeon auction. I wondered if he had considered taking some of her birds, since she had to find new homes for them before the Murphys moved. He laughed. "No way," he said, shaking his head. "I've got plenty." He mentioned that he and Joan would be vacationing in Tampa soon because their son had agreed to take care of the pigeons. Increasingly, Tampa is where a lot of pigeon guys go when they retire. Frank Greenhall told me that a subdivision near Tampa has been nicknamed Little Belgium because of all the pigeon fanciers who have moved in.

Maybe when they were down in Tampa, Matt said, he and Joan would look at real estate. On a day like this, with his team underperforming, breaking his heart, the idea of moving seemed more palatable, maybe even appealing. "I love my birds," he said, "but I always wonder why I'm doing this." He suddenly bolted to his feet, pointing past the maple tree. "I got a bird!" he yelled. I could see a dark shape gliding around the crown of the tree, spiraling downward; then the shape resolved into a bird, and it landed on top of the coop. The bird was silky and gray, with pink feet and bright, round eyes. It had just flown two hundred miles on instinct or memory or by magnetic pull, or perhaps it was drawn back these two hundred miles because it loved where it lived. The bird was calm, composed, as if it had spent the whole morning dozing or scratching for feed at home. "C'mon, c'mon," Matt called out, until the bird inched across the top of the coop and finally strutted past the electronic finish line, registering its return on the timer at 13:15:42. Matt took a huge breath and then grabbed his phone, punched in a number, and shouted, "Hey! Louie! I got a bird!"

Animal Action

According to the American Humane guidelines, no animal actor should have to work like a dog. For instance, if an ape is on a movie set for more than three consecutive days, the production must provide a play area or a private park where the ape can exercise and relax. When a bear is working on a film, anything that produces smells that might bother the bear—cheap perfume, strong liquor, jelly doughnuts— must be removed from the location. Only cats that get along with dogs can be cast in cat-and-dog movies. No individual fish can be required to do more than three takes in a day. Also, under no circumstances can an animal cast member be squished. This rule applies to all nonhuman actors, including cockroaches. Karen Rosa, the director of American Humane's Film and Television Unit, was discussing this particular guideline one day last summer. "If you show up on set with twenty-five thousand cockroaches, you better leave with twenty-five thousand cockroaches," she said. I wondered if she extended the same welcome to cockroaches at home. She shook her head. "A cockroach in my kitchen is one thing," she said. "A cockroach in a movie is an actor. Like any other actor, it deserves to go home at the end of the day."

The Film and Television Unit headquarters are in Sherman Oaks, about twenty minutes from Hollywood, in a squat concrete building shaded by a highway overpass and a stand of gnarled banyan trees. The place is as homely from the outside as an auto body shop, but inside, it is sunlit and lively, decorated with movie posters and a portrait of famous animal actor Francis the Mule. A wirehaired, baby-faced mutt named Lulu has the run of the office, and staff members wander in and out between visits to soundstages and locations, making a cheerful bustle.

There are thirty full-time and part-time field representatives of the Film and Television Unit, which officially monitors animals in all Screen Actors Guild productions. Keeping an eye on animal actors is a monumental undertaking. In the past twelve months, more than 1,400 SAG scripts included some kind of animal action, ranging from ants in a television picnic scene to movies featuring hundreds of horses. During the week I spent with Film and Television Unit staff, there were tigers doing insert shots for *The Last Samurai*; owls, cats, rats, and dogs working on *Harry Potter and the Prisoner of Azkaban*; a miniature horse doing a guest appearance on *That '70s Show*; full-size horses at work in *Around the World in 80 Days* and *Deadwood*; a frog shooting scenes for *A Cinderella Story*; some deer working on *Thumbsucker*; cats and dogs rehearsing for the sequel to *The Truth About Cats and Dogs*; and spiders auditioning for *Constantine*. The Film and Television Unit keeps track of all of these. Even fake animals and dead animals are the unit's responsibility. If animals used in a movie are frozen or stuffed or shown as a food product— say, a haunch of beef—the unit requires proof that they showed up on set that way.

Most of the people who work for the Film and Television Unit are former veterinary technicians or zookeepers or horse trainers. Many are graduates of the Moorpark College Exotic Animal Training and Management Program, in Moorpark, California, which bills itself as "America's Teaching Zoo." Even though the Film and Television reps spend their days reading scripts and visiting locations, they think of themselves as being in the animal business rather than in the movie business, much the way that barbers in the navy probably think of themselves as being in the hair business rather than in the boat business. The truth is actually somewhere in between. Being part of the Hollywood animal world is a slightly bizarre confection that familiarizes you with such tidbits as the fact that Cameron Diaz is really good with monkeys and that Wilma the alligator, after a long career in medium-budget films, is now a taxidermied entryway ornament at Brockett's Film Fauna, in Thousand Oaks. One morning, I asked a field rep who specializes in supervising movies featuring horses if she liked having a job where she got to know a lot of movie stars. She thought about it for a moment and then said, "You know, it's been great, because I feel really attached to some of them. There's Rusty, who is one of my favorites, and there's Johnny, and one I really, really like named Pumpkin."

>-<

Animals used to have a rotten time in Hollywood. Only the few animals who were stars got deluxe treatment. Rin Tin Tin, for instance, had his own valet and chauffeur, and Jackie the Lion, who appeared in silent films with Mae West, Mack Sennett, and Gloria Swanson, lived on a diet of prime beef and vanilla ice cream. But background animals were considered cheap, disposable props rather than living things. Horses got the roughest handling. They were tripped, shocked, raced into open trenches, and run ragged. To make a horse fall on cue, wires were strung around its ankles or threaded through holes drilled in its hooves, so the rider could just yank the wires and pull the horse up short. In 1924, six horses were killed during the filming of *Ben-Hur*. In 1935, a hundred and twenty-five horses were wire-tripped in *The Charge of the Light Brigade*, and twenty-five of them died or had to be euthanized.

In 1939, for the Henry Fonda movie *Jesse James*, a blindfolded horse was ridden onto a greased chute teetering on a cliff above Lake of the Ozarks and then was pushed out of the chute in order to get a shot of a cowboy on horseback jumping into the lake. The horse broke its back and had to be destroyed. Only the first frames of the shot were used in the film, but the entire sequence of the animal plunging toward the water—hunched, helpless, stiff-legged—is nightmarish. American Humane, which had been founded in the late nineteenth century as an animal- and child-welfare organization, reviewed the footage and circulated a report reproaching the movie industry for the way it treated animals. In response, the Motion Picture Producers and Distributors of America (which later changed its name to the Motion Picture Association of America) added a section to its production code, known as the Hays Code, prohibiting the use of tilt chutes and trip wires. American Humane opened a Hollywood office to enforce these new standards. Besides supervising the care of animals on sets, it also worked to promote animal actors. In 1951, it instituted the Performing Animal Top Star of the Year (PATSY) award. Francis the Mule was the first PATSY winner. In 1973, American Humane created the Animal Actors Hall of Fame. Lassie was the first inductee.

In retrospect, provisions for animal care on movie sets was a strange fit with the production code, which was created to monitor the moral content of films by laying out restrictions on nudity, kiss duration, and the use of risqué words like "hell" and "tomcat" onscreen. But somehow the treatment of animals got packaged in with it. In the 1950s, a series of Supreme Court rulings challenged the constitutionality of the Hays Code on First Amendment grounds. The end of the Hays Code had the unintended consequence of ending American Humane's oversight of animals on film sets. A few films continued to allow American Humane representatives to observe, but most did not. There were still hundreds of movies and television shows being made that featured animals—in fact, it was a boom period for Westerns—and, according to Rosa, standards of animal safety were even lower than in the years before the Hays Code was established. *The Missouri Breaks*, *Heaven's Gate*, and *Apocalypse Now*, for instance, all had incidents in which animals were killed during filming. *Heaven's Gate* featured real cockfights, and chickens were decapitated for the use of their blood.

In the late seventies, actors and crew members began agitating to have standards for animals on film sets reinstated. Roy Rogers wrote an opinion piece for the *Los Angeles Examiner* in support of monitoring the film industry. "Hollywood, once cruel to its animal actors, has learned the far-reaching value of a lump of sugar and a pat on the nose . . . My pet palomino, Trigger . . . the most perfectly trained equine in films today, has not been subjected to cruelty. He has been handled with kindness, intelligence and patience . . . After Trigger and I complete a scene I always have a chat with him. And I think he knows what I say. Gene Autry's horse, Champion; Tex Ritter's horse, Flash; and Bill Elliott's horse, Thunder, also probably know what Gene and Tex and Bill have said to them. These horses don't know cruelty." The agitation eventually got results. In 1980, the Screen Actors Guild/Producer Agreement was amended to include rules requiring the proper treatment of animals, and American Humane was once again authorized to oversee animal actors in film, television, commercials, and music videos, and to issue, or withhold, the trademarked end credit "No animals were harmed in the making of this film."

➤─◄

A lot of people think that American Humane oversees the content of movies instead of just keeping an eye on the way they're made. "We get tons of calls and emails complaining about what's in movies," Karen Rosa said. "People don't understand that we're not telling producers what the movie should be about. We're just watching to see how it gets done." After a mouse was stomped to death onscreen in *The Green Mile*, the Film and Television Unit received dozens of complaints, although its website explained that only stuffed and computer-generated mice were used in the stomping scene. Sometimes, though, even the Film and Television Unit staff are fooled. After supervising the production of *O Brother, Where Art Thou?*, Rosa and her staff watched a final cut of the movie and were horrified to see a scene of a cow being hit by a truck. When she called the producers to object, they were delighted, because the scene was computer generated, and they figured that if they'd fooled the Film and Television Unit, they had done a good job. The movie got an "Acceptable" rating from American Humane. The review on the American Humane website goes to great lengths to explain the scene: "One of the cows appears to be hit by the car and falls down. This sequence was accomplished by attaching a cable to the car so that no contact was ever made with the animals. In fact, the car is never less than 25 feet away from the cows. When the cable is pulled, the car comes to a hard stop, creating the effect of hitting an object. The cow was actually computer generated in post-production."

American Humane's authority extends only to SAG productions. Independent and foreign films are outside its reach. Even though following its guidelines can be very expensive, most producers want the "No animals were harmed" end credit and a positive review on the American Humane website, which is viewed by almost half a million people a month. Before releasing Pedro Almodóvar's *Talk to Her* in this country, Sony asked American Humane to review it, even though the studio knew that it would not get a "No animals were harmed" end credit, because the movie includes actual bullfighting scenes. It was an unusual circumstance. The bullfighting scenes were "documentary"—that is, they were shot at the graduation ceremony at a bullfighting school in Spain that was taking place regardless, and not a fight that was staged for the purposes of the film. Also, bullfighting is not considered animal cruelty in Spain. Still, there was no doubt that animals were harmed in the scene. The bulls shown are real, and they did die. "We gave it a 'Questionable' rating," Rosa said. "There wasn't really anything else we could do."

➤•◄

The Film and Television Unit has an annual budget of just $1.5 million, which used to be raised through grants and donations. Since 1991, all of its funding has come from the Screen Actors Guild, which counts directors and producers among its members. This means that the American Humane reps are subsidized by the very people they are monitoring and sometimes forcing to spend money they probably don't want to spend. As dictated by American Humane guidelines, proper care for worms on a set can cost thousands of dollars a day, while using them in a shot and then tossing them out costs nothing. Several reps told me of incidents in which a producer growled at them about the money that their safeguards were costing. Rosa waves off the question of conflict. "The industry should support us," she said. "They have lots of money and we don't. We shouldn't have to compete for grant money that should be going to neutering programs and shelters." The budget is skintight, plus the number of productions that the Film and Television Unit oversees has grown every year, particularly since the expansion of cable, streaming, and independent films.

In the past, when a movie being produced outside this country had to be monitored, American Humane subcontracted with local humane associations. In one such instance, a family film called *Running Free* shot in 1999 in South Africa was supervised by the Animal Anti-Cruelty League of Johannesburg. That group vouched for the animals' treatment, but it also reported that four horses had died during filming and that shock collars were used to control others. American Humane gave the movie a "Believed Acceptable" rating, which is one notch below "Acceptable." Partly as a result of what happened on *Running Free*, the Film and Television Unit now uses only field reps it has trained. It sends reps around the world to cover locations and has employees on call in Australia and England. Rosa hopes eventually to add reps in Africa and Europe. "We have to keep up," she said. "This work is very high-profile. It sets a standard. And we have to keep current on new information. Right now, I'm looking into the new science that's coming out on whether fish feel pain in their lips. It's always been assumed that they don't, so we've permitted the use of barbless hooks in fishing scenes. If it turns out that they do actually feel pain, we'll have a lot of people in the industry pissed off when we tell them they no longer can put a real fish on a hook."

>-<

Overseeing a film like *Soccer Dog: European Cup* is a pretty soft assignment for a Film and Television Unit rep. The movie involved no snakes being milked (not allowed by American Humane guidelines); no chickens stacked in containers that forced the birds to defecate on one another (not allowed); no six-horse hitches in front of cannon fire; no arachnids having their physical characteristics permanently altered; and no apes required to perform near an animatronic object or a person in a clown costume to which the apes had not been first allowed to become accustomed (all forbidden). Unlike movies such as *Far and Away*, which had a thousand horses in a single shot that took three weeks to set up, or *The Horse Whisperer*, which had such difficult horse scenes that the Film and Television Unit field rep spent a year consulting with the producer before shooting even started, *Soccer Dog: European Cup*, the sequel to *Soccer Dog*, is a low-key family film with what the reps call "moderate action," requiring nothing more demanding than having the leading dog bounce a ball on its nose. The precautions necessary for the dogs would be considerably less expensive and complicated than those for, say, flies or maggots, which have to be accounted for after each shot.

The person assigned to monitor the movie was Netta Bank, a graduate of the Moorpark program, who has been with American Humane for twelve years. Bank is small and trim and has dark pixie-cut hair. She lives in Simi Valley with a parrot and five dogs, four of whom are decommissioned actors (one had a role in *As Good as It Gets*). In truth, though, Bank is more of a monkey person. Her major at Moorpark was sheep, parrots, baboons, and pigtail macaques. She once was a contestant on *To Tell the Truth*, impersonating her hero, the orangutan specialist Biruté Galdikas. "If there's a chimp job, they think of me first," Bank likes to say. She has worked on dozens of movies, some chimp and some not, and carries around an alphabetical list of them, which starts with *Anger Management* and ends with *What Lies Beneath*, *Wild Bill*, and *Wolf*.

This particular day was the fourth of the *Soccer Dog* shoot. We were on an elementary school playing field in the Los Angeles suburb of Rancho Palos Verdes, which for the purposes of the movie was standing in for a small town in Scotland. After driving to the set, Bank put her folding director's chair, her shade umbrella, and her snacks in a grassy area near the animal trainer's truck. Then she started filling out American Humane paperwork, which requires a scene-by-scene accounting of what the animals did, how they were induced to do it, and what safety precautions were in place. Another field rep, Ed Lish, had dropped by to watch some of the filming. He was on his way home from checking on Johnny, a horse starring in *Deadwood*. Lish is an American Humane officer as well as a Film and Television Unit rep, so he was dressed in a khaki uniform and was carrying a badge. He grew up on a ranch in Idaho and likes working with horses. "I hate doing the chimp jobs," Lish said. "They scream too damn much. Dogs are fine, too, although the worst job I ever did was that musher movie *Iron Will*. Have you ever been around sled dogs? Those dogs are the goddamn fightingest dogs I've ever seen."

The stars of *Soccer Dog*, however, were a couple of pacifists. The lead was played by a mongrel with searching green eyes named Chip. A nervous cairn terrier named Ernie played the bad guy. Roger Schumacher, the dogs' owner and trainer, had worked with American Humane on a batch of other movies, including *The Grinch*, *Annie*, *The Hulk*, *Benji: Off the Leash*, *S.W.A.T.*, and *Kill Bill*. Schumacher has been part of the Hollywood animal world his entire life. His father was an animal trainer, and Roger started working professionally with dogs in 1972. Like most of the people who procure animals for movies and television, Schumacher owns almost all the animals he uses. He has a kennel of twenty-five dogs. Most of them, including Chip, are rescues from animal shelters. Schumacher worked on the first *Soccer Dog* movie and had encouraged the producer to select Chip for the sequel.

Usually, producers hire a trainer first and the animal second, which is the equivalent of hiring an agent and acting coach first and the actor second, but in the animal acting business it makes sense. When it comes to casting, producers sometimes let the trainer choose the animal. Other times, though, the producers have a request so precise and improbable that it sounds like a punch line. One trainer told me that a producer recently asked him to find a long-haired dachshund that knew how to run on a treadmill. "It was so frustrating," the trainer said. "I already had a Jack Russell who knew how to do it! But the producer was stuck on the idea of a long-haired dachshund. What could I do?" If the trainer doesn't already own the kind of animal the producer wants, he or she will sometimes swap animals with another trainer. Earlier in the week, I had been talking to someone in the Hollywood animal business who was working on a movie that needed pigeons. He specialized in primates, so he borrowed pigeons from a colleague who was big in birds. He said it had worked out nicely, because a few weeks later the bird guy needed to borrow some of his baboons.

When we arrived on the *Soccer Dog* set, Chip was getting ready for a scene that required him to walk up a ramp and open the door of a Port-a-Potty. Then he was supposed to look in the Port-a-Potty and make sure there weren't any bad guys inside, and then step inside, letting the door slam behind him. Bank examined the Port-a-Potty and the ramp and determined that they were safe for Chip. She made a few notes and then settled into her chair. Schumacher ran through the scene with Chip and then told the director that they were ready to go.

On the first take, Chip went up the ramp too quickly—a tendency that Schumacher had told me was Chip's greatest limitation as an actor. The second take didn't work, because the door caught a breeze and swung open rather than shutting behind him. Then the director realized that the camera was catching Chip at an unflattering angle. "We're going to have to reset a little," he said to the cinematographer, pointing to Chip's tail. "Can we avoid making this too much of an anus shot, please?"

On the third take, Chip nudged the door open, paused as if he were really considering whether to go in or not, and then stepped inside. The door flapped shut behind him. "Perfect," the director called out. "Nice work, Chip."

While the next shot was being set up, Schumacher came over to talk to Bank. He was leading a fat yellow Labrador retriever that he was training for the upcoming James Brooks movie *Spanglish*. Unlike Chip, who was the backup in *The Grinch* and *Annie*, or Ernie, who had a long-running role on *George Lopez*, the Labrador retriever was not a professional actor. He was on loan from a private owner, an arrangement that animal trainers do not favor, but he was the only dog Schumacher could find with the kind of sweet, goofy face that Brooks was looking for.

"Be sure to write down that I beat my dogs, Netta," Schumacher said.

"You know I will," Bank answered. "I'm writing an incident report on you, Roger."

The fat Lab burped. "Let's go," Schumacher said to the dog. He said he needed to teach the dog to walk backward, so he planned to start working on it while the crew was moving equipment for the next shot. Ernie was resting in a crate in Schumacher's truck, and Chip was playing nearby with Schumacher's daughter. Ordinarily, Chip is a white dog with tan patches, but for the movie he had been dyed blond. He is a small, fluffy creature with a teddy bear face, long legs, and ears that fold over at the tips, like little paper airplanes.

Suddenly, one of the extras ran over and put her arms around him.

Bank jumped to her feet. "Don't handle the dog," she said in a loud voice.

"But I'm a professional masseuse," the woman said. "I just wanted to give him a massage."

"Do not handle the dog," Bank repeated. "He's working."

"I think he knows I'm a masseuse," the woman said, looking crestfallen.

"Maybe so," Bank said. "But he's working."

Where's Willy?

It was a hell of a time to be in Iceland, although by most accounts it is always a hell of a time to be in Iceland, where the wind never huffs or puffs but simply blows your house down. This was early in August, and it was stormy, as usual, but the summer sun did shine a little, and the geysers belched blue steam and scalding water, and the glaciers groaned as they shoved tons of silt a few centimeters closer to the sea. On the water, the puffins frolicked, the hermit crabs frolicked, and young people bloated with salmon jerky and warm beer barfed politely into motion-sickness buckets on the ferry sailing across Klettsvik Bay.

The young people were on their way to an annual songfest and drinkathon on the Westman Islands, a string of volcanic outbreaks off Iceland's southern coast. During the trip, they spoke in Icelandic about Icelandic things, like whether they had remembered bottle openers and bandannas, and then they turned greenish and stopped talking as the boat lurched up and down the huge cold waves. After two hours or so, the waves settled and the boat slowed and glided into Heimaey Harbor, which is ringed by cliffs of old lava that are as holey as Swiss cheese. Dozens of trawlers and knockabouts bobbed at their moorings, nudging the docks and making that clanging sound that is guaranteed to make you feel lonely.

We sailed past a row of white buoys strung across the mouth of a small bay, marking off a section of water. A few of the young people, gummy-mouthed and bleary-eyed, roused themselves and gazed out the portholes.

"Hey! Keiko!" one girl exclaimed, pointing at the buoys.

"Huh?" another mumbled, looking where the first one was pointing. "Keiko?"

"Willy! Free Willy!"

"Oh, *Keiko*!" the others said, pushing up to the window, yanking one another's sleeves and gawking at nothing but the empty inlet, the glassy water, the blank, looming cliffs. "Keiko! Oh, yeah! Oh, *wow*!"

＞•◀

The whale was not there, of course. He had left Iceland in early July, after taking a watery journey with his human overseers to look at other whales—his kin, if not his kith—that had stopped near the Westman Islands for a midsummer feast. Keiko had seen wild whales before—he was originally one himself—but he had been reintroduced to them only two years ago, after spending twenty years in captivity. He had watched the visiting whales from a shy distance at first and a bolder one later, but he'd always returned to the boat that had led him out to open water. Back at his private pen in the harbor, that buoyed-off section of the ocean the young people had noticed, an international staff of humans would massage his fin, scratch his tongue, and compose press releases detailing his experiences at sea.

In July, however, Keiko ventured closer to the whales than he usually did. Then, quite unexpectedly, instead of coming back to the boat, he followed the wild whales when they headed off past Lousy Bank, past the Faroe Islands, onward to—well, honestly, who knows? Whales keep their own counsel. The truth about them is that they come and go, and you can't really know where they've gone—unless by chance you had previously fished them out of the water, drilled holes in their dorsal fins, and hung radio tags on them. Only a madman would suggest that drilling a hole in a whale's dorsal fin is easy. The whales that visit Iceland every summer, that Keiko decided to hang out with, hadn't been drilled. This is why no one was sure where they were heading late in July.

But Keiko—his name means "lucky one" in Japanese—is the most watched whale in the world. He has both a satellite tag and a VHF transmitter. He also has three nonprofit organizations vested in him, along with millions of spectators, all waiting to see if this famous, accomplished, celebrated whale, who has lived most of his life as a large pet, will take to the wild. Every day that Keiko is on his own, his location is tracked by satellite, relayed over the Internet, and then plotted on a marine chart in the Free Willy/Keiko Foundation offices in the Westman Islands, a row of neatly penciled X's tracing his arcing route through the sea.

What is known about Keiko is this: he is an *Orcinus orca*, commonly called the orca or killer whale. Weighing as much as ten thousand pounds, the orca is the largest member of the dolphin family—big mouth, big teeth, big appetite. Like humans, orcas can kill and eat almost anything they choose. What they usually choose is herring, salmon, or cod, but some orcas prefer to eat sea lions, walruses, and other whales. They have been known to neatly skin a full-grown minke whale, bite off its dorsal fin, and eat only its tongue, a behavior that has been construed as epicurean wastefulness or perhaps a reenactment of an Aztec virgin sacrifice. Orcas seem to have no taste for humans. Only three people have ever been killed by captive killer whales, and two of those deaths involved the same whale, SeaWorld's Tillikum; he held his victims underwater to drown them but did not eat them afterward. Orcas are found in every ocean on the planet. They have enjoyed relative invulnerability from hunting because they are not valued for oil (they are twenty times less blubbery than sperm whales) and their meat is far less tender and flavorful than that of minke whales. They are fiercely smart and remarkably educable. They are also handsome, outfitted in black and white with a grayish saddle patch; they are more attractive than, say, the transcendent horribleness, the blank ghastliness, the strange and awful portentousness of a gigantic white whale. Therein lies the killer whale's greatest vulnerability, namely its suitability for being displayed and taught to perform silly tricks that are all the more marvelous because of the orca's reputation as a ruthless assassin.

>--<

In 1964, the Vancouver Aquarium commissioned an artist to make a life-size orca sculpture for its grounds. In the interest of accuracy, the aquarium hired a fishing company to kill an orca to use as a model. The fishing company harpooned an orca, but the animal survived the assault, so the aquarium decided to make the best of the screw-up and used the live whale for display rather than making the sculpture.

The Vancouver staff named the whale Moby Doll. She was the first orca ever held in captivity. She died after only eighty-seven days in the aquarium, but it was enough time for observers to realize how intelligent she was. Since Moby Doll's misadventures, more than 130 orcas have been captured for display around the world. Many of them were captured around Iceland, until 1989, when the country halted all whaling. It is harder these days to obtain an orca for display. Currently, there are about 50 orcas in aquariums and amusement parks around the world, and their scarcity has made them each worth a million dollars or more.

>--<

Keiko's beginnings were humble. He was born near Iceland, around 1977 or 1978. He was captured in 1979, while he was still a youngster. For the first few years of his captivity, he lived in a down-in-the-mouth aquarium outside Reykjavik that raised most of its operating capital by catching and selling orcas to other aquariums. In 1982, the Reykjavik aquarium sold Keiko to Marineland, a park in Niagara Falls, Ontario. It wasn't a good fit; the other, older whales at Marineland bullied Keiko mercilessly. After three years of trying to help him get along with the other whales,

Marineland gave up and sold Keiko to Reino Aventura, an amusement park in Mexico City.

The whale facility at Reino Aventura was too small, too shallow, and too warm for an orca. There were also no other whales at the aquarium to keep Keiko company. He wallowed. His fitness deteriorated: he had the muscle tone of a wet noodle and could hold his breath for only a measly three minutes. He wore down his teeth by gnawing the concrete around his tank. He spent much of his time swimming in nihilistic little circles and had a profound lethargy that some saw as foretokening an early death. He developed a droopy dorsal fin, which was symptomatic of nothing but made him look very sad. In spite of all of these shortcomings, he was much adored by visitors to the park. He, in turn, appeared to be very fond of children and cameras, and acted as if he was delighted by their attention.

>-<

Except for Dino De Laurentiis's 1977 disaster epic, *Orca*, Hollywood has shown little interest in cetacean films. Into this void, a screenwriter named Keith Walker wrote a script about a mute orphan boy who lives with nuns and befriends a whale at an amusement park. In Walker's original script, the boy is silent until the end of the movie, when he releases the whale into the ocean while crying out, "Free Willy!" Walker submitted the script to the producer Richard Donner, an environmentalist and an animal lover, who liked the script's intentions and suggested to his wife, the producer Lauren Shuler Donner, that she and her partner, Jennie Lew Tugend, develop it. Tugend and Shuler Donner thought that the story was too sugary. They revised the script, making the boy a juvenile delinquent, the whale a petulant malcontent, and the amusement-park operator a penny-pinching crook, but they kept the climax of the whale's "Free Willy!" release.

Once Warner Bros. agreed to underwrite the project, Tugend and Shuler Donner began auditioning the killer whales of the world to find one to play Willy. Twenty-one of the twenty-three orcas in the United States belong to SeaWorld. The company's executives were horrified by the script's message of whale emancipation and told the producers that none of its orcas were available to appear in the movie. Shuler Donner and Tugend looked further. In Mexico, at Reino Aventura, they found Keiko, who was definitely available for movie work. They also realized that Reino Aventura's dilapidated facility would be perfect to use as the film's fictional dilapidated facility. The park's owners didn't seem bothered by having their whale and their park appear in a pro-wild, anti-captivity movie.

Free Willy was shot on a lean budget of $20 million. It had a cast of mostly unknowns. The star was a child actor named Jason James Richter, who was twelve years old—just a few years younger than Keiko. No one imagined what a success the movie would become or what message audiences would draw from it. Shuler Donner did have an inkling that something was afoot when an audience member handed her ten dollars after an early screening and said, "Here, use this money to save the whales."

Free Willy pulled in huge audiences right from the start. It was a smash with kids, who insisted on seeing the movie over and over and over (thus answering the movie's tag-line question, "How far would you go for a friend?"). It had a walloping gross of $154 million. A message at the end of the movie directed people interested in saving whales to call Earth Island Institute, an environmental group, at 1-800-4-WHALES. The resulting torrent of calls blew the minds of everyone involved—the executives at Warner Bros., the producers, the people at Earth Island Institute. It was not just the number of calls that surprised them. What they hadn't anticipated was that many of the callers were asking very specifically what had happened to the whale who played Willy in the movie.

"We had no clue that this interest from moviegoers would involve Keiko as an individual," David Phillips, of Earth Island Institute, says. "Up until that point, he was just a prop in the movie. Of course, everyone who worked on the film had fallen in love with him. The cast was in love with him. Everyone who gets near him gets Keiko virus."

Despite his movie fame, Keiko was still languishing in his crummy little pool at Reino Aventura in Mexico. The owners of the park didn't want to part with him, but they recognized that he was in poor health, and possibly even dying. He was even more sluggish than before and had become infected with a real virus—a papillomavirus that was causing acne-like irritation around his armpits. The park owners had previously tried to find Keiko another home. They had offered him to SeaWorld, but SeaWorld hadn't wanted a warty whale. But now, with his movie acclaim, everybody wanted him. Michael Jackson sent representatives to Mexico, hoping to acquire Keiko for his ranch. Conservation groups wanted him for this or that aquarium. Scientists asked to bring him to Cape Cod for research.

With the support of the movie's producers, David Phillips formed the Free Willy/Keiko Foundation, with the mission of rehabilitating and eventually releasing Keiko into the wild. Reino Aventura's owners chose the foundation over other suitors. They agreed to give Keiko to the Free Willy/Keiko Foundation for free, but the foundation had to pay for moving him. Whale-moving expenses are considerable. More than a million people had already contributed to the cause, but the amounts donated were usually modest, raised at Free Willy bake sales and by kids breaking open their piggy banks. UPS offered to pay for Keiko's flight out of Mexico. Still, someone had to cover the cost of the shipping container as well as other travel incidentals, which would be at least $200,000.

Shuler Donner brought several bulging bags of letters to Warner Bros. executives. These were letters demanding to know whether Willy had really been set free and, if he hadn't, what Warner Bros. was going to do about it. What Warner Bros. did about it, eventually, was to give a million dollars to the Free Willy/Keiko Foundation. The Humane Society of the United States contributed another million. Then telecommunications tycoon Craig McCaw put in a million, through the Craig and Susan McCaw Foundation. "Craig's not really an animal person," McCaw's spokesman, Bob Ratliffe, told me not long ago. "He's an environmentalist and is interested in the health of the oceans, and—well, long story short, Craig gave the million bucks. And then he gave another one and a half million to build a tank for Keiko in Oregon. His intention was never to be as involved as he became, but he really kind of bonded with Keiko. He went swimming with him. He was actually on the whale's back, and—well, long story short, he got very involved."

>-<

Mexican children cried bitterly when Keiko was loaded onto a UPS truck and taken away in January 1996, and who could blame them? Reino Aventura used to allow kids to hold birthday parties in Keiko's tank, but now he was leaving for good, traveling thousands of miles north to the Oregon Coast Aquarium. A documentary film about Keiko's new chapter featured his Reino Aventura trainers, who in the film appeared nearly hysterical when discussing his departure, saying he was not just a whale or a job but their closest friend. The truck carrying him to the C-130 Hercules cargo plane moved at a solemn pace with a police escort, as if it were the Popemobile. More than a hundred thousand people lined the streets at dawn to say goodbye. In Newport, Oregon, the depressed, gray seaside town where Keiko's new home was situated, there were more crowds and more tears—Willy was almost free! The Free Willy/Keiko Foundation had built a gorgeous new $7.3 million tank for him there, hired a staff of six to care for him and get him ready for the big, wide world. Throughout Oregon, Keikomania erupted. Local news reported on his arrival around the clock, and television crews set up Keiko cams. The newspapers in Oregon printed special sections about the whale, with instructions on how to fold a broadsheet into a whale-shaped cap.

"It was like New Year's Eve when Keiko arrived," Ken Lytwyn, the senior mammalogist at the Oregon Coast Aquarium, said recently. He sounded wistful. "I've worked with dolphins and sea lions and even other killer whales, but Keiko was . . . different. There was really something there."

By every measure, Keiko thrived in Newport. His skin cleared up. He gained two thousand pounds. He tasted live fish for the first time since infancy. He had toys to play with and a television set on which he watched cartoons. His caretakers found his personality more Labrador retriever than orca. He was cheerful, affectionate, eager to please—the sort of killer whale who, if you were in the tank and he swam over to see what you were doing, would take care to not accidentally crush you to death. Attendance at the struggling aquarium rose to an all-time high, and all those visitors, with their demands for snacks and souvenirs and motel rooms and gasoline, buoyed every enterprise around.

>—◄

Wouldn't it have been great if Keiko could have stayed in Newport forever? He was by then twenty-one years old, a middle-aged piebald virgin living as good a life as captivity could offer. But the plan had always been to free Willy, even though a captive killer whale had never been set free before. It's always a long-shot proposition to reintroduce captive animals to the wild, and Keiko was hardly an exemplary candidate for release. He had been confined for so long, and had become so accustomed to human contact, and was so much more a diplomat than a killer that it was hard to imagine him reverting to natural orca behavior, such as chewing holes in walruses and beating schools of salmon to a pulp with his terrible, awesome tail.

>—◄

When would Keiko be ready to take the next step toward freedom? Criteria had been set up, and benchmarks had been established to determine his fitness for freedom. Was he eating live fish? Could he swim great distances? Could he hold his breath under water for a long time? Even with these benchmarks to guide the conversation, right-minded people might disagree. In fact, right-minded people could even litigate, as the Oregon Coast Aquarium did, in 1997. The aquarium, extremely fond of its blubbery sugar daddy, sued the Free Willy/Keiko Foundation to prevent the foundation from moving Keiko to Iceland, where the foundation planned to pour him into the actual ocean, or rather, an open-water pen in Heimaey Harbor. The aquarium's position was that Keiko was not ready to leave. The foundation's position was that (a) Keiko was indeed ready to leave, and (b) he belonged to the foundation, not the aquarium. Relations grew ugly, then hideous. In early October 1997, the board members of the aquarium requested an independent evaluation of Keiko's health. A few days later, the Oregon Veterinary Medical Examining Board announced that it would investigate Keiko's care and the legality of his custody arrangements. There was talk in the Free Willy camp of moving Keiko to a pen in Oregon's Depoe Bay as a compromise. Finally, a blue-ribbon panel of experts was formed to analyze Keiko's well-being and whether he could be successfully released to the wild. To the dismay of the Oregon Coast Aquarium, the panel announced that in its opinion, Keiko was ready and able to go. The run of million-visitor years at the aquarium would soon end.

Even after the panel's declaration, there were skeptics who believed that the effort to free Keiko was doomed. Some of those skeptics happened to be employed by SeaWorld, which had been picketed to free their own orcas in the wake of *Free Willy*. The SeaWorld contingent warned that the poor whale would get frostbite if he was exiled to dark, cold, miserable Iceland—in spite of the fact that Keiko was born in Iceland and that killer whales teem in the waters around Iceland. Perhaps SeaWorld was looking for cover when challenged about releasing its own orcas. But even whale people—free-whale people, that is, who very much wanted Keiko to be liberated—had doubts. Keiko, they suggested, was already ruined. It was too late to teach him what a wild whale needs to know. He repeatedly demonstrated an alarming preference for frozen fish over fresh, suggesting that his tastes had become completely corrupted by his two decades in a fishbowl. A conspiracy theory circulated in the most radical anti-captivity ranks that SeaWorld might actually be behind the free-Keiko efforts. The theory suggested that SeaWorld supported the move to free Keiko because they knew he would flounder. This would make the release of captive animals seem unwise, and possibly even unkind, which might inoculate amusement parks and zoos around the world against an upwelling of liberationist sentiment.

Skepticism was not the only impediment to moving Keiko to his ancestral home. Consider this: Icelandic fishermen view whales as annoying and gluttonous—big, fat fish vacuums that consume commercial seafood product by the ton. The Icelandic government had asked the International Whaling Commission to allow regulated whaling again, and the nation had just received its first shipment of Norwegian whale meat in fourteen years. Now imagine that you are David Phillips, of Earth Island Institute. You represent a telecommunications billionaire, the Humane Society, and Ocean Futures Society, an environmental group founded by Jean-Michel Cousteau, and you have to approach various Icelandic ministries for permits to construct a million-dollar pen in the harbor as well as organize a fleet of boats, helicopters, airplanes, and a crew of scientists, veterinarians, and animal trainers, for the nurture and eventual discharge of one Keiko, aka Willy, a delicious, edible whale. The insult of having a whale, especially a whale being so coddled, in a safe haven in Icelandic waters would not even be offset by the comfort of cold cash, since Keiko would not be on display in Iceland. There would be no Icelandair travel packages to visit Keiko, no hotel revenue, no admission fees, no photo ops. Keiko would live in a huge pen in the harbor where he would be accessible only by boat, and the only visitors permitted would be his caretakers, as he was slowly weaned from human contact to ready him for life among his brethren.

"The opposition from the Ministry of Fisheries was fierce," Phillips said to me. "This program for Keiko was antithetical to everything they do. There is very little by way of whale-conservation awareness in Iceland, and a lot of hostility toward anything at all coming from the U.S. So, we started looking at other locations, in Ireland and in England, too.

But Iceland was Keiko's home waters and really the best place for him, and, after a long series of complexities, we finally got it approved."

➤◄

So Keiko would head to Iceland from Oregon. There was another flight to pay for ($370,000 to fly him to Iceland), another pen to build ($1 million), a staff to recruit and equip and pay. The annual costs of the project in Iceland were estimated at $3 million. If Keiko never learned to live on his own, the foundation could conceivably be looking after him for thirty more years (his natural life span), at a cost of $90 million. "Along the way, this had become a different kind of project," Bob Ratliffe, of the Craig and Susan McCaw Foundation, explained. "It was involving planes and helicopters and big boats and major expenses." But, Ratliffe said, the McCaws had made a commitment to the whale, and they did have a desire to help try to achieve something people thought couldn't be achieved.

Keiko's flight on an air force C-17 was booked. Gallons of diaper-rash ointment to moisturize the whale during the long flight were procured. Familian Industrial Plastics was contracted to build the new pen. The staff of fifteen was lined up. By September of 1998, it was all ready. The goodbyes were again tearful. Keikomania had rolled on, unabated, since the day the whale arrived in Newport, and two more Willy movies had come out— *Free Willy 2: The Adventure Home*, and *Free Willy 3: The Rescue*. Although these used computer-enhanced footage of wild whales and animatronic models rather than a real Willy, they further incited whale devotion.

"I went to his tank and told him goodbye and good luck," Ken Lytwyn, the Oregon Coast Aquarium mammalogist, recalls. "I would love to see the release work, but, because of who Keiko is, the kind of individual he is, I don't think it will. I was really sad when they said he was going, but it wasn't my call."

➤◄

Ah, the Westman Islands! So raw, so rugged, ripped so recently from the earth's dermis! In fact, the youngest landmass on earth may be the little rock pile called Surtsey, the southernmost Westman Island, tossed up above sea level only thirteen years before Keiko was conceived. As recently as 1973 a volcano erupted right in the middle of Heimaey, increasing the island's landmass by 20 percent. To make a living, people in the Westman Islands fish and they fish and they fish, and a few of them service the small but steady tourist economy. Slogans in the Westmans range from the somewhat inexplicable "Westman Islands, Capri of the North" to the more explicable "Ten Million Puffins Can't Be Wrong." Everywhere you look in the Westmans, you see dozens of these stout, clownish black-and-white puffins: nesting in lava outcroppings, teetering on cliffs, plopping like stones into the sea. Every August, the baby puffins sail out of their nests to make their first trip on the ocean but instead crash-land in town, seduced by the lights of human civilization. This magical visitation and potential avian catastrophe is known locally as *pysjunaetur*—the Night of the Pufflings—and children and visitors await it every summer, armed with cardboard boxes for the rescue effort. In the morning, the rescued puffin babies are released at the water's edge. When fully grown, puffins are enjoyed in the Westmans roasted, smoked, or sliced thin, like carpaccio.

The whale was not unwelcome in Iceland when he arrived, in September of 1998, even though you couldn't see him unless you drove up to the ledge across the harbor and looked through a telescope that the foundation had installed; and even though not many local people got jobs on the project; and even though the Keiko merchandise—the shot glasses and aprons and tea cozies decorated with his distinctive black-and-white face—wasn't flying off the shelves in the souvenir shops. He was met with what was becoming the standard greeting in Keiko's life—several hundred accredited representatives of the media. And of course there were scores of ebullient schoolchildren, many of whom had first seen *Free Willy* when an Icelandic hot dog company gave a VHS tape of the movie away with every purchase of a six-pack of franks. Everyone was fond of Keiko and admired him for his gentle-giant-ness, for being the good egg who tolerated being crated and shipped hither and thither, for suffering the strange, fickle circumstances of his life with a sort of martyred calm. If anyone thought that the money being spent on his rehabilitation was an insane extravagance, they didn't blame it on the whale. It wasn't his fault that he was captured to begin with and stuck in a lousy tub in Mexico. It wasn't his fault that he became a ten-thousand-pound symbol of promises kept (or not) and dreams achieved (or not) and integrity maintained (or not) and nature respected (or not). It also wasn't his fault that he didn't know how to do whale things like blowing a bubble net to trap herring, and it wasn't his fault that he'd been torn from the bosom of his family at such a young age that now he was a little afraid of wild whales, and that they, in turn, viewed him as a bit of a freak.

Moving the Keiko project to Iceland wasn't easy. The storms were endless—wild, white, end-of-the-world storms, with screaming winds and waves so high and stiff that they looked set with pomade. A whopping squall hit Heimaey just two weeks after Keiko arrived. The net that formed his pen, held in place with what the staff called "the big-ass chain"—each link weighed five hundred pounds—broke apart and had to be rebuilt and re-anchored. Keiko's living quarters were splendid, but all the maintenance and care for him had to be done by boat, since the land that formed the bay around him was a sheer ridge of petrified lava. A crust of grass grew on the lava, and every summer local farmers ferried their sheep out to spend the season grazing there. The staff agreed to restrain Keiko when the sheep were floated back and forth, since no one could guarantee that a killer whale wouldn't have a taste for mutton.

Throughout the next three years Keiko's caretaking staff turned over again and again, because it was lonely and cold in Iceland, even if you were crazy in love with your whale. Then the stock market deflated. This would not ordinarily be a matter of much concern to a whale, but Craig McCaw's company, Nextel, saw its stock price fall from a high of more than eighty dollars a share to somewhere around ten. McCaw wasn't crying poorhouse, but it was concerning. Moreover, he had turned his attention to his other undertakings—some land-based conservation efforts, some world-peace initiatives with Nelson Mandela. At the end of 2001, word went out that the $3 million annual underwriting for Keiko from the Craig and Susan McCaw Foundation would soon end.

>-<

It was such an irony, in a way—just as everything in Keiko's life has been an irony—that the funding dried up just as the project was starting to accomplish what it had set out to do. In the summer of 2000, Keiko began taking supervised "walks" out of his pen into the ocean. The staff would lead him into open water, stopping whenever Keiko wanted to take a look around. At first, when Keiko saw wild whales, he did a spy-hop to get a good look at them, but he always swam back to the staff boat and followed it home. The next year, when he saw wild whales, he dallied a little longer, and more than once he stayed with the wild whales for a brief time when the staff boat inched away.

Meanwhile, though, the budget for the project was cut from more than $3 million a year to $600,000. The helicopter and pilot that McCaw had provided were furloughed. The lovely Free Willy/Keiko Foundation offices in Heimaey were consolidated into one drab waterfront space, a former grocery store (which had, conveniently enough, a huge freezer for Keiko's herring).

Despite Keiko's progress in testing the open waters, there was still no irrefutable evidence that he would ever want to leave his bay pen permanently. During the winter, when the wild whales were gone, he stayed in his pen full-time, and he was the same tractable fellow as always, ready in a minute to put his big wet rubbery head in your lap. Even if he was getting an idea of what wildness was, he was still a bit of a baby, and daintier than you might think a killer whale should be. Once, the trainers instructed Keiko to fetch something, anything, from the bottom of the bay. They expected him to bring up something like a boulder, but instead, he presented them with a tiny puffin feather. When he accidentally dropped the feather, he dived back down and brought up the same feather. Another time, doing the same fetching exercise, he brought up a little hermit crab that blithely scurried up and down the long row of his teeth, evidently oblivious to the fact that it was inside the mouth of a killer whale. When seagulls stole his food, Keiko would get angry, but he usually just grabbed them, shook them a bit, and spit them out.

>-◄

Really, though, just how big a baby was he? There were plenty of people who wondered whether Keiko was being held back. "I worry about the trainers," David Phillips said. "Just who is more dependent on whom?" It wasn't simply that Keiko provided jobs for them, which would disappear if he went free; it was the emotional attachment. One of his trainers carried pictures of Keiko rather than of her children in her wallet.

But if Keiko didn't leave—that is, if he didn't join a whale pod and learn how to hunt, eschewing the easy life of a Hollywood retiree—he would have to be funded with new money from somewhere. Whoever contributed to the Keiko project now would have to do it knowing that he or she would possibly be underwriting not a magnificent mammal's colossal leap to freedom but an ongoing day-care program for an aging whale.

>-◄

Then, on July 7, 2002, Keiko was gone like a shot. That morning, his trainers had led him out to the waters near Surtsey, where several pods of killer whales were rounding up a ration of herring. Keiko headed over to the whales and this time he didn't turn back, even when the boat pulled away. Days went by, and he was still loitering with the whales. The staff sailed out and checked on him, noted that he was getting on nicely, and then slipped away without his noticing. More days went by. The summer was in full bloom. The sun hung in the sky until close to midnight; the ice creaked and melted; the sheep, now so heavy with wool that they looked like four-legged snowballs, clipped the grass down to the rock on the cliffs surrounding the empty bay pen. In late July, a huge storm muscled in on Heimaey. For days it was too rough to send anyone out on the water to check on Keiko. The satellite was still transmitting coordinates from his radio tag, but there was no way to tell whether he was still with the wild whales and thriving, or floundering around, lost and alone.

By the time I got to Heimaey, Keiko had been gone for almost a month. I went down to the office the morning I arrived, during the three-hour window of the satellite feed from his tags. The foundation office is one large room across from the harbor. It is outfitted with a miscellaneous array of cast-off desks, boating magazines, foul-weather gear, and a large photograph of a loaf of bread that one of the staff members had baked in the still-warm crater of Heimaey's volcano. A handful of people wandered in and out: Fernando Ugarte, a Mexican scientist with a master's degree in the killer whales of Norway; John Valentine, an American whale-training consultant, in town from his home in Thailand; Colin Baird, a Canadian now running the Heimaey office; Michael Parks, a marine-operations coordinator, who is from Oklahoma but lives in Alaska; a Danish whale scientist; a sailor from Ireland; and three Icelandic staff members, one of whom was an awesomely musclebound former Mr. Iceland. Charles Vinick, the executive vice president of Ocean Futures, had flown in from the group's Paris office to oversee the effort to figure out where Keiko had gone. Naomi Rose, a marine-mammal scientist with the Humane Society, had also just arrived on what had been planned as a trip to check Keiko's physical fitness.

"It looks like he's spent all this time with wild whales," Vinick said. "To me that's, like, wow."

Michael Parks was plotting the satellite information on a marine chart. "He's south today," he said. "Jesus Christ, he's here." He was pointing to a spot southeast of Surtsey, several inches off the chart.

"He's making the decisions now. He's in charge," Vinick said. "He could be gone for good." People drifted over to examine the chart. It looked as though Keiko was traveling sixty or seventy miles a day and was now too far away to reach by the project's fast workboat. It was decided that three people would take a sailboat in Keiko's general direction. This would put them out of regular radio range, making it impossible to receive the updated satellite coordinates. But one of the staff people knew a company in Reykjavik that rented satellite telephones that would work at such distances, and he arranged to have one flown from Reykjavik to Heimaey—or conveyed by ferry, if fog, which rolled in regularly, kept the island airport closed. Then another group would convey the phone out to the sailboat. Vinick also wanted to hire a private plane to fly overhead, but none would be available for a couple of days. Once the crew on the sailboat sighted Keiko—that is, if they sighted Keiko—they would either leave him alone, if he seemed to be eating and keeping company with other whales, or lure him back to the pen, if he seemed distressed or despondent or hungry. By the time all the arrangements were made, everyone seemed a little exhausted, as if they had laid out plans for an armed invasion.

We took a boat out in the harbor to check on the pen. On the deck of the equipment shed was a dead puffin, probably blown sideways by the storm. Inside the shed, someone had posted a list of possible new behaviors to teach Keiko, which included "Pec slap and swim," "Bubble-blow underwater," and "Swallow Jim in one piece." A crew of divers was scheduled to start cleaning the seaweed off the net in preparation for winter, although now it seemed like a bootless task, given that Keiko might never come back.

But it was a good day, all things considered. The Humane Society had just announced that it would take over managing and funding the project, and Craig McCaw's ex-wife, Wendy, said she would contribute $400,000 for Keiko's care. In the afternoon, the fog thinned, flights made their way to Heimaey, and the rented satellite phone arrived. As we loaded gear onto the workboat, a gray-faced local woman, wearing a man's overcoat and red galoshes, hollered from the dock, "How's my Keiko? Is our star still out there?"

>–◄

Call me slightly disappointed. Who wouldn't want to have seen the great black-and-white whale? Who wouldn't want to scratch his tongue, look into that plum-size eye, take a turn around the bay pen on his back? All I saw of whales in Iceland were two humpbacks who dived a few feet from the workboat, flourishing their tails like ladies' fans. As it turned out, Keiko was far away by then. He swam to Norway, where he panhandled from picnicking families and romped in Skaalvik Fjord. What a choice! In the entire world, the only country that allows commercial whaling is Norway. Norwegians are not sentimental about whales, and in fact, while Keiko was there, a member of Bergen's Institute of Marine Research suggested that it was time to stop the madness and put Keiko to death. But the children in Skaalvik Fjord who swam on his back and fed him fish reportedly found him delightful, as has everyone who has ever known Keiko. He played with them for a night and a day, the luckiest whale in the world, and the great shroud of the sea rolled on as it rolled five thousand years ago.

Carbonaro and Primavera

O ne thing will never change: Carbonaro must always be on the right. Five years from now, ten years, even twenty, if all goes well, Carbonaro will still be on the right and Primavera on the left, the two of them yoked together, pulling a spindly plow across the loamy fields in the hills outside Cienfuegos, Cuba. Oxen are like that. They are absolutely rigid in their habits, intransigent once they have learned their ways. Even when a working pair is out of harness and is being led to water or to a fresh spot to graze, the two animals must be aligned just as they are accustomed. Otherwise, they will bolt, or at the very least dig in and refuse to go any farther until order is restored, each ox in its place.

Carbonaro and Primavera were not always a pair. Twenty years ago, Primavera was matched up and trained with an ox named Cimarrón. They worked side by side for two decades. But Cimarrón was a glutton. He broke into the feed one day and ate himself sick; he died happy from incurable colic. It was an enormous loss. An ox costs thousands of pesos and must be coddled along until the age of two and then requires at least a year of training before he can be put to work. It is especially difficult to lose half of a working pair, since you have to find a new partner who fits the temperament and strength of your animal, and above all, you have to find an ox who can work on the now vacant side. Primavera would work only on the left. He could be matched only with a partner who was used to working on the right. It was a lucky thing to find Carbonaro, a right-sider and a pretty good match in terms of size, although to this day he is a little afraid of Primavera and hangs back just a bit.

➤◄

For a long while, oxen had seemed part of the Cuban landscape. Huge, heavy-bodied creatures, their necks rise in a lump of muscle, their gigantic heads tapering into teacup-size muzzles. They are homely animals with improbably slim legs and a light tread, their whip-thin tails flicking in a kind of staccato rhythm, the rest of their being unmoving, imperturbable, still. Everyone in Cuba used to work their land with a pair of oxen.

But then cheap Soviet oil came to Cuba, and then came chemical fertilizers, and then, most important, came tractors. In fact, during the 1960s and 1970s more tractors were being sent to Cuba from the Soviet Union than the farmers could use. Sometimes when the Agriculture Ministry called the farming cooperatives to announce the arrival of more tractors, it was an event of such little distinction that no one even bothered to go to the port to pick them up. During that time, the time of plentiful tractors, hardly anyone wanted oxen. With a heavy tractor a farmer could rip through a field at five or six times the speed he could with an ox team. Tractors seemed so much more modern, and so much simpler, than dealing with the complicated politics of a flesh-and-blood team of animals. The pivot to tractors was so complete that hardly anyone was raising or training oxen anymore. With such a windfall of tractors, no one imagined that oxen would ever again be anything other than a quaint anachronism.

➤◄

Even during the time of abounding tractors, Humberto Quesada preferred using Primavera and Cimarrón—and then, of course, Carbonaro. Humberto is an independent sort of man. His grandfather was brought to Cuba as a slave and was put to work on a sugar plantation of seventy thousand rich acres owned by a Massachusetts family. Humberto's father was a slave on the plantation, too, and as a child Humberto worked beside him in the fields, so that he could learn how to do what he assumed he'd grow up to do, namely be a slave on the plantation. Even though the Quesadas were slaves, they were mavericks. Humberto's sister Ramona, a tiny woman with tight curls and a dry laugh, married the son of white farmers down the road from the plantation. It was a scandal at the time, but it yielded a happy fifty-year marriage that became the warm center of the joined families.

And Humberto went his own way, too. After the Castro revolution emancipated him from his destiny of slavery, he became a truck driver. He still kept a hand in farming. It was different from the old days, because after the revolution he was farming his own land. The plot he owned was a piece of the old plantation. Ownership of the land was the key to his freedom. "The land is the foundation of everything," he told me. "If you have land, you always have something." He was encouraged to join a farming cooperative, but like many Cuban farmers, he chose to work alone. "There's always a lazy person in a group, so I don't like being part of groups," he explained. He held fast to his piece of property and resisted each time the government tried to take little bits of it away. Recently the government wanted to build a health clinic on his land. But the official in charge of the appropriation realized that the magnificent sweet potatoes he regularly enjoyed were grown on Humberto's farm, so he changed his mind and said Humberto should have *more* land, not less.

➤•◄

Once or twice over the years, Humberto rented a tractor to work his fields, but he didn't particularly like it. "The tractor presses too hard," he explained. "The land ends up flattened, like a Cuban sandwich." Even when everyone else was using tractors and chemicals, and growing only sugar, Humberto did things differently. He fertilized naturally, the way his father had taught him. He cultivated tomatoes and corn and lettuce and beans and those magnificent sweet potatoes rather than just sugar. And he plowed with oxen, appreciating their stalwart nature and the way they barely disturbed the land beneath their hooves.

When the Soviet money ran out, the battalions of tractors across Cuba rattled to a standstill. The scarcity of gas made them useless. Suddenly, oxen—quaint, anachronistic oxen—were again worth their weight in gold. It was a lucky farmer who had never given them up, who still had a working team, who could still plow and plant even in the worst moments after the Soviet collapse. Luckier still was a farmer who had diversified with such crops as corn and tomatoes rather than being seduced by the money that had seemed as if it would flow forever from sugar, the price of which was crashing.

In such a moment a man like Humberto no longer seemed a throwback. Now in his eighties, slightly lame, wizened, Humberto is everything the new Cuban farmer needs to be: small-scale, efficient, diversified, organic, and, most important, invulnerable to the ups and downs of Cuba's gasoline economy, which once depended entirely on Soviet goodwill and has since come to rest precariously on Venezuelan largesse. Most of the imported oil in Cuba these days comes from Venezuela, and because of the good relationship between Fidel Castro and Hugo Chávez, Venezuela's president, the price had long been especially favorable. But Chávez was nearly overthrown in April of 2002, and when he regained his footing, he suspended the shipments of oil to Cuba. Across Cuba, gasoline prices rose by as much as 20 percent. It was a very good time to have an ox.

>-<

One recent morning Humberto went by to say hello to his sister, who lives with her extended family on another piece of the old plantation property. It was a brilliant, breezy day. Outside Ramona's little cottage a couple of chickens were worrying the dirt, and a litter of piglets were chasing around in a pile of hay. The cottage is tidy, old, and unadorned.

There is something timeless about it, as if nothing here, or nearby, has changed in twenty or thirty or fifty years.

Of course, nothing much *has* changed in the countryside. The elemental facts, the worries over sun and water and whether the seeds have germinated and the eggs have hatched, don't ever change. In Cuba there is a persistent sense of immediacy, a sense that the country is on the brink of newness and change, a sense that the future is unfurling now. Even so, the countryside has a constancy, a permanence. These days Humberto feels like a rich man. He said that everyone he knows is going crazy looking for oxen, and that you have to barter for them or apply to the government, and that anyone who still knows how to train a team—a skill that was of course considered obsolete when the tractors prevailed—is being offered a premium for his talents. He grinned as he said this, pantomiming the frantic gestures of a desperate man looking high and low for a trained plowing team.

>–•–◂

Someday, no doubt, the tractors will start up again, and the hills beyond Cienfuegos and the fields outside Havana and the meadows in Camagüey and Trinidad and Santiago de Cuba will be plowed by machines faster than the fastest team could dream of. Then, once again, oxen won't be golden anymore. They will be relics, curiosities. But this is their moment, just as it is Humberto's moment, a time when being slow and shrewd and tough is paying off.

After we'd talked awhile, Humberto got up and headed down the drive and over to his barn. A few minutes later he reappeared, leading the two oxen, who were walking side by side. He stopped in the yard near the cottage and brought the animals to a halt and stood beside them, his hand resting lightly on Primavera's neck. The oxen shuffled their feet a little and looked sidelong at the cottage, the chickens, a curtain ruffling in the breeze in Ramona's entryway. Humberto's straw hat was tipped back, and it cast a lacy shadow across his face. He leaned a little against the animal's warm gray shoulder and smiled.

Lifelike

As soon as the 2003 World Taxidermy Championships opened, the heads came rolling in the door. There were foxes and moose and freeze-dried wild turkeys; mallards and buffalo and chipmunks and wolves; weasels and buffleheads and bobcats and jackdaws; big fish and little fish and razor-backed boar. The deer came in herds, in carloads, and on pallets: dozens and dozens of white-tailed and roe; half deer and whole deer and deer with deformities, sneezing and glowering and nuzzling and yawning; chewing apples and nibbling leaves. There were millions of eyes, boxes and bowls of them, some as small as a lentil and some as big as an egg. There were animal mannequins, blank-faced and brooding, earless and eyeless and utterly bald; ghostly gray antelopes and spectral pine martens and black-bellied tree ducks from some other world. An entire exhibit hall was filled with equipment, all the gear required to bring something dead back to life: replacement noses for grizzlies, false teeth for beavers, fish-fin cream, casting clay, upholstery nails.

The championships were held in April at the Crowne Plaza Hotel in Springfield, Illinois, the sort of comfortably appointed place that seems more suited to regional sales conferences and rehearsal dinners than to having stuffed wolves stacked in the corridors and people crossing the lobby shouting, "Heads up! Buffalo coming through!" A thousand taxidermists converged on Springfield to have their best pieces judged and to attend such seminars as Mounting Flying Waterfowl, Whitetail Deer—From a Master!, and Using a Fleshing Machine. In the Crowne Plaza lobby, across from the concierge desk, a grooming area had been set up. The taxidermists were bent over their animals, holding flashlights to check problem areas like tear ducts and nostrils, and wielding toothbrushes to tidy flyaway fur. People milled around, greeting fellow taxidermists they hadn't seen since the last world championships, held in Springfield two years ago, and talking shop:

"Acetone rubbed on a squirrel tail will fluff it right back up."

"My feeling is that it's quite tough to do a good tongue."

"The toes on a real competitive piece are very important. I think Bondo works nicely, and so does superglue."

"I knew a fellow with cattle, and I told him, 'If you ever have a calf stillborn, I'd really like to have it.' I thought it would make a really nice mount."

That there is a world taxidermy championship at all is something of an astonishment, not only to the people in the world who don't know how to use a Dan-D-Noser and Soft Touch Duck Degreaser but also to taxidermists themselves. For a long time, taxidermists stayed a bit under the radar. Taxidermy, the three-dimensional representation of animals for permanent display, has been around since the eighteenth century. It was first brought into popular regard by the Victorians, who hankered for tokens of exotic travel and especially any representations of wilderness—the glassed-in miniature rain forest displayed on the tea table; the mounted antelope by the front door. The original taxidermists were upholsterers who tanned the hides of hunting trophies and then plumped them up with rags and cotton, returning them to their original shape and size. Those early taxidermied animals were stiff and simple, and their faces were fairly expressionless.

The practice spread from Europe to this country and became popular here, too. By 1882 there was a Society of American Taxidermists, which held annual meetings and published scholarly reports, especially on the matter of preparing animals for museum display. As long as taxidermy served to preserve wild animals and make them available for study, it was viewed as an honorable trade, but most people were still discomfited by it. How could you not be? It was the business of dealing with dead things, coupled with the questionable enterprise of making dead things look like living things. In spite of its scientific value, it was often regarded as almost a black art, a wholly owned subsidiary of witchcraft and voodoo. By the early part of the twentieth century, taxidermists such as Carl E. Akeley, William Temple Hornaday, and Leon Pray had refined techniques and begun emphasizing artistry. But the more the techniques of taxidermy improved, the more it discomfited. Instead of the lumpy moose head that was so artless that it looked fake, there were mounts of pouncing bobcats so immaculately and exactly preserved that they made you flinch.

For the next several decades, taxidermy existed in the margins. There were a few practitioners here and there, often self-taught, and usually known only by word of mouth. Then in the late 1960s, a sort of transformation began. The business started to seem cleaner and less creepy—or maybe, in that messy, morbid time, popular culture started to again appreciate the messy, morbid business of mounting animals for display. An ironic reinterpretation of cluttered, bourgeois Victoriana and its strained juxtapositions of the natural and the man-made was in full revival—what hippie outpost didn't have a stuffed owl, or a moose head draped with a silk shawl? Once again, taxidermy found a place in the public eye. Supply houses concocted new solvents and better tanning compounds, designed lightweight mannequins over which skins would be stretched, and produced modern formulations of resins and clays. Previously, an aspiring taxidermist could only hope to learn the trade by apprenticing or by taking one of a few correspondence courses available, but taxidermy schools began opening. In 1971, the National Taxidermist Association was formed (the old society had moldered long before). In 1974, a trade magazine called *Taxidermy Review* began sponsoring national competitions. For the first time, most taxidermists had a chance to meet one another and share advice on how to glue tongues into jaw sets or accurately measure the carcass of a squirrel.

>-<

Competitions were an opportunity for taxidermists to compare their skills and see who in the business could sculpt the best moose septum or could most perfectly capture the look on a prowling coyote's face. Taxidermic skill is a function of how deft you are at skinning an animal and then stretching its hide over a mannequin and sewing it into place. Top-of-the-line taxidermists usually sculpt their own mannequins. Otherwise, they buy a ready-made polyurethane-foam form and tailor the skin to fit. Body parts that can't be preserved (ears, eyes, noses, lips, tongues) can be either store-bought or handmade. How good a mount looks—that is, how alive it looks—is a function of how assiduously the taxidermist has studied reference material (photographs, drawings, and actual live animals) so that he or she knows the particular creature literally and figuratively inside and out.

To be good at taxidermy, you have to be good at sewing, sculpting, painting, and hairdressing, and mostly you have to be a little bit of a zoology nerd. You have to love animals—love looking at them, taking photographs of them, hunting them, measuring them, casting them in plaster of Paris when they're dead so that you have a reference when you're, say, attaching ears or lips and want to get the angle and shape exactly right. Some taxidermists raise the animals they most often mount. That way, they can just step out in the backyard when they're trying to remember exactly how a deer looks when it's licking its nose. This has become especially important because modern taxidermy emphasizes mounts with interesting expressions, rather than the stunned-looking creations of the past. Taxidermists seem to make little distinction between loving animals that are alive and loving ones that are not. "I love deer," one of the champions in the white-tailed division said to me. "They're my babies."

Taxidermy is now estimated to be a $570 million annual business. It is made up of small operators around the country who mount animals for museums, for decorators, and mostly for the thirteen million or so Americans who are recreational hunters and on occasion want to preserve and display something they killed and are willing to shell out anywhere from $200 to mount a pheasant to several thousand for a grizzly bear. There are state and regional taxidermy competitions throughout the year. The world championships are held every other year. There are two taxidermy magazines; a score of taxidermy schools; and three thousand daily visits to Taxidermy.net, where taxidermists can trade information and goods with as much good cheer as you would find on a knitting website:

"I am in need of several pair of frozen goat feet!!! Thanks! —Tim"

"Hi Tim! I have up to 300 sets of goat feet and up to 1000 set of sheep feet per month. Drop me an email at frozencritters.com . . . or give me a call and we can discuss your needs."

"I have a very nice small raccoon that is frozen whole. I forgot he was in the freezer. Without taking exact measurement I would guess he is about twelve inches or so—very cute little one. Will make a very nice mount."

"Can I rinse a boar hide good and freeze it? —Bob"

"Bob, if it's salted, don't worry about it!"

"Can someone please tell me the proper way to preserve turkey legs and spurs? Thanks!! —Brian"

"Brian, I inject feet with Preserv-It . . . Enjoy!"

>‑◄

The word in the grooming area at the championships was that the piece to beat was Chris Krueger's happy-looking otters swimming in a perpetual circle around a leopard frog. A posting on Taxidermy.net earlier in the week declared, "EVERYTHING ABOUT CHRIS KRUEGER'S MOUNT KICKS BUTT!!!" Kicking butt, in this era of taxidermy, requires having a mount that is not just lifelike but also artistic. It used to be enough to do what taxidermists disdainfully call "fish on a stick" displays. Now a serious competitor worries about issues like flow and negative space and originality.

Another one of this year's most serious contenders was Ken Walker's giant panda. It had artistry and accuracy going for it, along with the element of surprise. It looked 100 percent pure panda, but you can't go out and shoot a panda, obviously, so everyone was dying to know how Walker had done it. The day the show opened, Walker was in the grooming area, gluing bamboo into place behind the panda's back paws, and a crowd had gathered around him. Walker works as a staff taxidermist for the Smithsonian. He is a chatty, shaggy-haired guy whose hands are always busy. One day, I saw him holding a piece of clay while waiting for a seminar to begin, and within thirty seconds or so, without actually paying much attention to it, he had molded the clay into a little mink-like creature.

"The panda was actually pretty easy," he was saying to the crowd around him. "I just took two black bears and bleached one of them. I think I used Clairol Basic bleach. Then I sewed the two skins together into a panda pattern." He took out an Oral-B toothbrush and fluffed the fur on the panda's face. He added, "Two years ago, at the world championship, a guy came in with an extinct Labrador duck. I was in awe. I thought, what could beat an extinct duck? And I came up with this idea." He said he thought that his panda would get points for creativity alone. "You can score a ninety-eight with a perfectly mounted squirrel, but it's still a squirrel," he said. "So that means, I'm going with a panda."

"What did you do for toenails, Ken?" someone asked.

"I left the black bear's toenails in," he said, pointing to the animal's feet. "They looked pretty good."

Another passerby stopped to admire the panda. He was carrying a grooming kit, which contained Elmer's glue, brown and black paint, a small tool set, and a bottle of Suave mousse. "I killed a blond bear once," he said to Walker. "A two-hundred-pound sow. Blond as can be. Whew, she made a beautiful mount."

"I'll bet," Walker said. He stepped back to scrutinize the panda. "I like doing re-creations of these endangered animals and extinct animals, since that's the only way anyone's going to have one. Two years ago, I did a saber-toothed cat. I got an old lioness from a zoo and bleached her."

Walker had entered the panda in the ReCreation (Mammal) division, one of the dozens of divisions and subdivisions and sub-subcategories at the competition. They ranged from the super-specific ("Whitetail Deer Long Hair, Open Mouth Division") to the sweepingly colossal ("Best in the World") and would share in $25,000 worth of prizes. (There is even a sub-sub-subspecialty known as "fish carving," which uses no natural fish parts at all; it is resin and wood sculpted into a fish form and then painted.) Nearly all the competitors are professionals, and they publicize their awards wherever possible. For instance, instead of ordering just any Boar Eye-Setting Reference Head out of a taxidermy catalogue, you can order the Noonkester's #NRB-ERH head sculpted by Bones Johnson, which was, as the catalogue notes, the 2000 National Taxidermist Association Champion in the Gameheads category.

➤◄

The taxidermists take the competition very seriously. During the time I was in Springfield, I heard conversations analyzing such arcane subjects as exactly how much a javelina's snout wrinkles when it snarls, and which molars deer use to chew acorns as opposed to which ones they use to chew leaves. These topics are important because the ultimate goal of a taxidermist is to make the animal look exactly as if it had never died, as if it were still in the middle of doing ordinary animal things like plucking berries off a bush or taking a nap. When I walked around with the judges one morning, I heard discussions that were practically Talmudic in their specificity, about whether the eyelids on a bison mount were overdetailed, and whether the nostrils on a springbok were too wide, and whether the placement of whiskers on an otter appeared too deliberate.

"You do get compulsive," a taxidermist in the exhibit hall explained to me one afternoon. At the time, he was running a feather duster over his entry—a bobcat hanging off an icicle-covered rock—in the last moments before the judging in his category would begin. "When you're working on a piece, you forget to eat, you forget to drink, you even forget to sleep. You get up in the middle of the night and go into the shop so you can keep working. You get completely caught up in it. You want it to be perfect. You're trying to make something come back to life."

I said that his bobcat was beautiful, and that even the icicles looked completely real. "I made them myself," he said, sounding proud. "I used clear acrylic toilet-plunger handles. The good Lord sent the idea to me while I was in a hardware store. I just took the handles and put them in the oven at four hundred degrees." He tapped the icicles and then added, "My wife was pretty worried, but I did it on a nonstick cookie sheet."

➤·◄

So who wants to be a taxidermist? "I was a meat cutter for fifteen years," a taxidermist from Kentucky said to me. "That whole time, no one ever said to me, 'Boy, that was a wonderful steak you cut for me.' Now I get told all the time what a great job I've done." Steve Faechner, who is president and chairman of the Academy of Realistic Taxidermy, in Havre, Montana, started mounting animals in 1989, after years spent working on the railroad. "I had gotten hurt, and was looking for something to do," he said. "I was with a friend who did taxidermy and I thought to myself, 'I have got to get a life.' And this was it." Larry Blomquist, who is the owner of the World Taxidermy Championships and of *Breakthrough*, the trade magazine that sponsors the competition, was a schoolteacher for three years before setting up his business. There are a number of women taxidermists (one was teaching this year's popular seminar on Problem Areas in Mammal Taxidermy), and there are budding junior taxidermists, who had their own competition division for kids fourteen and under.

The night the show opened, I went to dinner with three taxidermists. They had driven to Springfield from their homes in Kentucky, Michigan, and Maryland. They were all married, and all said their wives complained when they found one too many antelope carcasses in the family freezer. They worked full-time mounting animals. Most of their commissions were for deer, for local hunters, but they all got occasional safari work from people who had shot something in Africa. When I mentioned that I had no idea that a person could make a living as a taxidermist, they burst out laughing, and the guy from Kentucky pointed out that he lived in a small town and there were two other full-time taxidermists in business right down the road from him.

"What's the big buzz this year?" the man from Michigan asked the other two taxidermists.

"I don't know. Probably something new with eyes," the guy from Maryland answered. "That's usually where you see the big advances. Remember at the last championship, those Russian eyes?" He was referring to glass animal eyes that had a reflective paint embedded in them, so that if you shone a light, they would shine back at you, sort of like the way real animals' eyes do. The men discussed those Russian eyes for a while, then talked about the new fish eyes that had been introduced recently, which have photographic transfers of actual fish eyes printed on plastic lenses. We happened to be in a restaurant with a sports theme, and there were about a hundred televisions on around the room, broadcasting dozens of different athletic events, but the men never glanced at them, and never stopped talking about their trade. We had all ordered barbecue ribs. When dinner was over, all three of them were fiddling around with the bones before the waitress came to clear our plates.

"Look at these," the man from Kentucky said, holding up a rib. "You could take these home and use them to make a skeleton."

>-<

In the seminars, the atmosphere was as sober and exacting as a tax-law colloquium. "Whiskers," one of the instructors said to the group, giving them a stern look. "I pull them out. I label them. Please be aware that there are left whiskers and there are right whiskers. If you want to get those top awards, you're going to have to think about whiskers." Everyone took notes.

In the next room: "Folks, remember, your carcass is your key. The best thing you can do is to keep your carcass in the freezer. Freeze the head, cast it in plaster. It's going to really help if your head is perfect." During the breaks, the group made jokes about a T-shirt that had been seen at one of the regional competitions. The shirt said "PETA" in big letters, but when you got up close you saw that PETA didn't spell out People for the Ethical Treatment of Animals, the bane of all hunters and, by extension, all taxidermists; it spelled out "People Eating Tasty Animals." Chuckles all around, then back to the solemn business of Mounting Flying Waterfowl. "People, follow what the bird is telling you. Study it, do your homework. When you've got it ready, fluff the head, shake it, and then get your eyes. There are a lot of good eyes out there on the market today. Do your legwork, and you can have a beautiful mount."

It was brisk and misty outside. The antler vendors in the parking lot looked chilled and miserable. The modest charms of Springfield, with its mall and the Oliver P. Parks Telephone Museum and Abraham Lincoln's tomb, couldn't compete with the strange and wondrous sights inside the hotel. The mere experience of waiting for the elevator—knowing that the doors would peel back to reveal maybe a man with a moose, or a bush pig, or a cougar—was much more exciting than the usual elevator wait in the usual Crowne Plaza hotel. The trade show was a sort of mad tea party of body parts and taxidermy supplies, gadgets for pulling flesh off a carcass, for rinsing blood out of fur—a surreal carnality, but all conveyed with the usual trade-show earnestness and salesmanship, with no irony and no acknowledgment that having buckets of bear noses for sale was anything out of the ordinary.

"Come take a look at our beautiful synthetic fur! We're the hair club for lions! If you happen to shoot a lion who is out of season or bald, we can provide you with a gorgeous replacement mane!"

"Too many squirrels? Are they driving you nuts? Let us mount them for you!"

"Divide and Conquer animal forms—an amazing advance in small-mammal mannequins, patent pending!"

➤◄

The big winner at the show turned out to be a tiny thing, a mount of two little tree sparrows building a nest. It had been submitted by a strapping German named Uwe Bauch. Bauch had grown up in the former East Germany and had long dreamed of competing in an American taxidermy show. His piece was precise and lovely, almost haunting, since the more you looked at it the more certain you were that the birds would just stop building their nest, spread their wings, and fly away.

Early one morning, before I left Springfield, I took a last walk around the competition hall. It was quiet and uncanny, with hundreds of mounts arranged on long tables throughout the room. The deer heads clustered together, each in a slightly different pose and angle, looking like a kind of animal Roman forum caught in mid-debate. A few of the mounts were a little gory—there was a deer with a mailbox impaled on an antler, another festooned with barbed wire, and one with an arrow stuck in its brisket. One display, a coyote whose torso was split open to reveal a miniature scene of the destruction of the World Trade Center, complete with little firefighters and rubble piles, was surpassingly weird. Otherwise, the room was biblically tranquil, the lion at last lying down with the Corsican lamb, the family of jackdaws in everlasting, unrequited pursuit of a big green beetle, and the stillborn Bengal tiger cub magically revived, its face in an eternal snarl, alive-looking although it had never lived.

Lion Whisperer

O ne recent morning, Kevin Richardson hugged a lion and then checked something on his phone. The lion, a four-hundred-pound male with paws the size of dinner plates, leaned against Richardson's shoulder during the hug and gazed magnificently into middle space. A lioness lolled a few feet away. She yawned and stretched her long body, then swatted idly at Richardson's thigh. Without taking his eyes from his phone, Richardson shrugged her off. In the meantime, the male lion completed his moment of contemplation and began gnawing on Richardson's head.

If you were present during this scene, which unfolded on a grassy plain in the northeast corner of South Africa, this would be the moment when you would make note of the sturdiness of the security fence that stood between you and the pair of lions. Even so, you might still take a step back when one of the lions turned its attention away from Richardson and, for a chilling instant, locked eyes with you. Then, considering that Richardson was on the other side of the fence, you would begin to understand why so many people place bets on when he will be eaten alive.

Kevin Richardson was first referred to as the "lion whisperer" by a British newspaper in 2007, and the name stuck. There is probably no one in the world with a more intimate and unusual relationship with wild cats. One video of Richardson frolicking with his lions has been viewed on YouTube more than twenty-five million times and has collected more than eleven thousand comments. The scope of reactions to the video ranges from awe to respect to envy to bafflement. "If he does die, he will die in his own heaven doing what he loves," one man posted. "This guy chilling with lions like they're rabbits," observed another. Thousands of the comments are just wistful versions of "I want to get to do what he does."

The first time I saw one of Richardson's videos, I was transfixed. Every fiber in our being tells us not to cozy up with animals as dangerous as lions. When someone defies that instinct, it seizes our attention like a tightrope walker without a net—the anticipation of disaster has an irresistible pull. How did Richardson manage this illogical intimacy, and why did he do it? Is he a daredevil with a higher threshold for fear than most people who has, so far, been lucky? That might explain it if he were dashing in and out of a lion's den on a dare, performing a version of seeing how long you can hold your hand in a flame. But it's clear that Richardson's lions don't plan to eat him, and that his encounters with them aren't desperate scrambles to stay a step ahead of their claws. They snuggle up to him, nap on him, lean against him, as lazy and compliant as house cats. His lions aren't tame. He is the only person they tolerate peaceably, and they would probably attack any other person who came close (and in 2018, one of them did kill a visitor). The lions simply seem to have accepted Richardson on some special terms, as if he were an odd, furless, human-shaped member of their pride.

>-<

How we interact with animals has preoccupied philosophers, poets, and naturalists for ages. With their parallel but unknowable lives, animals offer us relationships that exist in the realm of silence and mystery, distinct from the relationships we have with others of our own species. We are all capable of having a rapport with domesticated animals, but anyone who can have a relationship with wild animals seems exceptional, and perhaps a little crazy. Some years ago, I read a book by the writer J. Allen Boone. The book detailed Boone's bond with a variety of creatures, including a skunk and a German shepherd named Strongheart, who had a brief career in Hollywood. Boone was proudest, though, of the friendship he said he had developed with a housefly he named Freddie. Whenever Boone wanted to spend time with Freddie, he "had only to send out a mental call" and Freddie would appear. According to Boone, he and Freddie kept each other company during household chores and often listened to the radio together. Like Richardson's lions, Freddie wasn't tame. No one else could approach him so closely. When an acquaintance of Boone's insisted on visiting Freddie in order to experience this special connection, Boone reported that the fly sulked and refused to be touched.

Befriending a housefly, or a lion, raises the question of what it means when we bond across species. Does it mean something beyond the amazing fact that it has been accomplished? Is it a mere oddity, a performance that signifies nothing important once the novelty has worn off? Does it violate something fundamental, namely, the natural order in which wild things eat us or sting us or at least avoid us, rather than snuggle with us? Or are such rare, extraordinary kinships valuable because they remind us of a continuity with living creatures that we easily forget?

➤◄

Because of his great naturalness with wildlife, you might assume that Kevin Richardson grew up in the bush. Instead, he is a product of a Johannesburg suburb with sidewalks and streetlamps and not even a square inch of jungle. The first time he saw a lion was when he was on a first-grade field trip to the Johannesburg Zoo. (He says he remembers being impressed by the lion, but also thinking it odd that such a magnificent animal existed in such reduced circumstances.) He found his way to animals anyway. He was the kind of kid who kept frogs in his pockets and baby birds in shoeboxes. He swooned over books like *Memories of a Game Ranger*, Harry Wolhuter's account of forty-four years as a ranger in Kruger National Park.

Richardson was a rebellious youngster, a hell-raiser. He is now forty years old, married, and the father of two young children, but he still has an energy and impishness that makes it easy to picture him as a joy-riding teenager, rolling cars and slamming back beers. During his wild adolescence, animals were pushed to the margins of his life. He came back to them in an unexpected way. In high school, he dated a girl whose parents included him on family trips to national parks and game reserves. Those trips reignited his passion for wildlife. He decided he wanted to become a veterinarian. When he didn't get accepted to veterinary school, he got a degree in physiology and anatomy instead.

After college, he worked as a physical trainer. He became friendly with one of his clients, a retail baron named Rodney Fuhr. Like Richardson, Fuhr was keen on animals. In 1998, Fuhr bought a faded tourist attraction near Johannesburg called Lion Park, and he invited Richardson to visit. Richardson says he knew very little about lions at the time. His first trip to the park was a revelation. "I met two seven-month-old lion cubs, Tau and Napoleon," he says. "I was mesmerized and terrified, but most of all, I had a really profound experience. I visited those cubs every day for the next eight months."

➤◄

I spent time with Richardson in South Africa's Dinokeng Game Reserve, which is now home to a wildlife sanctuary that bears his name. While I was there, I gave up all hope for uninterrupted sleep. The lions on the reserve wake up early, and their roars rumble and thunder through the air when the sky is still black with night. Richardson wakes up early, too. He is dark-haired and bright-eyed, and has the handsome, rumpled look of an actor in an aftershave commercial. His stamina is impressive. When he isn't running around with lions, he likes to ride motorcycles and fly small planes. He admits to having a hearty appetite for adrenaline and a tendency to do things to an extreme. He is also capable of great tenderness and loves cooing and sweet-talking to his lions. On my first morning at the reserve, Richardson hurried me over to meet two of his favorite lions, Meg and Ami, whom he has known since they were cubs at Lion Park. "Such a pretty, pretty, pretty girl," he murmured to Ami. It was like listening to a little boy whispering to a kitten.

In 1966, when Lion Park first opened, it was revolutionary. Unlike typical zoos of that era, with their small, bare animal enclosures, Lion Park allowed visitors to drive through a large property in which the wildlife wandered loose. The park's array of African plains animals included giraffes, rhinoceroses, elephants, hippopotamuses, wildebeests, and a variety of cats. These species had once thrived in the area. But Lion Park was adjacent to the heavily populated sprawl of Johannesburg, where most of the land was developed for housing and industry, so it didn't stand a chance to stay wild. Anything that wasn't built up was divvied up into cattle ranches. Between the houses, the factories, the fences, and the farmers, the large animals were driven from the region. Lions, in particular, were long gone.

They once enjoyed the widest global range of almost any land mammal on earth, but lions now live only in sub-Saharan Africa, except for a small population in India. In the last fifty years, the number of wild lions in Africa has dropped by at least two-thirds, from 100,000 or more in the 1960s (some estimates are as high as 400,000) to perhaps 32,000 today. Apart from one species of tiger, lions are the largest cats on earth. They hunt large prey, so a thriving lion ecosystem needs vast open territory where that prey can flourish. Lions are apex predators—in other words, they are at the top of the food chain and aren't hunted by any other predators. What accounts for their disappearance in South Africa, in part, is that they have been killed by farmers when they've ventured onto ranch land. But more important, they have been squeezed out of existence as open spaces have vanished and there is no prey for them. In most of Africa, far more lions live in captivity than in the wild.

The land that Lion Park encompassed, like the land around it, was barren. No large animals still existed on it. The park had to be stocked with lions, so Fuhr bought a pride of retired circus lions who had probably never seen a natural environment in their lives.

The safari drive at Lion Park was immediately popular. But it was a distant second to a park feature known as Cub World, where visitors were allowed to get out of their cars and enter an enclosure where they could hold and pet lion cubs. No one could resist it. Unlike a lot of other animals that could easily kill us—alligators, say, or poisonous snakes—lion cubs are adorable, with soft faces and snub noses and round ears. Part of the thrill of holding them is the disconnect between their fierceness as adults and their docility as cubs.

Once they get to be around six months old, though, lion cubs are too big and strong to be held. At Lion Park, these adolescents would graduate to being part of the "lion walk," where, for an additional fee, visitors could stroll beside them in the open. By the time lions are two years old, however, they are too dangerous for any such interactions. Every now and then, a few of the aged-out cubs might join the park's "wild" pride. But the real problem is a mathematical one. To keep the very popular Cub World stocked, you need lots of cubs. Then they grow up, and in a short amount of time, there are more adult lions than the park can accommodate.

Richardson spent as much time as he could at Cub World. He discovered he had a knack for relating to the animals. His connection seemed different and deeper than what the rest of the staff had with the animals. The lions appeared to respond to his confidence. Richardson invented his own version of lion language and would roar and howl along with them. Lions happen to be the most social of big cats. They live in groups and collaborate on hunting, and they are extremely responsive to touch and attention. Richardson played with the cubs as if he were another lion, tumbling and wrestling and nuzzling them. He got bitten and clawed and knocked over frequently, but he felt the animals accepted him as one of their own. The relationship sustained him. "I can relate to feeling so alone that you are happiest with animals," he says. He was most attached to Tau and Napoleon, and to Meg and Ami. He began spending so much time at the park that Fuhr eventually gave him a job. He was thrilled to be with his lions full-time.

>-<

At first, Richardson didn't give much thought to what became of the lions that had aged out of Cub World and the lion walk and weren't added to the park's adult pride. He says he remembers someone mentioning, vaguely, that the surplus lions were sent to a farm nearby. He admits that he let naiveté and willful denial keep him from pursuing the subject further. One thing is certain. None of the Cub World animals—or any cubs from similar petting farms that began popping up around South Africa, following Lion Park's success—were successfully introduced to the wild. Because they had been handled since birth and hadn't learned hunting skills, these lions were not fit for living independently. What's more, even if they were somehow able to adjust to a wild life, there was nowhere for them to be released. South Africa's wild lions live in national parks, where they are monitored and managed to ensure that they have sufficient range and prey. Each of the national parks already has as many lions as it can comfortably hold. There is simply no spare room at all, no space for more adult lions. This situation underscores a troubling realization: Taking care of Africa's lions shouldn't focus on increasing the lion population but instead accept that there are probably too many lions for the dwindling habitats. Lions are not in short supply. Space for them to live in the wild, however, is.

>-<

Some of the surplus lions from petting facilities like Lion Park end up in zoos and circuses. Others are sent to Asia, where they are slaughtered, and their bones are used in folk medicine. Many are sold to one of the roughly 180 registered lion breeders in South Africa, where they are used to produce more cubs. Cub-petting is a profitable business, so there is a constant need for new cubs, since each cub can be used for only a few months. Critics charge that these cub breeders take newborns away from their mothers shortly after birth, so that they can breed the females again immediately, rather than wait for them to go through the long process of nursing and weaning. Most of the approximately six thousand captive lions in South Africa live on breeding farms, cycling through pregnancy over and over again.

The rest of the extra adult lions from places like Lion Park end up as trophies in commercial hunts. The commercial hunt facilities operate in such a way as to guarantee hunters a trophy. The lions are contained in a fenced area, so they have no chance to escape, and sometimes they are sedated so the hunters have an easier shot at them. The fee to shoot a male lion in one of these "hunts" is up to $40,000. It costs around $8,000 to bag a female. Trophy hunting is big business in South Africa. It brings in nearly $100 million a year in revenue. Close to one thousand lions are killed in such hunts each year. The majority of the hunters come from the United States.

In an email, Fuhr acknowledged to me that cubs raised at Lion Park for the petting facility had ended up as trophies in canned hunts when they aged out of the petting and walking concessions. He added that he was sorry it had happened. He said that more recently he instituted new policies that "ensure the best that is possible [and] that no lions end up at hunting operations." He didn't explain where they would end up instead.

>-<

One day several years ago, Richardson arrived at Lion Park for work and went to look in on Meg and Ami. They were gone. He tracked down the park manager, who told him that Meg and Ami had been sold to a breeding farm. Richardson was furious. He managed to convince Fuhr to arrange for their return. Once the arrangements were made, Richardson decided to go retrieve the lionesses himself. It was the first time he had seen a lion breeding farm. He was shocked by the sight of hundreds of lionesses crowded into narrow corrals like cattle. It was his moment of reckoning. He finally understood that cub-petting was the root of the problem. It provided financial incentive to breed captive lions, and it produced scores of semi-tame cubs that had no reasonable future anywhere. He was part of a system that was dooming endless numbers of animals. He wanted no part of it anymore, but he wanted to keep the lions he was close to.

➤·◄

Richardson had begun to attract international attention by that time, thanks to a television special that featured him playing with one of his lions. This attention put him in an untenable position. He was known for celebrating the magnificence of lions. But demonstrating his unusual ease with them might seem to glorify the possibility of taming them. He also was working at a facility that contributed to their commodification through the cub-petting program. He felt directly responsible for the thirty-two lions, fifteen hyenas, and four black leopards that he cared for at Lion Park. He began imagining a scenario in which he convinced Fuhr to let him have them. But even if Fuhr would part with them, Richardson had no place to take them. "I started thinking, 'How do I protect these animals?'" he says. He didn't have an answer.

Around this time, Fuhr began working on a film called *White Lion*. The plot centered on an outcast lion that was facing hardship on the African plains. Richardson was coproducing it with Fuhr and was managing the animal actors. He suddenly had a notion: he suggested to Fuhr that he would trade his producing fee for half-ownership in his menagerie. To Richardson's delight and surprise, Fuhr agreed. Richardson scrambled to arrange suitable housing for the animals. He managed to find a farm nearby where he could house them. As soon as the film was done, he moved his group of animals from Lion Park to the farm. For a while, he continued working at Lion Park, even though he was beginning to feel more and more uncomfortable with his association with the place. Eventually, his relationship with Fuhr derailed and he left the job.

➤·◄

Richardson saw the rupture with Fuhr and his departure from Lion Park as a perfect chance to reinvent himself. He had become famous because of his ability to tame lions. Now, he decided, he wanted to work on behalf of keeping wild ones wild. All the while, though, he wanted to keep demonstrating his singular relationship with his animals—the snuggles, the hugs, the romps he had with the lions. The message was confusing, because it suggested that the ultimate relationship with a wild animal was intimate and familiar rather than arm's length. Richardson says he is aware of the contradictions inherent in what he's doing. His defense is that his lions are exceptional, on account of the exceptional circumstances in which they were raised, petted, and babied by all the visitors at Lion Park. He says he doesn't want them to be seen as a model for future lion-human interactions.

"If I didn't utilize my relationship with the lions to better the situation of all lions, it would just be self-indulgent," Richardson says. "But my 'celebrity,' my ability to interact with the lions, has meant I've had more impact on lion conservation." He believes that helping people appreciate the animals—even if it's in the form of fantasizing about hugging one—will ultimately motivate them to oppose hunting and support protection.

➤·◄

A few years ago, Richardson met Gerald Howell. Howell and his family owned a farm that abutted Dinokeng Game Reserve, which is the largest wildlife preserve in the Johannesburg area. Some time back, in a very unusual gesture, the Howells and many nearby farmers took down the fences between their properties and the park. This meant that any wild animals in the area could stroll across the combined property: effectively, it added huge amounts of land to the 46,000-acre reserve. Now, instead of farming their land, the Howells run a safari camp for visitors to Dinokeng.

After they met and formed a relationship, Howell offered Richardson a section of his farm where he could permanently house his animals. Richardson was elated. He built shelters and enclosures on the Howell farm. Then he moved his lions and hyenas to what he hopes will be their permanent home.

➤◄

There was rain in the forecast the week I visited Richardson. Every morning, the clouds draped down, swollen and gray. Still, the weather was fair enough for taking a lion out on a walk. Richardson's animals live in simple, spacious enclosures. They aren't free to roam at will, because they wouldn't mix well with Dinokeng's population of wild lions. Richardson tries to make up for their limitations by taking them out in the park frequently, letting them roam under his supervision. It's a strange mix of freedom and captivity. "In a way, I'm a glorified jailer," he says. "But I try to give them the best quality of life they can possibly have." After a lion-roar wake-up call, Richardson and I left the safari camp and drove across Dinokeng's rumpled plains of yellow grass and acacia trees and black, bubbling termite hills. Bush willows that had been uprooted by foraging elephants were piled like pickup sticks beside the road. In the distance, a giraffe floated by, its head level with the treetops.

That day, Richardson said, it was Gabby and Bobcat's turn for a walk. We drove to the lion enclosures. As soon as the animals saw Richardson's truck pulling in, they crowded up to the fence, pacing and panting, the way the family dog might when he sees someone reach for his leash. The lions seemed to radiate heat; the air pulsed with the tangy scent of their sweat. Richardson unlocked the gate and entered the enclosure. "Hello, my boy," he said, ruffling Bobcat's mane. Bobcat blinked slowly and deeply, shifting just enough to allow Richardson room to sit down. Gabby, who is excitable and rascally, flung herself on Richardson, wrapping her massive front legs around his shoulders. "Oof," Richardson said, struggling to keep his balance. "Okay, yes, hello, hello my girl." He tussled with Gabby for a moment and then pushed her down. Then he checked an app on his phone that showed him where Dinokeng's eight wild lions had congregated that morning. Each of the wild lions at Dinokeng has a radio collar that transmits its location. On the app, the lions show up as little red dots on a map. This is essential information for Richardson. Lions, in spite of their social nature, are ruthlessly territorial, and fighting among rival prides is one of the leading causes of death among wild lions. "We definitely don't want to run into the wild lions when we take these guys out for a walk," Richardson said. "Otherwise, that would be curtains. A bloodbath."

After deciding on our course, Richardson loaded Gabby and Bobcat into a trailer. We headed into the park, the truck jangling and clattering in the ruts in the road. Guinea fowl, their blue heads bobbing, strutted in manic circles in front of us, and a family of warthogs scampered by, bucking and squealing.

At a clearing, we rolled to a stop. Richardson climbed out and opened the trailer. The lions jumped down, landing without a sound, and then bounded away. A herd of waterbuck grazing in the scrub caught their scent and spun to attention, flashing their white rumps. They froze, staring hard, moon-faced and vigilant. Occasionally, Richardson's lions have caught prey on their walks, but most of the time they stalk but then lose interest, and come running back to him. The prey they stalk the most often is the tires on the truck, which apparently are wonderful if you're looking to chew on something squishy. Richardson often has to shoo them away when they set upon the tires.

I watched the animals trotting away. I asked Richardson why they don't just take off once they are let loose in the park. "Probably because they know where they get food, and just out of habit," Richardson said. Then he grinned and added, "I'd like to think it's also because they love me." We watched Gabby move toward the herd of waterbuck. She inched along and then exploded into a run. The herd scattered. As soon as they were out of her reach, she wheeled around and headed back toward Richardson. She heaved herself at him, three hundred muscular pounds going full speed. Even though I had seen him embrace his lions many times, and had watched all the videos of him in many such energetic encounters, and had heard him explain how he trusts the lions and they trust him, my heart lurched, and for a split second the sheer illogic of a man and a lion in a warm embrace rattled around in my head.

Richardson cradled Gabby for a moment, saying, "That's my girl, that's my girl." Then he dropped her down and tried to direct her attention to Bobcat, who was rubbing his back against an acacia tree nearby. "Gabby, go ahead," he said, nudging her. "Go, go, my girl, go!"

Gabby headed back to Bobcat. Then the two of them trotted down the path, away from us, small birds bursting out of the brush as they passed by. They moved quickly, confidently. For a moment it looked as if they were on their own, lording over the landscape. It was a beautiful fantasy. These were lions who had grown up in an amusement park, being petted by tourists. And even if they forsook their relationship with Richardson and ran off, they would soon come to the fenced perimeter of the park, and their journey would end. Those constraints are not just present here in Dinokeng. All of South Africa's wilderness areas, and most throughout Africa, are fenced in, and all of the animals in them are, to some extent, managed—their roaming is contained, their numbers are monitored. The hand of humanity lies heavily on even the farthest reaches of the most remote-seeming bush. Humankind has ended up mediating almost every aspect of the natural world, muddling the notion of what being truly wild can really mean anymore.

>--<

Rain began to dribble down from the darkening sky. A light wind picked up, scattering bits of brush and leaves. Richardson checked his watch. It was time to head home. He hooted to the lions. They heard him call and almost immediately circled back. Each of them took a swipe at the truck tires and then, unprompted, hopped into the trailer for the ride home. Once they were locked in the trailer, Richardson handed me a treat for Gabby. He told me how to offer it to her. I held my hand flat against the bars of the trailer, my heart banging against my ribs. She pressed against the bars and scooped the meat away from my hand with her tongue. After she swallowed, she fixed her amber eyes on me, took my measure, and then slowly turned away.

➤◄

Richardson would like to make himself obsolete. He imagines a world in which we do not meddle with wild animals at all, and we no longer create misfits that are neither wild nor tame, out of place in any context. In such a world, lions would have enough space to be free, and places like his sanctuary wouldn't be necessary. He says that if cub-petting and canned hunting were stopped immediately, he would give up all of his lions. He says this, it seems, to demonstrate his commitment to abolishing the practices of cub-petting and canned hunting. But it's more hypothetical than possible, because those enterprises aren't likely to be stopped anytime soon. In reality, no matter what happens, his lions will be dependent on him for the rest of their lives. They have known him since they were a few months old. Most of them are now middle-aged or elderly, ranging from five to seventeen years old. A few, including Napoleon, the first lion who enchanted him at Cub World, have died.

He told me that he had no plans to acquire young lions, so at some point all of his animals will be gone. Sometimes, though, in spite of your firmest intentions, plans change. That's the way of the world. A few months ago, Richardson was contacted by a lion rescue organization, which had seized two malnourished lion cubs from a theme park in Spain. The organization hoped Richardson would provide a home for the cubs. At first, he said no, in keeping with his vow to not acquire any more lions. But eventually he relented. He knew the cubs would never be entirely healthy and would have a hard time finding another place to go. In a blink of an eye, he had two new lion cubs.

He is pleased with how the cubs have thrived since they arrived. When we stopped by the lion nursery one day, it was clear how much Richardson loved being near them. Watching him with lions is a strange and marvelous sort of illusion—you don't quite believe your eyes, and you're not even sure what it is that you're seeing, but you are thrilled by the mere sight of it and the possibility that it implies, that we can peaceably live with wild things.

The cubs, George and Yame, tumbled on the ground, clawing at Richardson's shoes and chewing on his laces. Richardson wrestled with them and scratched their itchy spots. "After them, that's it," he said, shaking his head. "Twenty years from now, the other lions will have passed away, and George and Yame will be old. And I'll be sixty." He started laughing. "I don't want to be jumped on by lions when I'm sixty!" He leaned down and stroked George's belly. He sighed and said, "I think I've come a long way. I don't need to hug every lion I see."

The Rabbit Outbreak

Most rabbits have, in their skill set, the ability to pretend that they're healthy even when they're quite sick. It's sort of the inverse of playing possum, but done for the same purpose, namely, to deflect attention from predators, who would consider a sick rabbit easy pickings. As a result of this playacting, rabbits often die suddenly—or what appears to be suddenly—when, in fact, they've been sick for a while.

This past February, a pet rabbit being boarded overnight at the busiest rabbit veterinary practice in New York City, the Center for Avian and Exotic Medicine, died. The fact that this rabbit had seemed chipper but then expired without warning was chalked up to the rabbit habit of feigning good health. Later that evening, another rabbit at the clinic died. The coincidence of the additional death was strange, especially because the first rabbit that died was elderly, and the second was young. A third rabbit that died at the clinic that same night was middle-aged. Even though this rabbit was known to have had an abdominal mass that compromised her well-being, there had been no reason to think she was about to perish. Two deaths might have been a fluke. Three seemed ominous.

The clinic's staff wanted to get the remaining fifteen or twenty rabbits out of the building immediately, but many of the owners were away and unable to retrieve them on short notice. This group of owners happened to include Alix Wilson, the clinic's medical director. Wilson was on vacation; her own rabbits, Captain Larry and Dolly, were boarding at the clinic while she was away. In the meantime, as a precaution, the staff threw out all the clinic's rabbit food and bedding, in case something in them had poisoned the three rabbits. Within several weeks, eight more rabbits that had been at the clinic in February succumbed. Captain Larry was thriving. But Dolly, a medium-size lop that Wilson had just adopted to keep Larry company, died.

>-<

One of the lagoviruses of the virus family Caliciviridae causes a highly contagious illness called rabbit hemorrhagic disease. RHD is vexingly hard to diagnose. An infected rabbit might experience vague lethargy, or a high fever and difficulty breathing, or the rabbit might exhibit no symptoms at all. Regardless of the symptoms, though, the mortality rate for RHD can reach a gloomy 100 percent. There is no treatment for it. The virus's ability to survive and spread is uncanny. It can persist on dry cloth with no host for more than a hundred days. It can withstand freezing and thawing. It can thrive in a dead rabbit for months, and on rabbit pelts, and in the wool made from Angora rabbit fur, and in the rare rabbit that gets infected but survives. The virus can travel on birds' claws and flies' feet and coyotes' fur. Its spread has been so merciless and so devastating that some pet owners have begun referring to it as "rabbit Ebola."

According to the United States Department of Agriculture, RHD is a "foreign animal disease": one that is "an important transmissible livestock or poultry disease believed to be absent from the United States and its territories that has the potential to create a significant health or economic impact." All foreign animal diseases are "reportable." This means that any incidence of the disease needs to be reported to a state animal-health official. In most places, that's the state veterinarian, who, like a governor, oversees local policy. (Many animal issues are decided at the state level.) The disease must also be reported to the USDA and to the World Organisation for Animal Health, which is headquartered in Paris and tracks viruses globally.

Alix Wilson, the veterinarian, was familiar with RHD, and she wondered in passing whether it might have been responsible for the deaths at her clinic. "But then I thought, No, impossible," she said recently. "Rabbit hemorrhagic disease isn't in New York City." Her staff sent tissue from one of the dead rabbits to a lab at Cornell University, which subsequently transferred it to the federal foreign-animal-disease lab, on Plum Island, in New York. When the diagnosis came back as a variant of the virus, called RHDV2, Wilson was astonished. The clinic immediately stopped taking in any rabbits, and began a deep cleaning, which included replacing ceiling tiles and discarding thousands of dollars' worth of equipment that couldn't be sterilized. Todd Johnson, the USDA's emergency coordinator for New York and New Jersey, helped oversee the cleanup, and a veterinary epidemiologist and an intern from the department contacted 155 owners of rabbits that had been in the clinic during the previous few months, in an effort to identify Rabbit Zero. The bewildering thing was that, as it turned out, rabbits had already been dying of RHDV2 in Washington State, and soon were dying in other states, including Arizona, Texas, New Mexico, and Nevada.

➤◄

The RHD virus was originally identified in 1984, in Jiangsu Province, China. First, it killed Angora rabbits being raised commercially for wool. Then it burned through pet rabbits and rabbits farmed for meat, all of which are members of the same species, *Oryctolagus cuniculus*, or what is commonly known as the European, or domestic, rabbit. During the initial outbreak in China, some 140 million rabbits were killed by the virus. The disease soon ravaged rabbit populations elsewhere in Asia, and then in Europe, the United Kingdom, Australia, and the Middle East.

There were only a handful of cases of the original variant of RHD in this country, and they were quickly contained. Still, the majority of rabbit products—meat, fur, skins, and live rabbits—imported to the United States came from countries where the disease had been widespread. The USDA decided to classify it as a foreign animal disease, but a department report written in 2002 warned that RHD "has emerged as a growing concern for the rabbit industry following outbreaks in 2000 and 2001."

➤◄

In the universe of human-animal relations, rabbits occupy a liminal space. They are the only creatures we regularly keep as pets in our homes that we also, just as regularly, eat or wear. Fitting into both the companion-animal category and the livestock category means that rabbits are not entirely claimed by either. A number of animal statutes—particularly felony-cruelty provisions—apply to dogs and cats, but not to rabbits. Laws protecting livestock, such as the Humane Methods of Slaughter Act, don't cover rabbits, even rabbits being raised for meat, because the USDA does not officially recognize them as livestock. There is probably no other animal that is viewed as diversely, and valued as differently, by its various partisans. Simply being a rabbit person doesn't mean that you look at rabbits the same way as another self-identified rabbit person. Any of the almost twenty thousand members of the American Rabbit Breeders Association (ARBA) are just as likely to be raising a prized Jersey Wooly that sleeps in their bed and is primped for rabbit shows as they are to have hundreds of caged rabbits that will end up as stew.

A few years ago, a lawyer named Natalie Reeves, who volunteers at a rabbit shelter and has lectured on rabbit law at the New York City Bar Association, was having trouble untangling the hair of her pet long-haired rabbit, Mopsy McGillicuddy. She found an Internet group for long-haired-rabbit owners. She posted about Mopsy's hair troubles, and expected she would receive tips on conditioners and brushes. On the site, she noticed that a common response to similar problems was to kill the rabbit and start fresh with another.

>-◄

Rabbits are everywhere among us. They live on every continent except Antarctica, in a wide range of environments. They have been domesticated for hundreds, if not thousands, of years. There have even been noteworthy rabbit booms. During the Victorian era, the most sought-after, bidded-up bunnies were a domestic breed, the Belgian hare, which was, quite unironically, developed to look like a wild rabbit. Belgian hares had sleek, black-ticked chestnut fur, comically long ears, and long bodies. They were the spitting image, in fact, of Peter Rabbit, who debuted in Beatrix Potter's *The Tale of Peter Rabbit* in 1902, in the thick of Belgian hare mania.

A shipment of six thousand Belgian hares that arrived in the United States from Europe in 1900 attracted interest from tycoons including the Rockefellers, the du Ponts, and J. P. Morgan, who considered them an equity investment. (They were indeed a good investment: a male Belgian hare sold for $5,000, the equivalent of more than $150,000 today.) According to the Livestock Conservancy, nearly every large American city soon had a Belgian hare club. Fans in Los Angeles alone had sixty thousand Belgians.

Rabbits being rabbits, the number of Belgian hares grew exponentially, and the market for them, inflated by their seeming scarcity, eventually buckled. People moved on to other breeds, and superfluous Belgians began to disappear. By the 1940s, there was a worry that they might even become extinct.

Rabbits have an unusual history with viruses. The first virus ever deliberately used to eradicate a wild animal population was myxoma virus, which causes myxomatosis, a disease fatal to domestic rabbits. It was deployed in 1950 in Australia, where a dozen or so domestic rabbits released on a hunting estate in 1859 had outperformed all mathematical modeling and become many hundreds of millions. The spread of rabbits in Australia was the fastest-known spread of any mammal on earth. The rabbits wreaked ecological disaster as they ate their way across the country. Shooting them made only a temporary dent in their numbers. Myxoma virus was introduced in the hope of controlling the population. It soon killed an estimated five hundred million rabbits. (In parts of Australia, probably as a result of this population explosion and fear that it could repeat itself, it is still illegal to have a pet rabbit.)

Two years after the release of myxoma in Australia, a doctor in France who was annoyed by rabbits stealing vegetables from his garden caught two of them in the act and injected them with myxoma. The rabbits bolted, and survived just long enough to transmit the virus to other rabbits. The disease eventually bloomed across Europe and the United Kingdom, killing almost every rabbit in its path. Eventually, a myxomatosis vaccine was developed, and after wiping out most of the rabbits in Europe, the disease was more or less brought under control.

>-◄

Myxomatosis did make its way to the United States, but for some reason it never got much of a foothold here. Had it established itself, it would have been disastrous, because at that time, in the middle of the last century, rabbits were a significant food source. Most people associate rabbit meat with European diets, but it was once a staple in this country. There were many huge commercial rabbit farms in the United States, and rabbit meat was readily available in supermarkets. The biggest processor was (and still is) Pel-Freez. The company was founded in 1911 by a man who was given a pet rabbit that happened to be pregnant, and, according to Pel-Freez's corporate history, he turned "the dilemma into an opportunity." Rabbit meat, which could be cooked like chicken, was appealingly high in protein and low in fat. Back then, rabbit was also much cheaper than beef. And raising rabbits is easy; anyone can do it in the backyard. A rabbit can give birth every thirty days. A young rabbit reaches what is known as "fryer age" in just sixty days. Even during their heyday as a market product, though, rabbits weren't treated like other livestock. Because the USDA doesn't classify them as such, it has never required rabbit meat to be inspected or graded.

After the Second World War, the demand for rabbit meat began to decline. The number of cattle being raised domestically nearly doubled around that time, so beef, which had previously been something of a luxury, became affordable. The cattle industry, which brings in some $70 billion a year, began promoting beef as the patriotic mainstay of the American dinner table. In the same years, factory farming made chicken ubiquitous. Soon, chicken became the white meat of choice, and rabbit was marginalized as an occasional dish.

Eric Stewart, the executive director of the American Rabbit Breeders Association, lays some of the blame for the decline of rabbit meat on Bugs Bunny. Created in 1940, Bugs, a sassy, man-size gray-and-white rabbit, had a leading role in the Warner Bros. cartoons *Merrie Melodies* and *Looney Tunes*. In 1960 Bugs's star turn, *The Bugs Bunny Show*, was launched; it ran on network television for the next forty years. Stewart believes that the generations that had grown up watching Bugs Bunny could not stomach eating rabbit.

In addition to the impact of Bugs, pet-rabbit ownership suddenly surged. It got a huge boost in 1981, with the publication of a book called *Your French Lop: The King of the Fancy, the Clown of Rabbits, the Ideal Pet*. The author, a rabbit owner named Sandy Crook, made the case that pet rabbits could be perfect house pets, just like cats and dogs. Rabbits could be kept inside, rather than relegated to a hutch in the backyard, because they could be trained to use a litter box. Many people consider *Your French Lop* to be the foundational text of the house rabbit movement. Furthering the movement, another best-selling manifesto, Marinell Harriman's *House Rabbit Handbook: How to Live with an*

Urban Rabbit was published four years later. The number of rabbits kept as house pets has grown ever since.

✦

We don't know exactly how many rabbits there are in the United States, but we do know that they are the third-most-popular pet in the country, ranking just behind dogs and cats. Among small pets, they are the most popular, ahead of hamsters, guinea pigs, and mice. The USDA estimates that there are more than 6.7 million pet rabbits, but the total number of domestic rabbits would depend on whether you're counting only pet rabbits or including rabbits raised for slaughter. Further complicating matters is the category of rabbits raised as, say, a 4-H project, which, once the project is done, might segue from pet to meat.

Rabbit-related activities are also on the bounce. There are about five thousand ARBA-sanctioned rabbit shows each year. The largest show attracts more than twenty-five thousand rabbits. There are rabbit fashion shows, which are especially popular in Japan. One show in Yokohama has featured rabbits dressed like Sherlock Holmes, Amelia Earhart, and Santa Claus. In New York City, pet owners regularly hold rabbit play-dates in Central Park. Throughout the country, owners organize rabbit speed dates, which are opportunities for rabbits to meet and see if they like one another, a necessary process if an owner is thinking of getting a second, or third, or fourth. The typical American owner has more than one rabbit, so speed dating is important, because rabbits, despite their prodigious ability to multiply, don't always get along.

✦

Within five years of the emergence of the original form of rabbit hemorrhagic disease in China, a vaccine protecting against RHD had been developed. A number of manufacturers produce vaccines against this strain, including Filavie, in France; HIPRA, in Spain; and Merck, which is headquartered in New Jersey but made the vaccine only for the European market. The vaccine was never made available in the United States. After all, there were only a few RHDV1 cases here, and they seem to have originated elsewhere. One in Pennsylvania, for instance, was thought to have come from an Oktoberfest party where imported rabbit meat was served. If the meat was infected, the virus could have spread to vegetables prepared in the same kitchen; the vegetable scraps were then fed to rabbits who later developed RHDV1.

Most countries affected by RHDV1 began offering the vaccine, and within a few years the spread in Europe appeared to have been tamped down. But in 2010, rabbits in France began dying of what turned out to be a mutated version of the virus. The vaccine for the original virus was ineffective against the new strain; this was RHDV2. Soon, RHDV2 was rampant throughout Europe and Australia. In England, the spread was so vigorous that parents were advised not to let their children bury their dead rabbits in the garden; the practice, "while comforting to children, may help circulate rabbit virus." The mortality rate of the new variant appeared to be slightly lower than that of the original. At first this seemed like good news. But, in fact, RHDV2 was even more efficient at spreading, in the sense that more infected rabbits were surviving, and, because they might not show any symptoms, they weren't being isolated and could pass along the disease. Vaccines guarding against RHDV2 were soon developed. (In some cases, they were produced in combination with the vaccine that prevents RHDV1.) By 2016, they were available across Europe, and vaccinating rabbits for both variants became common.

Initially, the new variant of the virus, like the original, seemed to stay away from the United States, except for a few isolated cases. But in July 2019, a pet Norwegian Dwarf male on Orcas Island, near Seattle, developed a bloody nose and then died. A veterinarian who examined the rabbit was aware of RHD, and knew that bloody noses are a symptom, so she called the Washington State Department of Agriculture to report the rabbit's death. Susan Kerr, an education and outreach specialist in the department, was alarmed when she heard of the veterinarian's report, because she knew there was an ongoing RHDV2 outbreak in British Columbia. The rabbit's body was sent to a lab for a necropsy, to determine what had killed it.

While waiting for those results, Kerr's coworkers began receiving calls from a number of people on San Juan Island, which is about a dozen miles southwest of Orcas Island. The callers were noting that the island's rabbits seemed to have disappeared. As it happens, San Juan Island is famous for its rabbits. In the 1930s, a commercial breeder on the island was going out of business and released its three thousand rabbits into the wild when it closed up shop. These rabbits multiplied and became a tourist attraction. Rabbit hunting on the island was so celebrated that, in the sixties, *Sports Illustrated* ran a story about it, titled "Hippity Hop and Away We Go." By 1971, San Juan Island, which covers just fifty-five square miles, was home to an estimated one million feral domestic rabbits.

Kerr's department also began receiving calls from a few other nearby islands reporting rabbit deaths. Something, clearly, was afoot. The lab soon confirmed that the Orcas Island rabbit had died of RHDV2. Kerr then got news that most of the 145 rabbits at a facility on the Olympic Peninsula, across Puget Sound from the islands, had died in a three-week period. Their symptoms sounded like RHDV2. The virus was traveling. As a precaution, rabbits and rabbit products were banned from the ferry system that services Puget Sound.

A colleague of Kerr's posted about the outbreak on an online animal-health newsletter and was inundated with requests from owners who knew that a vaccine existed, asking how they could get their rabbits inoculated. But the vaccine for RHDV2, like the vaccine for the original virus, was available only overseas. No companies had a license to distribute it in the United States. The USDA opposed importing it, except for limited special circumstances. One reason the USDA held back is that attempts to produce the vaccine on cell lines in a laboratory, in accordance with USDA rules, have failed. Merck produces a vaccine in cells, but it's a live, genetically modified vaccine, which is not permitted in this country. The other companies that currently manufacture the RHD vaccine produce it by infecting live rabbits with RHD. When those rabbits die, vaccines are made from their livers. According to a spokesperson for Filavie, one rabbit yields several thousand vaccine doses.

The USDA also maintained that vaccinating some rabbits would make it difficult to distinguish between sick rabbits and those with antibodies produced by the vaccine, so you might end up mixing them and inadvertently spread the virus that way. Whatever the merits of these arguments, the rabbit community found the department's mulishness infuriating. Some people said that it reflected the department's bad attitude toward rabbits, treating them as disposable goods, easily replaced. Others thought that the USDA simply didn't want to manage all the paperwork required to bring a vaccine from overseas, or maybe just didn't want to acknowledge that the virus was present in the United States.

The USDA finally agreed to consider requests for the emergency importation of limited amounts of the vaccine, but only if veterinarians applied first through their state veterinarians. Leaving the question of the vaccine to the states, though, meant that there could be fifty different decisions on it—a patchwork of guidelines for a disease that would travel with no regard to borders. A number of veterinarians said that they were interested in applying to import the vaccine, but, once they discovered the headaches involved, most of them gave up. Alicia McLaughlin, one of the medical directors of the Center for Bird and Exotic Animal Medicine, in Bothell, Washington, was the first veterinarian in the country to obtain the vaccine. (She ordered it from Filavie.) She, too, had heard about the RHDV2 outbreak in British Columbia, so she started researching how to get the vaccine well before the USDA finally made its ruling. By that time, McLaughlin had a list of several hundred clients who had requested it. "I knew the virus would get here eventually," she said recently. "Once it was in British Columbia, it was just a matter of time."

To get the vaccine, she first applied to the Washington state veterinarian for permission; was shuttled for a month between the state agriculture department and the USDA; had to manage language and time-zone barriers; and then had to hire a customs broker, at her own expense, to shepherd the vaccines across borders. Finally, more than four months after she applied, she received five hundred doses of Filavac VHD K C+V, which protects against both RHDV1 and RHDV2. By the time McLaughlin was finally able to administer the vaccine to her clients, in April 2020, concerns over COVID-19 had meant that she could offer only curbside service, and she had to struggle to find personal protective equipment, which she needed, because she was interacting with patients and handling their animals.

>--<

The Center for Avian and Exotic Medicine, in Manhattan, had to be thoroughly sanitized after its RHDV2 outbreak. To be absolutely sure that it was uncontaminated, Alix Wilson, the veterinarian, brought two rabbits to live at the clinic. The rabbits would serve as sentinels. Because the virus is so contagious, the rabbits would almost certainly come down with RHDV2 if it was still in the facility. "No one wants to bring animals in to die," she said. "But it's one sure way in veterinary medicine to prove that a cleanup has worked." To her relief, the rabbits survived. Wilson then applied to import the vaccine and received a rejection letter from the USDA saying that "without evidence of widespread infection," the risk was too low to justify her request, especially since, as the department maintained, household rabbits have no contact with others.

There had been a few days' delay between the first rabbit deaths at the clinic and when the clinic announced the diagnosis. Some of the clinic's patrons were furious. According to Wilson, though, the clinic couldn't have done it any faster, since it had to wait to hear the results of the necropsy. The fact is that even the mention of RHD panics rabbit owners. Thousands have joined a Facebook group to exchange knowledge, vent, and worry. Useful information is interlaced with dread. One concern is whether it's even safe to let a veterinarian know if you think that your rabbit might have RHD, since the veterinarian is obliged to report it to the state veterinarian. The fear—which, according to the New Mexico state veterinarian, Ralph Zimmerman, is mostly justified—is that, if your rabbit does have the virus and you have other rabbits, you will be required to "depopulate"; that is, you will have to euthanize them. There is also persistent chatter that the vaccine actually caused the disease—that RHD is part of a global plot to rid the world of rabbits. Recently, a member of the Facebook group proposed that rabbit owners sue Australia, perhaps conflating the past use of myxoma virus there with the outbreak of RHD. "No," another member replied, "we cannot sue Australia."

>—◂

Just as the clinic in New York was reopening after being sanitized, someone came across thirty dead rabbits near Fort Bliss, Texas. Unusual numbers of dead rabbits were also found in Arizona, New Mexico, and Colorado. Along with pet rabbits and a small rabbit-meat industry, the Southwest has large populations of wild black-tailed jackrabbits and cottontails. Although they resemble domestic rabbits, these are different species entirely; they can't interbreed with domestic rabbits, nor are they susceptible to all of the same diseases. Wild rabbits seemed immune to RHDV1. But RHDV2 made a cross-species leap, and in March 2020, jackrabbits and cottontails throughout the Southwest began dying in droves. "I've gotten reports that it's in the thousands," Zimmerman said. "I'm sure next I'll be hearing that it's in the tens of thousands." Zimmerman has scraped together money from New Mexico's state budget to import five hundred doses of the vaccine, which he will distribute to veterinarians around the state. He assumes that those doses will go to "high-dollar breeding animals."

But nothing can help the wild rabbits. Some vaccines, such as the one for rabies, can be distributed to wild animals by putting them out as food, but the vaccine for the RHD virus has to be given by injection and repeated every year. The concern is not only that many wild rabbits could be lost; what happens to them reverberates in other animals, including foxes and bobcats and wolves and hawks, since rabbits are their chief protein source. "Once those predators run out of rabbits," Zimmerman said, "cats and poodles will become their preferred food." Or, if there aren't enough wayward cats and poodles to go around, they'll starve.

In the past three months, RHDV2 has shown up in seven western states. Now that it has jumped to wild rabbits, most veterinarians I've spoken to believe that the virus is here to stay, and that the USDA should change its designation from a foreign animal disease to one that's endemic. There have been a few lucky breaks. For instance, the big rabbit shows scheduled for the spring, which would have brought together tens of thousands of rabbits—a recipe for contagion—were canceled because of COVID-19. Nevertheless, RHDV2 is advancing unabated.

The National Assembly of State Animal Health Officials, which represents all state veterinarians, recently formed a working group to evaluate the vaccine and make recommendations to the public. The group hasn't released its report yet, but recently I got an email from Annette Jones, the California state veterinarian, who is the vice president of the assembly, saying, "Yes, we should have [the vaccine] available . . . we are hoping a manufacturer steps up and applies to USDA for a license." No American manufacturer has applied so far, but at least one has contacted the American Rabbit Breeders Association to feel out interest. "It's hard to get these companies interested in rabbit medicine," a veterinarian told me. "All the money is in cats and dogs." The fact that people tend to own rabbits in multiples makes the economics of selling the vaccine complicated. Pet owners with one or two rabbits might not shy away from an annual vaccination that could cost thirty dollars or so, but many rabbit owners have ten or twenty or two hundred rabbits, so the cost becomes prohibitive.

Cost and availability aren't the only challenges. "I'm worried that there is the controversy that a bunny died to make the vaccine," Alicia McLaughlin told me, sighing. "This vaccine is the only option we have at the moment, so it's frustrating." The House Rabbit Society, a rabbit rescue and education organization, posted a letter on its website pointing out that rabbits die in the manufacturing process of the vaccine. In conclusion, it urged members to consider whether "the RHDV2 vaccines are right for you and your family." Natalie Reeves had been eager to vaccinate her rabbit, Radar, as soon as possible. She has never skimped when it comes to her rabbits—she spent thousands of dollars on veterinary care for Mopsy McGillicuddy, her rabbit with the tangled fur, treating her for lymphoma. "I just learned information tonight that is very disturbing," she wrote me in an email, after reading the House Rabbit Society letter about the manufacture of the vaccine. "I don't know whether I could in good conscience vaccinate my rabbit, knowing that I would be contributing to the death of others."

As RHDV2 is poised to become endemic in the United States, the vaccine, which is the one thing that might stop it, is now caught up in the contradictions of rabbits. When I first spoke to Reeves, she had mentioned that rabbits are the most discriminated against of all domestic animals. They are ridiculed for their lustiness; viewed as expendable; lumped in with oddball animals like chinchillas and prairie dogs; always subject to the question of whether they're pets or meat. She rued that the vaccine was just one more example of the peculiarity of rabbits' place in the world. Would dog owners be expected to use a medicine that was produced by killing a dog? Once again, rabbits seem to be betwixt and between. As Ralph Zimmerman put it, "Rabbits are just a real conundrum."

The Perfect Beast

One recent morning, inside a renovated camel barn, across town from the White House, and just past a refrigerator on which a form was posted listing portions of bamboo and something called "Leaf Eater Food, Gorilla," four adult humans sat with their gazes fixed on a bank of video screens on which absolutely nothing was happening. Everyone in the room was delighted. The images being transmitted were of two creatures in an enclosure in an adjoining room. One of them looked like a large, fuzzy soccer ball—its shape, proportions, and black-and-white markings were reminiscent of a MacGregor Classic Size 5. The other was the considerable bulk of a middle-aged female *Ailuropoda melanoleuca*, a giant panda, named Mei Xiang. Mei and the cub, which was born in late summer and is named Bao Bao, were both sound asleep. Except for the slightest flutter of fur rising and falling with their breath, they were absolutely motionless. The audio feed from the enclosure was more nothingness, just a low rushing whoosh made by air passing over a microphone. The observers were nevertheless transfixed as the pandas continued their deep, still sleep. Minutes ticked by. On the screen, one paw flicked, and then the animals resumed their pure repose. The hypnotic appeal kept everyone in the room almost as immobile and silent as the pandas, all eyes on the screens. "Great morning," one of the observers finally murmured. "Everything is just perfect."

>--<

Whatever strange twists and bends evolution took to create the giant panda worked devilishly well to result in an animal that is irresistible. Even inert, pandas have charisma. That morning, as I sat in the control room of the National Zoo's Panda House, Mei and the cub offered little more than that one slight flick of a paw and, a few minutes later, one small adjustment of their sleeping positions, and yet I had to be dragged away from the screens when it was time to go. The number of people who have volunteered to monitor the cameras and log each minute of the baby panda's life—a job that could define the word "tedium"—far exceeds the number needed. It is easy to enumerate the elements that contribute to the panda's allure. Take one part overly large, childlike head; add big eyes (made to appear bigger by black eye patches), rounded ears, chunky build, and snazzy fur. Add the fact that pandas rarely kill anything. Add their usual posture—sitting upright, bamboo stalk in hand, expression Zen-like, or bumbling along pigeon-toed, wagging their short, flat tails—and you have built the perfect beast. As Brandie Smith, a curator of mammals at the National Zoo, likes to say, pandas are the umami of animals; they are simply delicious. It seems that humans have the equivalent of panda taste receptors that leave us besotted at the mere sight of one, even when it is sound asleep, curled up in a ball, doing nothing other than being a panda.

If pandas were simple, they might not be as marvelous. Instead, pandas are peculiar, persnickety. They are a one-off, limited-edition animal model that has guarded many of its secrets, in spite of the fact that it has been scrutinized by zoologists for decades. Even the basic question of what they are—whether they are more bear or more raccoon or something else altogether—is still tossed around. A study in 1985 by Stephen O'Brien of the National Cancer Institute used molecular analysis to definitively classify pandas as members of the bear family. But they are weird bears. Unlike other bears, for instance, they are not hunters. (Instances of a panda eating another animal are so unusual as to be newsworthy; when a panda in China was spotted scavenging the carcass of a goatlike animal, it made headlines for days.) Unlike all other bears, pandas do not hibernate. They do not make bearlike sounds. Smith showed me a video of Bao Bao being examined by zoo veterinarians, and the sound she made was exactly like a teenage girl whining, "Owwww! Owwww!" in a nasally, high-pitched voice. As an adult, Bao Bao will bleat like a Merino sheep.

In the meantime, Bao Bao will grow one of the few functionally opposable thumbs in the animal kingdom. She will use her thumb to strip leaves off her beloved bamboo. When she is mature, she will have a once-a-year estrus, which will last one to three days, during which she will show the only flicker of interest in other pandas she will ever demonstrate. The fact is that the pandas we adore so much simply don't adore one another. (They hardly tolerate each other's company.) After her brief coupling up, the panda will have a hormonal surge that will seem to indicate that she's pregnant, but the surge occurs whether she is pregnant or not. This makes it nearly impossible to tell the difference between a real panda pregnancy and a "pseudo-pregnancy" until the day a cub is born (or not) approximately four months later, which is why there always seems to be such breathless anticipation when a captive panda reaches the end of what might be a real gestation. It's a lot like a royal baby watch, but with one major difference. When the Duchess of Cambridge is pregnant, there's no question that she's pregnant; a panda, on the other hand, keeps you guessing. In short, the panda is the classic mystery wrapped in an enigma, delivered in the most endearing package in the world.

➤◄

These days, captive pandas are made, not found. Mei's cub, for instance, is the happy result of artificial insemination. Even though Mei Xiang and the zoo's male panda, Tian Tian, have intercourse now and then, they aren't very good at it, so the zoo veterinarians inseminate Mei for insurance each time she is in estrus. In a small, crowded room across the zoo property from the panda enclosure, the reproductive physiologist who did the actual insemination, Pierre Comizzoli, showed me several small metal tanks that contain frozen sperm from many species at the zoo, including samples from Tian Tian, Bao Bao's father. In another of the panda's many oddities, it produces very hardy sperm. Unlike, say, bull semen, panda semen does well when it's cryopreserved at minus 200 degrees Celsius. Strangely enough, that hardy sperm produces one of the tiniest babies in the animal world, proportionately speaking: a 250-pound panda delivers a cub that is about the size of a stick of butter, and as fragile and helpless as a china doll.

>-<

Are pandas some sort of evolutionary mistake? Their scarcity sometimes makes it seem that way, and so does their eccentricity—the finicky diet, the fleeting day of fertility, the tiny cubs. But that's not quite so. Their diet is one-note, but that one note happens to be among the most abundant forms of vegetation on the planet. Still, bamboo is an odd choice, and scientists have determined that it actually wasn't the panda's first choice of meals. Panda ancestors were carnivorous distant cousins of hyenas, saber-toothed cats, and badgers. Pandas' digestive tracts are designed for meat: they don't have the long, redundant stomach system of grass-eaters like cows. As a result, they eat a lot of bamboo, but they don't digest it very well. So why not stick with meat? Apparently, in the course of evolving, pandas lost the taste receptor for high-protein foods. They simply weren't attracted to meat anymore. Scientists aren't sure why this happened. Whatever the reason, the result was an appetite for leafy greens, and fortunately, the pandas' range was covered with bamboo forests that kept them nourished, even though an adult has to eat bamboo almost constantly to maintain its body weight.

The panda's brief window of breeding is vexing to zoo staff trying to get their pandas pregnant, but in the wild, pandas have had no trouble reproducing. They are a species way off in the margins, but these were comfortable margins—that is, until development began its squeeze on their habitat. The newest surveys of China's wild panda population are rumored to contain good news. The number of animals in the large preserves appears to be growing. This suggests that pandas are not a misfit species, dwindling because of their own bad engineering, but instead, a special animal so finely in tune with its environment that any change puts the species in jeopardy.

>‒<

We are so smitten with the pandas we are able to see in captivity that it's easy to forget the ones we don't see, the wild ones that carry on in their solitary, bamboo-crunching way, almost entirely hidden from view in the snowy folds of China's mountains. At the Smithsonian Conservation Biology Institute in Front Royal, Virginia, I met with a few of the dozen or so researchers who spend their time worrying about those pandas. According to David Wildt, the head of the species survival team, it is a sometimes thankless and often unglamorous task. Much of the time, after trekking through hard terrain in lousy weather, researchers end up seeing lots and lots of panda feces but no pandas. There is much to learn even from that, but it couldn't compare with the pleasure of encountering one of these almost magical animals, especially in its own domain. The strange equation of evolution has created an unusual animal like the panda, as well as having induced in humans a powerful desire to look at pandas, however we can.

>‒<

Sometimes, of course, the scientists in the field do get lucky. One of the researchers I met at Front Royal was a man named Dajun Wang, a research scientist at Peking University. Dajun trained with the Smithsonian and collaborates with the species survival team. He spends most of his time tracking pandas on the preserves in western China. He was explaining to me that wild pandas' elusiveness is a matter of their hard-to-navigate habitat and their solitary behavior, rather than any fear of humans. In fact, they don't actually seem to mind humans very much.

As Dajun was talking about this, he began to grin, and then he told me about one female panda that he had tracked that had become particularly comfortable in his presence. She was so relaxed that one spring morning, as she was walking near Dajun with her cub, she stopped and indicated that she wanted him to babysit the cub so she could head off to feed. Another scientist filmed this episode of Dajun providing panda child care. Watching the video, which is now posted on YouTube, you will be struck not only by the amazing sight of a panda cub tumbling and frolicking with Dajun, but also by the look of utter joy on Dajun's face as he scratches the cub's belly, extracts the sleeve of his jacket from the cub's inquisitive grip, and then, at one point, hoists the cub up in the air and waltzes with him for a moment.

"That," Dajun writes on the YouTube page, "was best time in my life."

Lost Dog

On August 6, 2003, Stephen Morris parked his car at the Atlanta History Center, expecting to spend the next half an hour or so edifying himself and his nephew on the particulars of the Civil War. It was the beginning of what would turn out to be a very bad day. At first, though, everything seemed fine. Morris is a sinewy guy in his fifties with a scramble of light-brown hair and the deliberative air of a nonpracticing academic. He was in the thick of completing his doctoral dissertation, a biography of William Young, a seventeenth-century composer in the court of the Archduke of Innsbruck. Morris's teenage nephew was visiting from British Columbia, and Morris had taken a break from his dissertation to show his nephew the highlights of Atlanta. Morris's wife, Beth Bell, a square-shouldered, dry-witted epidemiologist whose specialty is hepatitis, didn't join them because she was at her job at the Centers for Disease Control and Prevention. She is a senior investigator at the CDC; that day, she was knee-deep looking into a salmonella outbreak among attendees of jam-band concerts.

Morris found parking at the History Center easily enough. The open-air three-story garage there is small, but it had plenty of available spaces. A sign above the entrance reads, forebodingly, "Help Us Keep Your Vehi-

cle Safe While You Are Here. Please Remove All Valuables from Vehicle."
But, warning aside, the History Center is in a prosperous, bosky section
of Atlanta called Buckhead, where people and vehicles are generally out
of harm's way. Morris and Bell's car, a dinged-up but serviceable 1999
Volvo station wagon, was not the sort to attract much attention anyway.
The only noteworthy things about the car were its contents: Morris and
Bell's dog, Coby, a black border collie with an artificial hip and a missing
tooth, and a rather nice viola da gamba that Morris was looking after in
his capacity as a rental-program director of the Viola da Gamba Society
of America.

August 6 was a hot, soupy day. On Coby's behalf, Morris left the car
with its windows up and its doors locked but with the engine running
and the air conditioner on. He took an extra ignition key with him. This
is a common bit of animal husbandry in southern climates if you want
to leave your dog in a parked car and don't want to return to find him
cooked. An unoccupied but idling car with the ignition key inserted, sitting in a relatively empty parking garage, might present to a certain kind
of person an irresistible temptation. But if anyone saw such a person in
the vicinity, he didn't make an impression.

Morris and his nephew wandered through the cool white halls of the
museum, did a quick appraisal of the War Between the States, and then
got ready to leave. They walked back to the garage and couldn't find
the car. At first, they thought they had misremembered where they'd
parked it. They looked through the whole garage and came back to where
they were absolutely sure they had left it. There was no question that the
Volvo, the viola da gamba, and the dog were gone. All that marked the
spot was a glittering blue sprinkle of broken glass.

Around eighty cars are stolen in greater Atlanta every day. It is a steady
but not exceptional number, putting the city's rate of disappearing cars
a little behind Houston's and a little ahead of Seattle's. Besides the car,
most of the auto thefts reward the perpetrator with nothing more than
the typical car contents—maybe a couple of cassette tapes, some fast-

food flotsam, or a clutch of exhausted air fresheners. Stephen Morris and Beth Bell's car, though, included its unusual booty of dog and viola da gamba. It is quite likely that the thief never even noticed these contents. He was probably too excited about finding a car with a key in the ignition to take stock.

Morris and Bell were upset about losing the viola da gamba (it was a good reproduction of a fifteenth-century instrument and worth thousands of dollars). They were not happy about losing their car. But those were trifling concerns compared with how they felt about losing their dog. In the report that Morris filed with the police once they arrived at the History Center, he didn't even mention the viola da gamba, but he brought up Coby's kidnapping a number of times.

>-◄

Generally speaking, people love their dogs. Morris and Bell are especially devoted to Coby because they have nursed him through a variety of misadventures. They first spotted him at a sheepherding event they came across when they were out bicycling in the Georgia countryside. They were instantly smitten and asked the breeder if the dog was available; she told them she had already promised him to someone else. Bell checked back with her a few days later, just in case the other prospective owners had changed their minds. It was the breeder who had changed her mind: she decided that she wanted the puppy for herself. Morris and Bell persisted, and after a day of serious pleading, the breeder agreed to sell Coby to them.

As he grew up, Coby developed full-blown dysplasia in his hips and needed a $4,000 surgery to replace one of them. When he was two and a half, he busted a tooth playing catch. Sometime later, he caught a stick wrong, and it jammed down his throat a few millimeters from his windpipe. Coby's vet, who saved him from the stick mishap, likes to describe him as a dog with nine lives. In his current life, at least, Coby is a bushy-haired, prick-eared dog with tensed shoulders, an arresting stare, and an avid fetch-centric attitude. His dedication to retrieving bounceable rubber objects is so inexhaustible that it is exhausting. He has worn a deep, dusty path in Bell and Morris's yard between where they like to stand when they throw his Kong toy and where he likes to lie in wait for it. Thanks to Coby, Morris has developed a hot pitching arm and a firm way of saying, "That will do, Coby," when he runs out of energy to keep throwing.

>-<

So here was the problem with the dog in the stolen car. A dog on foot can travel only about five miles an hour, but a dog in a car can travel at sixty or seventy miles an hour. In one scenario, in which, say, Coby jumped out of the car and walked away from the History Center, a perimeter of his possible whereabouts could have been plotted according to his likely pace. If he was in the car, though, there was no way of knowing where he might be. Within an hour or two, he could have been crossing into Alabama or South Carolina or Tennessee.

Epidemiological science was of some help in Coby's disappearance. That evening, a number of Bell's CDC colleagues joined her and Morris and set out to search the thirty-three acres of the History Center and the surrounding area. "We were in the hypothesis-generation stage of the investigation," Bell said. "We first developed the hypothesis that Coby might still be at the History Center." Bell postulated that the guy who had taken the car did not actually want a dog, that his interest was solely in the car, and consequently, it would stand to reason that as soon as he noticed Coby, he would have let him out. Her secondary postulation was that when the thief broke the window to get into the car, Coby had escaped. Both premises had Coby still in the History Center area.

This led them to the Tullie Smith Farm, an antebellum homestead on the grounds of the History Center. The homestead features maidens in muslin churning butter and dipping candles, and also features a small herd of sheep. Border collies love sheep. Direct line of reasoning! The crew of epidemiologists headed straight for the it. No Coby. They returned the next day, too. "We looked around and didn't see Coby, but we stopped everyone who passed us," one of the searchers told me. "We got some interesting responses. We approached one older woman and asked her if she had seen the dog, and she said no. Then she said that she had just lost her family and she asked us if we'd seen them."

The search party continued their efforts. They hung some hastily made posters on light poles. They checked around trash cans and dumpsters, places a hungry dog might go. They flagged down cars driving past on nearby West Paces Ferry Road. They crisscrossed the History Center's Mary Howard Gilbert Memorial Quarry Garden and its Victorian Playhouse and its Swan Woods Trail. They searched until eleven at night on Wednesday, and most of the day Thursday, but there was no dog, and no sign of the dog.

>-<

In all sorts of circumstances, dogs go missing. They slip out the door with trick-or-treaters; they burrow under fences; they take off after unattainable squirrels and pigeons. Some dogs are repeat offenders. Recently, I heard the story of Huey and Dewey, a pair of Shetland sheepdog siblings from Massachusetts who took strong exception to an examination by a veterinarian and ran away. After forty-three days, Huey was found by a dog-search volunteer, but Dewey, alas, was gone for good. A year and a half after that first walkabout, Huey took strong exception once again, this time to a visit to a kennel. She was found eighty-nine days later, a few feet from where she'd escaped.

Sometimes a dog that is presumed lost forever unexpectedly reappears. A certain Doberman pinscher from San Francisco, capable of standing on its head, vanished. Three years went by. His owner found him when by chance she overheard a waiter in a restaurant saying that his roommate's new dog, a Doberman, had the ability to stand on its head; it was her missing Dobe.

According to the American Pet Product Manufacturers Association's count, in 2003 there were sixty-five million pet dogs in this country. An estimated ten million go astray every year. About half of those are returned. Others end up in new homes under assumed names or are killed by cars or by other misadventures. Many, though, disappear without a trace.

Dog-identification contraptions are a gigantic subset of the supergigantic $34.3-billion-a-year pet-care industry. In addition to tags shaped like hearts and stars and fire hydrants, available in aluminum, gold, steel, or with rhinestones, to be worn dangling from a collar, there is a brisk business in microchip tags, which are grain-size data-bearing devices that are implanted under the skin between an animal's shoulder blades. Microchips were introduced in the early eighties. Avid Identification Systems, of Norco, California, one of the largest microchip companies in the world, has more than eleven million pets in its international database. HomeAgain, another major microchip supplier, has its chips in close to three million animals. GPS Tracks, a Jericho, New York–based company, introduced the world's first global-positioning system for dogs, a fist-size transmitter called a GlobalPetFinder, which attaches to the animal's collar and transmits its exact location every thirty seconds to a cell phone or computer. Before the device was even officially announced, the company had a waiting list of more than three thousand customers. "One night, it was pouring rain, my dog had run away, the kids were hysterically crying, and I thought, this *has* to stop," Jennifer Durst, the founder and CEO of GPS Tracks, said recently. "If they have LoJack for cars, why can't there be a LoDog for dogs?"

➤◄

Coby, regrettably, had neither a microchip implant nor an early release prototype of GlobalPetFinder. He wasn't even wearing his rabies tag, which is another way a lost animal can be identified. Coby usually wears his rabies tag attached to a nylon collar printed with his name and phone number, but Bell and Morris take it off every night so that Coby can sleep in the nude. They put his collar on every morning. That particular day, unfortunately, Morris hadn't put Coby's collar on yet because he expected that the History Center trip would be brief, and he assumed that Coby would be safely cosseted in the car. This meant the dog was now at large as well as anonymous, and anything that could identify him and help him be sent back home was in a basket by the back door of Bell and Morris's sprawling split-level in a suburb of Atlanta.

After Wednesday night's fruitless search, Bell decided that it was time to accelerate into an outbreak investigation—that is, to apply the same techniques she uses when analyzing something like, for instance, a wave of illness among methamphetamine users in Wyoming. She and Morris blast-faxed Atlanta-area animal shelters, local rescue groups, and nearby veterinarian offices. They listed Coby on many of the almost countless Internet lost-pet sites, including PetFinder, Pets 911, Pets Missing in Action, FindFido, Petznjam, K9Finder, Dog Tracer, and Lassie Come Home. They made hundreds of posters. On Thursday they hung the posters in high-volume, highly animal-sensitive areas like the parking lots of pet stores. They also hung them along Peachtree Road, which cuts diagonally through northeast Atlanta and is lined with the city's busiest restaurants and bars. Bell reasoned that it was one of the few places in the city where people travel on foot—in other words, at a speed slow enough to allow for a close reading of a lost-dog poster.

They got responses immediately. A woman about an hour's drive away in northern Gwinnett County called to say that she had found a dog loosely fitting Coby's description. Bell and Morris drove up to take a look at the dog, but he turned out to be a border collie someone else had lost. A woman called from Alabama, but by her description, the dog she had found was a small white poodle. The phone kept ringing. Some of the calls reported dog sightings, some offered advice, many were from people who had also lost dogs and just wanted to commiserate. Bell and Morris were flooded with emails:

Hi, this is Amy . . . I'm so sorry to hear about this tragedy.
Maybe the thieves put him out in Buckhead, but who knows?
Wonder why the dog was left in a car on a HOT summer
day??????
I'm sorry your dog is missing, what a sad story.

➤◄

On Thursday and Friday, Bell and Morris visited animal shelters around Atlanta to make sure that Coby wasn't waiting among the errant terriers and beagles in the city pound, or the pit bulls and hounds languishing in shelters outside of town. Bell realized that it was also, unfortunately, time to start checking with the city employee who was assigned the unpleasant task of cataloguing each day's roadkill. "When you're searching for something, you never know what you're going to find," she said recently. "But I know from my work that you do have to ask the question."

One other question was whether to look for help elsewhere. The cohort of people with lost pets is large and forms a significant and often free-spending market to be served. One of the best-known lost-pet detectives in the country, Sherlock Bones, got into the business on a price-per-pound basis. Fed up with a job in the insurance industry, Bones, whose civilian name is John Keane, decided to start his own business. He wasn't sure what kind of business to pursue until he happened to see an ad for a lost Chihuahua. Keane said that the ad was an epiphany.

"There was a thousand-dollar reward for that Chihuahua," he told me recently. "I thought to myself, 'That's five hundred dollars a pound.'" Keane started Sherlock Bones in 1976. He operates out of Washougal, Washington, and works on about five hundred lost dog cases a year. He used to do ground searches but now has moved on to just consulting and producing materials—primarily posters and mailers—for bereft owners. "Doing actual searches was very stressful," he said. We spoke on the phone while he was out for a morning walk with his own dog, a French Briard, and he was puffing lightly as he talked. "You're dealing with people in crisis," he went on. "It's a serious business, since after eight hours it is unlikely someone will find their pet themselves, unless they're very lucky. They need help from someone who has the right information. You don't go to a rabbi to learn how to play baseball." Keane said he specializes in dogs and cats. "I don't deal with infrequent animals," he said. "Although I did make up a poster for a lost llama once. He was named Fernando Llama."

Bell and Morris decided to call Sherlock Bones if they hadn't had any success finding Coby by Monday. In the meantime, they got in touch with a volunteer dog searcher named Debbie Hall, who belongs to a loose community of people across the country who trace lost pets for free. Hall helped them redesign their flyer for maximum impact. She suggested that they add a description of their car as well as the dog. She sent them extensive recommendations—eight long documents—on pet searches.

Hall and her husband live in southeastern Massachusetts. They have a Yorkie-Chihuahua mix and a Yorkie-poodle mix. They also have three parakeets, two of which they got as gifts and a third that is probably someone's lost pet, because it just showed up in their yard one day. An entire room in the Halls' house is taken up by pet-detective appurtenances—a rack of camouflage clothes, a few Havahart traps, and half a dozen notebooks detailing Hall's searches. Hall often stays out all night on cases. "It's a long-ass day," she explained, "but I love what I do. This is the one thing in my life that I'm good enough at to call my work." It has not been without its challenges. Someone pulled a gun on her while she was searching for a German shepherd in Virginia, and once she got trapped in her own six-foot Havahart trap. Worst of all, she has spent countless days mourning dogs that she found only after they had died. "It still hurts," she said, flipping to a page in her notebook about her first case, Tia, a runaway border collie who eventually was found drowned. "But I am always optimistic that you will find your dog."

Late Saturday night, three days after Coby had disappeared, Bell and Morris got a break. A young guy walking down Peachtree noticed one of their posters and called to say that he had been playing rugby in a park downtown a few days earlier and he had seen a dog there that looked like Coby. He told Bell that a man had been walking around the park with the dog, saying someone had just dropped it off.

First thing Sunday morning, Bell and Morris headed over to the park, a weary-looking plot of land in a hard-luck section of the city known as Old Fourth Ward. At the nearby Tabernacle Baptist Church and Mount Sinai Baptist Church, services were just ending, and congregants were pouring out of the building, so Bell and Morris stopped and asked them if they had seen the dog, but no one had. They left the church and walked down Boulevard, the wide road on the western edge of Old Fourth Ward, past men playing dice in minimart parking lots and loitering in front of signs saying, "Private Property Do Not Sit on Wall." They passed out flyers and asked after Coby.

"My brother has that dog," one of the men told Bell. "If you give me two dollars, I'll go get him." Someone else said he'd played catch with the dog but couldn't remember when or where.

Bell and Morris handed out more flyers. A young man passing them on the sidewalk took a flyer, walked away, and then turned on his heel and came back to talk to them. He introduced himself as Chris Walker and told Bell and Morris that he didn't know anything about the dog, but he did know something about their car. He said he had seen it near the park over the last few days, and he knew the guy who was driving it because they'd been in police detention together a few months earlier.

"This guy Chris was a true scientist," Bell said admiringly. "He didn't know the guy's name, but he recalled that there were only three other people in detention with him. One was Egyptian, one was elderly, and the third was the car thief. Consequently, all we needed to do was get the detention records, eliminate the Egyptian and the elderly person, and we would end up with the car thief's name."

Walker urged Bell and Morris to call the police right away. He seemed eager for them to corroborate his story. They called the police. Walker waited with them for almost an hour until a cruiser responded. Walker was disgusted that the police didn't have a computer in the car that could review detention records on the spot. He was so eager to have his tip substantiated that he accompanied Bell and Morris to a nearby precinct house to see if a police officer there would pull up the records. The officer wouldn't oblige them, but he did believe that Walker was telling the truth. He suggested that Morris and Bell contact Midtown Blue, an organization of police officers who do security work when they're off duty, which he thought might help them.

Morris and Bell gave Walker some reward money for his tip, but he seemed more interested in making sure that they followed up on his story. "Chris has the family curse," Walker's uncle Lee Harris told me when I visited him last summer. "People in this family will just bend over backward to help anyone in pain." Later that Sunday, after leaving Bell and Morris, Walker tangled with a police officer. On Monday, when he called Bell to find out if she'd found her car, he mentioned that he was calling from jail.

>-<

As astonishing as Walker's story seemed, Bell and Morris believed that he had indeed seen their car. Factoring in what the rugby player who had called them from Peachtree had told them, they began to suspect the car thief had let the dog out in the park. Bell and Morris made their way to the shallow slope near the playing fields and talked to a number of homeless people who sleep there under a small stand of oak trees, who they figured saw what came in and out of the park. The people they spoke to all remembered seeing Coby.

Some of those same people were still living in the park the next summer when I went to Atlanta to learn about Coby's story. I visited the park on a blistering, heavy day. Sound was bouncing here and there: someone was listlessly banging tennis balls against a wall, and muffled cheers and hollers from a soccer game at the far end of the park rose up in the sodden air. A man was sitting on a bench under a concrete pavilion in a sliver of shade, plunking on a guitar held together with duct tape. He told me that his name was Ben Macon. He said that he had been living in the park for ten years. He told me that he had spent several days with Coby. He described the dog precisely, down to Coby's striking stare and predatory crouch while playing catch.

"That dog was unbelievable," Macon said. "He was someone you could play with. He'd be your friend. You could tell he was a people dog." Macon strummed a little and then leaned on the guitar. "If I had a place of my own, I'd like a dog like that. But people with dogs, those are people who have good jobs." He paused for a moment and then added, "A dog like that gives you a warm feeling. I miss him."

>-<

On Sunday, Bell and Morris spent hours searching the park and going up and down Boulevard. Finally, they took a break from handing out flyers and hanging posters and went home to shower and eat. Shortly after they got home, their phone rang. The woman on the line said that on Saturday she and her partner had picked up a black male border collie with no collar as he chased a tennis ball across Boulevard. They had been trying to find his owner through rescue groups, with no success. At that moment, they were in their car with the dog heading to the veterinarian because they had decided to keep him. But at a stoplight on the way to the vet they had seen one of Bell and Morris's posters. The poster had probably been hung no more than an hour before they'd spotted it.

The caller, Danielle Ross, suggested that Bell and Morris meet them at the vet. When she got off the phone, Ross decided to say the name of the dog on the poster to the dog in her car, just to see if he responded. First, she mispronounced it, saying "Cobbie," like a corn cob. The dog, who looked reasonably healthy but was totally exhausted, didn't lift his head. Then she tried another pronunciation—"*Co*-bee"—and the dog sat up, alerted. By the time Ross arrived at the Pets Are People Too clinic, she knew that Coby was going home.

When Bell and Morris pulled into the parking lot of the vet clinic, they could see the dog through the front window. They knew instantly that it was Coby. As exhausted as he was, he raced to meet them at the door.

>•<

At home, they doted on Coby and kept going over the details of the coincidence that led him back to them. The phone rang. A police officer identified himself and said he had news for them. There had been an automobile accident; the driver had fled; the car, which the police had impounded, belonged to them. The next day, Bell and Morris went to the police station to claim the car. First, they were told that they were mistaken—that no car matching their car's identification numbers had been impounded. But then the officer checked the records again and determined that the police did in fact have the car. There wasn't much to retrieve because it had been totaled.

With both Coby and the car accounted for, Bell and Morris felt they might be on a streak. All they needed now was to find the viola da gamba. They decided to look in the phone book for pawn shops. There are nearly three hundred pawn shops in the Atlanta area, so they concentrated on ones near the park where Coby had spent his time. One of them, Jerry's Pawn Shop, listed musical instruments among its specialties.

Admittedly, it was a long shot. There are some ten thousand items pawned each month in downtown Atlanta alone, and it was just a series of conjectures that, one, the car thief would have decided to cash in the instrument, and two, he would have chosen to do it at a pawn shop, and three, he would have taken it to a shop near the park. But the logic seemed solid. Morris called Jerry's and asked after the viola da gamba. Yes, they had just gotten one from a fellow who had pawned it for twenty-five dollars. Bell and Morris raced to Jerry's.

The viola at Jerry's was, in fact, Morris's loaner. The man who pawned it? "Well, he didn't strike me as a viola da gamba player," Bill Hansel, who handled the transaction, recalled. According to Hansel, the man was youngish, in a hurry, and wanted to sell the viola da gamba outright rather than pawn it. Georgia law requires fingerprints and identification from anyone doing business with pawn shops. The police later traced the address that the non–viola da gamba player had provided. It turned out to be an empty house.

>-◄

At this point, the police certainly knew the thief's name. After all, it was on the pawn voucher and in the detention records from his previous lockup with Chris Walker, and there were fingerprints on the Volvo, the viola da gamba, the pawn voucher, and probably on Coby. But the man was still at large. Before the car was towed to a wrecking yard, Morris went through it one more time to see if there were any last belongings of his or Bell's still inside. There was nothing of theirs, but the thief had left behind some of his clothes, a bunch of computer parts, notes from his girlfriend, poetry he had written, and a stack of address labels bearing someone else's name.

Where Donkeys Deliver

The donkey I'll never forget was coming around a corner in the walled city of Fez, Morocco, with six color televisions strapped on his back. If I could tell you the exact intersection where I saw him, I would do so, but pinpointing a location in Fez is a formidable challenge, a little like finding GPS coordinates in a spiderweb. I might be able to be more precise about where I saw the donkey if I knew how to extrapolate location using the position of the sun, but I don't. Moreover, there wasn't any sun to be seen and barely a sliver of sky, because leaning in all around me were the sheer walls of the medina—the old walled portion of Fez—where the buildings are so packed and stacked together that they seem to have been carved out of a single huge stone rather than constructed individually, and they are clustered so tightly that they blot out the shrieking blue and silver of the Moroccan sky.

The best I can do, in terms of telling you where this took place, is to say that the donkey and I met at the intersection of one path that was about as wide as a bath mat and another that was slightly larger—call it a bath sheet. The Prophet Muhammad recommended that the minimum span of a road be the width of three mules, or about seven cubits, but I would bet that most of Fez's paths fall below that standard. The paths were laid out in the late eighth century by Idris I, founder of the dynasty that spread Islam in Morocco. They are so narrow that bumping into another person or a pushcart is no occasional accident. It is simply the way you move forward—your progress is more like that of a pinball than a pedestrian, bouncing from one fixed object to the next, brushing by a man chiseling names into grave markers only to slam into a drum maker stretching goat skin on a drying rack, then to carom off a southbound porter hauling luggage in a wire cart.

In the case of my meeting the donkey, the collision was low-impact. The donkey was small. His shoulders were about waist-high, no higher. His chest was tapered; his legs straight and slim; his hooves quite delicate, no bigger than a teacup. He—or she, perhaps—was donkey-colored, that is, a soft mouse gray, and had a light-colored muzzle and dark brown fur bristling out of his ears. The televisions the donkey was carrying, however, were big—boxy, bulky tabletop sets, not kitchen-counter portables. Four were loaded on the donkey's back, secured in a crazy jumble by a tangle of plastic twine and bungee cords. The remaining two were attached to the donkey's flanks, one on each side, like panniers on a bicycle.

The donkey stood squarely under this staggering load. He walked along steadily, made the turn crisply, and then continued up a smaller path, which was so steep that it had little stone stairs every yard or two where the altitude gain was especially rapid. I caught only a glimpse of the animal's face as he passed, but it was, like all donkey faces, utterly endearing, managing to be at once serene and weary and determined. There may have been a man walking beside him, but I was too transfixed by the sight of the donkey to remember.

This encounter took place a decade ago, the first time I visited Fez. Even amid the dazzle of images and sounds you are struck with in Morocco—the green hills splattered with red poppies, the gorgeous, tiled patterning on every surface, the keening call from the mosques, the balletic swirl of Arabic lettering everywhere—the donkey was what stayed with me. It was its stoic expression, of course. But even more, it was recognizing, in

that moment, the astonishing commingling of past and present—the enduring little animal, the medieval city, the pile of electronics—that made
me believe that it was possible for time to simultaneously move forward
and stand still. In Fez, at least, that seems to be true.

➤◄

Just a mile outside Casablanca's Mohammed V International Airport, on
the side of a four-lane high-speed roadway, underneath a billboard for a
cellular service provider, I saw a dark-brown donkey ambling along, four
huge sacks filled to bursting strapped to a makeshift harness on its back.
I had just arrived for my second visit to the country. I already could see
that there were donkeys everywhere in Morocco, that they operated like
little pistons, moving people and things to and fro, defying the wave of
modernity that was washing gently over the country.

In Fez, I saw donkeys trudging through the city carrying loads of
groceries, propane tanks, sacks of spices, bolts of fabrics, construction
material. The medina, which is the center of the city, may well be the
largest urbanized area in the world impassable to cars and trucks. In the
medina, anything that a human being can't carry or push in a handcart is
conveyed by a donkey, a horse, or a mule. If you need lumber and sacks
of cement to add a new room to your house in the medina, a donkey
will carry them in from the home improvement store outside the medina
for you. If you have a heart attack while building the new room on your
house, a donkey will serve as your ambulance and carry you out. If you
realize your new room didn't solve the overcrowding in your house and
you decide to move to a bigger house, donkeys will carry your belongings and furniture from your old house to your new one. Your garbage is
picked up by donkeys; your food supplies are delivered to the medina's
stores and restaurants by donkeys; when you decide to decamp from the
tangle of the medina, donkeys might carry your luggage out and carry it
back in when you decide to return.

In Fez, it has always been thus, and so it will always be. No car is small or nimble enough to squeeze through the medina's byways. Most motorbikes cannot make it up the steep, slippery alleys. The medina is now a UNESCO World Heritage site. Its roads can never be widened, and they will never be changed. Donkeys might carry in such modern amenities as computers and flat-screen televisions and satellite dishes and video equipment, but they will never be replaced.

When I came back from my first trip to Morocco, I realized I had fallen in love with donkeys in general, with the plain tenderness of their faces and their attitude of patient resignation and even their impenetrable, obdurate temperaments. In the United States, most donkeys are kept as pets. Their pessimism and obstinance almost seem comical. In Morocco, I realized that the donkeys' air of resignation was often coupled with a bleaker look of fatigue and sometimes despair, because in Morocco donkeys are work animals, and they are worked hard and sometimes thanklessly. But seeing them as something so purposeful—not a novelty in a tourist setting but an integral part of Moroccan daily life—made me love them even more, as flea-bitten and saddle-sore and scrawny as some of them were.

➤◄

I am not the first American woman to be fascinated by the working animals of the Fez medina. In 1927, Amy Bend Bishop, the wife of an eccentric, wealthy American gallery owner, passed through Fez on a grand tour of Europe and the Mediterranean. She became intrigued by the approximately forty thousand donkeys and mules working in the city. She was also disturbed by their poor condition. She decided to donate $8,000—the equivalent of at least $100,000 today—to establish a free veterinary clinic in Fez for the city's working animals.

The clinic was named the American Fondouk—*fondouk* is Arabic for "inn." After a stint in temporary quarters the clinic moved to a whitewashed compound built around a courtyard on the Route de Taza, a busy highway just outside the medina, where it has operated ever since. The Fondouk is well known in Fez, even among Fez's animals. Often creatures show up unaccompanied at the Fondouk's massive front gate, needing help. Somehow, they know they will find it at the Fondouk. Just days before I arrived, for instance, a donkey having some sort of neurological crisis stumbled to the clinic on its own. It is possible that these supplicants were abandoned at the door by their owners in the early hours before the Fondouk opened. But Fez and Morocco and the American Fondouk seem to be magical places. After spending just a few hours in Fez, the idea that animals find their way to the Fondouk's shady courtyard didn't seem unlikely to me at all.

The highway from Casablanca to Fez rushes past fields and farms, along the edge of the busy cities of Rabat and Meknes, rolling up and down golden hills and grassy valleys that are lush with yellow broom and chamomile in bloom, and, dotted among them, hot-red poppies. The highway looks new. It could be a freshly built road anywhere in the world, but as soon as you see several mules and donkeys trotting across overpasses as you zoom underneath, it is undeniably set in Morocco.

King Mohammed VI, who is based in Rabat, the capital, makes frequent visits to Fez. Some people speculate that he might relocate the capital there. The king's presence is palpable. The Fez that I encountered ten years ago, on my first visit, was dusty, crumbling, clamorous, jammed. Since then, the massive royal palace has been restored, and at least a dozen fountains and plazas now line a long, elegant boulevard where there used to be a dusty, buckling road. The royal family's interest in the city sparked new development. As I headed to the Fondouk, we passed a gaping excavation that will soon be the Hôtel Atlas Saiss Fès, and a score of billboards touting shiny condominiums with names such as Happy New World and Fez New Home.

The medina, though, looked exactly as I remembered it: the dun-colored buildings tight together, hive-like; the twisting paths disappearing into shadow; the crowds of people, slim and columnar in their hooded *jalabas*, hurrying along, dodging and sidestepping to make their way. It is rackety, bustling.

I chased after my porter, who was wheeling a handcart with my luggage from the car. We had to park outside the medina, of course; he found a spot near the beautiful swoop of Bab Bou Jeloud, the Blue Gate, which is one of the few entryways into the walled city. Just a moment after we got out of the car and passed under the gate into the medina, I heard someone shout, *"Balak, balak!"*—Make way, make way!—and a donkey carrying boxes marked AGRICO came up behind us, his owner continuing to holler and gesture to part the crowd. Within a few moments came another donkey, hauling rusty orange propane tanks. Then came another one. He was wearing a harness but carrying nothing at all, and he picked his way gingerly down one of the steepest little roads. As far as I could tell, this donkey was alone: there was no one in front of him or beside him, and no one behind. I wondered if he was lost or had broken away from his handler, so I asked my porter, who looked at me with surprise. The donkey wasn't lost, he explained. He was probably just finished with work and on his way home.

➤◄

Where do the donkeys of the medina live? Some live on farms outside the walls and are brought in for work each day, but many live inside the medina. Before we arrived at my hotel, the porter stopped and knocked on a door. From the outside, it looked like any of the thousands of doorways of any of the thousands of medina houses. The young man who answered the door led us through a sitting area, where it appeared he had been practicing electric guitar, to an adjoining low-ceilinged room, which was a bit damp but not unpleasant. The floor was strewn with fava beans and salad greens and a handful of hay. A brown goat nursing a puppy-size newborn kid sat in a corner, observing us with a look of cross-eyed intensity. The young guitar player explained that ten donkeys lived in the house. They worked in the medina all day and found their way home each night.

It is estimated that a hundred thousand people in Fez depend in one way or another on a donkey for their livelihood. A good donkey is prized but not sentimentalized. Every time I spoke to someone with a donkey, I asked the donkey's name, just out of habit. The first man I asked hesitated at my question and then answered, "H'mar." The second man I asked also hesitated and then answered, "H'mar." I assumed that I had just stumbled upon the most popular name in Morocco for donkeys, the way you might by chance meet several dogs in the United States named Riley or Tucker or Max. When the third person I asked told me his donkey's name was H'mar, I realized it couldn't be a coincidence, and then I figured out that H'mar is not a name—it's the Arabic word for "donkey." Every donkey in Fez is named Donkey. In Morocco, donkeys serve, and they are cared for, but they are not pets. One afternoon, I was talking to a man with a donkey in the medina and asked him why he didn't give his donkey a name. He laughed and said, "He doesn't need a name. He's a taxi."

>--<

I woke up early my first morning in Fez to try to beat the crowd to the Fondouk. The doors open at 7:30 a.m., and there is almost always a crowd of animals outside the gate by then, waiting to be examined. I have seen photographs of the Fondouk from the 1930s, soon after it had been established. It is remarkably unchanged. The Route de Taza is probably busier and louder now, but the handsome white wall of the Fondouk with its enormous arched wooden door is exactly as it was back then, and the throng of donkeys and mules at the front door with their owners, dressed in the same somber long robes that they still wear today, look like they could exist in any time at all. In those old pictures, an American flag is displayed on the Fondouk's walls, and it still is today.

At the time of my visit, the Fondouk's chief veterinarian was a silver-haired Canadian named Denys Frappier, who had come to the Fondouk planning to stay just two years, but fifteen years have now gone by and he has yet to manage to leave. Frappier lives in the staff residence, a pleasant house fashioned out of some old decommissioned stables. He shares his quarters with ten cats, nine dogs, four turtles, and a donkey. All of them are creatures who were either left at the Fondouk for care and never retrieved by their owners or were independent walk-ins who never walked out. The donkey is a tiny creature who does have a name, the Arabic word for "trouble." He was born at the Fondouk, but his mother died during birth. The owner had no interest in taking care of a baby donkey, so he simply never came to pick him up. An ill-built, knock-kneed animal with a huge head and a tiny body, Trouble was adopted by the veterinary students who were doing internships at the Fondouk. One of them used to let the newborn donkey sleep in her bed in the student dormitory.

Over time, Trouble has become the Fondouk mascot. He is given free rein. He likes to visit the exam room and sometimes snuffles through the papers in the office. When I arrived that morning, he was following Dr. Frappier around the courtyard, watching him on his rounds. "He is nothing but trouble," Dr. Frappier said, looking at the donkey with affectionate exasperation, "but what can I do?"

Before joining the Fondouk, Dr. Frappier had been the chief veterinarian of the Canadian Olympic equestrian team, where he tended to pampered performance horses worth $100,000 or more. His patients at the Fondouk are quite different. That morning's lineup included a bony white mule who was lame; a donkey with deep harness sores and one blind eye; another donkey with jutting hips and intestinal problems; a hamster with a corneal injury; a flock of three sheep; several dogs with various aches and pains; and a newborn kitten with a crushed leg. A wrinkled old man came in just behind me, carrying a mewling lamb in a paper shopping bag. By 8 a.m., another six mules and donkeys had gathered in the Fondouk's courtyard, their owners clutching little wooden numbers and waiting to be called.

The Fondouk's original mission was to serve the working animals of

Morocco, but long ago it began to dispense free care to all manner of living things. The only animals that were turned away were cattle, which are considered a luxury in Morocco, and therefore don't merit free care. Frappier also refused pit bulls. "I was tired of patching the pit bulls up just so their owners could take them out and fight with them again," Dr. Frappier explained as he was checking the hooves of the lame mule. The mule was poorly shod, as are many of the donkeys and mules in the medina. Instead of iron shoes, he was shod with rubber pads cut out of old automobile tires. The corners of his mouth were rubbed raw by a harsh bit. He would have looked better if he'd weighed another thirty or forty pounds.

It took Frappier several years to adjust to the poor condition of many of the animals here. At first, he was so discouraged that he put in a request to resign his post and return to Montreal. He stayed, and in time, he learned to differentiate between "dire" and "acceptable," which is the usual range he sees. The Fondouk has quietly pushed an agenda of better care, and in some part it has been successful. For example, it managed to convince mule and donkey owners that the common practice of sticking cactus thorns in their animals' harness sores didn't encourage them to work harder, and that rubbing salt in their eyes, which folklore claimed would make them walk faster, was not only ineffective but often left the animals blind.

There are animals everywhere you look in Fez, and in Morocco. Cats tiptoe around every corner. Dogs lounge in the North African sun. Even on the roaring roads of Casablanca, horse-and-buggies clatter alongside SUVs and sedans. Yet there are only twelve full-time veterinarians in Fez. Even though its care is free, the Fondouk is considered exceptional, and on two separate occasions the royal family of Morocco, which could certainly afford any veterinarian in the world, has brought its animals there.

Souk el Khemis-des Zemamra, one of Morocco's largest donkey markets, is held every Thursday on a fairground about two hours southwest of Casablanca. I wanted to see it, to be in the epicenter of the donkey universe in Morocco, where thousands of creatures are bought and sold and traded. After decades of leaving such markets to regulate themselves, the government recently began visiting Khemis-des Zemamra and the other large souks to take stock of the transactions and, most urgently, to levy sales tax on them. As a result, more of the trade migrated away from the souks toward word-of-mouth impromptu markets, out of reach of the tax man. The number of donkeys sold in Khemis-des Zemamra these days is perhaps a third less than what it was five years ago.

Still, the souks thrive. Besides donkeys, they sell every single food product and toiletry and household item and farm implement you could ever imagine, serving as a combination Agway, Wal-Mart, Mall of America, and Stop & Shop for the entire population for miles around. If you want chickpeas or hair dye or a fishing net or a saddle or a soup pot, you can find it at a souk. If you want a donkey, you will certainly find the one you want any Thursday morning in Khemis-des Zemamra.

I set out on the five-hour drive from Fez to Khemis-des Zemamra on a Wednesday night. The market starts at the crack of dawn. By noon, the sun is so punishing that the market empties out, leaving nothing but trampled grass and mud marked with wagon wheel tracks and hoof prints. I traveled to the souk with a young Moroccan man named Omar Ansor, whose father recently retired after working for twenty-five years at the American Fondouk. Omar's brother, Mohammed, has worked at the Fondouk since 1994.

Omar told me he loves animals, but he found my fascination with donkeys puzzling. Like many Moroccans, he considered donkeys tools— good, useful tools, but nothing more. Maybe to him, my enthusiasm about donkeys was like being enthusiastic about wheelbarrows. "A donkey is just a donkey," he said. "I prefer horses."

The drive took us past Casablanca, with its gritty air and smoking chimneys and thicket of apartment buildings, and then to El Jadida, a whitewashed resort town on a flat spread of pinkish beach, where we stayed the night. Thursday morning was warm and clear, the silky light spilling over wide fields of corn and wheat. All around us, donkeys and mules were at work in the fields, pulling irrigation machines and plows, shouldering heavily into their harnesses. Carts hurtled alongside on the shoulder of the road, just inches from the roaring traffic, groaning with large families and loads of bulging burlap bags, boxes, and miscellany. The animals pulling the carts moved snappily, as if the sound of the car traffic was egging them on.

We arrived just after 7 a.m. The fairground was already mobbed. We had no trouble parking in the motor vehicle section, because there were only a handful of cars and another handful of trucks. But the rest of the parking area was cluttered with wagons and carts and, tethered near them, scores of donkeys and mules—a few hundred of them at least. They were dozing, nibbling on the scraps of grass, swaying in place, hobbled by a bit of plastic twine tied around their ankles. These animals weren't the ones that were for sale. They were transportation, parked while their owners were shopping.

A roar floated over the fairground—the haggling of hundreds of buyers and sellers, and the smack and thump of boxes being opened, and the sound of sacks being slapped down to be filled, and the hollering of vendors, and a thunderous blast of Moroccan music playing off of an unattended laptop computer that was hooked to man-size speakers, beneath a tent made of fabric cut from a Nokia cell phone billboard. We walked through a section of the souk where sellers sat dwarfed by their piles of dried beans in baskets four feet wide, and past stalls selling fried fish and kebabs, the greasy, smoky air hanging, trapped, in the tents. At last we arrived at the donkey area. We had to pick our way through rows and rows of vendors selling donkey and mule supplies to get to the actual donkeys. A young man, deep furrows in his lean face, was selling bridle bits made of rusty iron; his inventory, which was certainly hundreds, if not thousands, of bits, formed a tangled stack three feet high beside him. Next to his mountain of bits, a family sat on a blanket surrounded by harnesses made of orange and white nylon webbing. Every member of the family, including the tiny children, was stitching new harnesses while they waited to sell the ones they had just made. A dozen stalls in the next row offered donkey saddles, which are V-shaped wooden forms that sit on the animal's back and support the cart shafts. The saddles were fashioned out of old chair legs and scrap lumber. The corners were nailed together with squares cut from old tin cans. They were rough-looking but sturdy, and they had thick felt padding where they would rest on the animal's skin.

>-<

The donkeys that were for sale were jammed in an area just past the saddle sellers. The interested buyers strolled among them, stopping to glance at one, size up another. There was much milling around, the crowd moving busily in and out of the clusters of donkeys. The donkeys, though, stood quietly, nodding off in the warming sun, absentmindedly chewing a bit of grass, idly flicking off flies. They were a rainbow of browns, from dusty tan to almost chocolate, some sleek and glossy-coated, others still carrying the last fuzzy patches of their winter coats. For someone who loves donkeys, it was an astounding sight.

I stopped near one dealer in the center of the field. He was in the middle of a transaction with a small woman who was shrouded head to toe in black fabric. She was trading an elderly donkey and some cash for a younger animal. The donkey dealer took her cash and then leaned down to tie a hobble on the old donkey. After the woman led her new young donkey away, the dealer turned to me and said he only had a moment to talk. He was having a busy day: he had brought eleven donkeys to the souk that morning and had sold eight of them already. His name was Mohammed, and his farm was nearby, just ten miles from the souk. He brought his donkeys to the fair in the back of a flatbed truck. Between the souk and word of mouth, he usually sells fifty or so donkeys a week. It's a steady business, he said, a longtime family business. His mother and his father, his grandparents and their grandparents, had all been donkey dealers.

"How old is this one?" I asked, patting the smallest of the remaining donkeys.

"He's three years old," the dealer said.

As he said this, a young man who seemed to be associated with him jabbed him in the side and said, "No, no, Mohammed, he's only one."

I was puzzled. "Is he three years old or one year old?"

"Uh, yes," the dealer said, navigating around my question. "And very strong." He leaned down and began untying the young or not-so-young donkey's hobble. "You will not find a better donkey here at the souk. Just give me fifteen thousand dirhams."

I explained that I lived in New York City, and that it didn't seem practical for me to buy a donkey in Khemis-des Zemamra. Moreover, the price—the equivalent of about $1,800—sounded exorbitant. Donkeys here usually go for less than seven hundred dirhams.

"Tell me, what is the price you want to pay?" Mohammed asked. He was a dark-skinned man with sharp features and a loud, chesty laugh. He untied the donkey and led him a few feet away, and then turned him in a circle, displaying his finest points. By now a crowd of other donkey sellers had gathered to observe the demonstration. I said that I was not trying to negotiate for a better price. I simply couldn't buy the donkey. As much as I would love to, it was more impractical than even I, an often-impetuous shopper, could possibly be.

"Then we'll make it twelve thousand dirhams," he said firmly, with a tone that sounded conclusive. "Very good."

By this time, the crowd had become emotionally invested in the idea that I might buy the donkey. A gaggle of little boys had joined the group. They giggled and jumped up and down with excitement, ducking under the donkey's head to glance at me and then dashing away. The donkey was unperturbed by the commotion. He seemed wise in that donkey way to the fleeting nature of the moment, and the inconsequential nature of the outcome; wise to the fact that whatever happened here, life would just roll on as it has for thousands of years, and that certain things like the hard work of animals and the mysterious air of the medina and the curious and contradictory nature of all of Morocco will probably never change.

I left without that small, sturdy donkey, who was undoubtedly named H'mar, but I know that if I return to that field in Khemis-des Zemamra years from now, I will find another brown donkey for sale with the exact same air of permanence and the exact same name.

Farmville

Chicken Chores

My day begins with chicken chores. I allow myself coffee, and then I tumble out of the house in my pajamas and a pair of muck boots, hauling a five-gallon container of water. Keeping animals, I have learned, is all about water. Who even knew that chickens drink water? I didn't, before I moved to my farm in the Hudson Valley and started husbanding chickens. They drink water, and a lot of it. A bigger, fancier farm might have a water line into its chicken coop, but mine doesn't, so I am the water carrier, lugging as much as I can lug from the spigot at the back of the house to the coop. In the summer, the birds guzzle everything they can get their beaks into, so I fill two five-gallon water dispensers for them, then make a third trip to fill a bowl with water that the ducks can slosh in. Discovery: water weighs a lot. Other discovery: no need to use free weights to tone your biceps when you're carrying ten gallons of water back and forth every day.

In the winter, the water situation gets more complicated, requiring heated stands for the water dispensers, and resulting in the slickest ice you have ever seen, made by the water the ducks (the world's sloppiest drinkers and swimmers) manage to splash around. When it rains, you would think my water-carrying chores would be less necessary, but the rain seems to plunk down everywhere except where it would be useful, and on top of that it kicks a mist of mud and gravel into the drinking trough. I have to dump out the dirty water in the rain and fill it up again.

There's a school of thought that in the modern world we don't do enough physical labor (see *Shop Class as Soulcraft: An Inquiry into the Value of Work*, by Matthew B. Crawford, for one good take on the subject). In my very informal poultry-oriented way, I have come to agree. Even at their messiest and most burdensome, these chicken chores please me. It's a concrete need—*water!*—to which I can respond specifically— *here you go, birds, water!*—and the cycle is complete. (Until they need water again, of course.) In so many endeavors, including writing, you are never truly done, and nothing is ever perfect. You are haunted always by the possibility that you could have done more and better. It is a relief sometimes to take on a task and see it through and know it to be wholly sufficient.

Deer Diary

Soon, the snow will melt, the grass will green up, and the fields will be filled again with toffee-colored deer—or, as we affectionately refer to them, Cloven-Hoofed Disease Vectors. From a distance, it is hard to see the tiny ticks that get a free ride on the deer, then drop off into the grass and try to catch an inbound express on a human ankle or animal belly. These ticks are quite often carrying bacteria. In my household alone, we've had two bouts of Lyme disease (me), one of ehrlichiosis (my husband), and one case of chronic Lyme (my dog). I can't even begin to count the friends and neighbors who have gotten one or both diseases, and some of them have become deathly ill.

Lyme is especially vexing, because its symptoms are so vague and diffuse. The first time I had it, I was initially (wrongly) diagnosed with gout, diabetes, a staph infection, a heart irregularity, and a broken toe. The second time, I had gone to the doctor because I was having a flare-up of carpal tunnel syndrome, and on a whim, I asked whether there was any chance that the pain in my arm was actually Lyme again. It was. Or, more correctly, my blood test showed that I did indeed have Lyme disease again, which might or might not have been making my carpal tunnel hurt, but since I have a history of carpal tunnel, I took the belt-and-suspenders approach of doxycycline for the Lyme and anti-inflammatories for the carpal tunnel.

There is not much to do about the ticks. You can spray something awful on your grass, but it's not very effective, and since infected ticks are everywhere in the Hudson Valley, where I live, I wouldn't be safe if I ever left home. Last year, I fell for the guinea fowl scam. It's rumored that these noisy, odd-shaped birds eat ticks by the bushel, so I bought nine of them, and after a period of cooping them up to win their loyalty I set them loose in my yard to clean up the ticks. In a day, the guinea fowl had all disappeared (my guess is that foxes are to guinea fowl what guinea fowl are, supposedly, to ticks). It was an emotional loss but not really a disease-control catastrophe, since everything I read after the birds flew the coop suggested that guinea fowl will eat any bug, and, despite the promotional campaign touting their skills as exterminators, there is no proof that they specifically seek out tiny deer ticks over anything bigger and juicier. Anyway, I realized there are so many ticks in our grass that I would have needed many more than nine guinea fowl to have had any effect at all.

Months after my great guinea fowl fiasco, I came out one morning to find Prince Charles, the male of the lost flock, back at my coop. I bought a female, whom I named Camilla, to keep him company, and the two of them now live in a fenced pen with my chickens, dining on grain and egg-layer pellets. They probably wouldn't recognize a tick anymore if it bit them. I'm not sure there's anything else to try on the tick front, so we just muddle through. We get blood tests whenever we have a Lyme-like symptom (a list so long and so general that it barely counts as a list), and we view the arrival of spring, when the ticks reappear, with a mixture of elation and dread.

Strangely enough, even though the deer are the gateway animal for this whole mess, I still love to see them rambling. They are such nuisances, really; besides giving safe harbor to ticks, they eat the prettiest plants in my garden, grind up the grass on their favorite paths, leave scat everywhere, and have managed to collide with my car twice, costing thousands in body work and scaring me half to death. And yet, I love them. I get excited every time I see one, even though I see them all the time. Their talent is in having those sensitive faces and the ballerina's poise that makes you forgive them almost anything.

Chicken TV

I'm bringing one of my chickens to Manhattan tomorrow, to be on an episode of *The Martha Stewart Show*, which Martha—a celebrated chicken keeper herself—is devoting to the subject of backyard chickens. My chickens are not seasoned travelers (note to self: maybe don't use the word "seasoned" when talking about pet chickens?) so I've been fretting about the whole enterprise, which will entail driving two hours from my house to the city and then spending several more hours in the studio while we tape the show.

For the last week or so, I've been auditioning to see which of my seven chickens would be the most camera-ready and most travel-friendly. My prettiest hen is a Silver Laced Wyandotte named Merry-Go-Round. She's plump and bosomy, covered with a craze of black and white stripes, and has a brilliant red wrinkly comb. She'd look great on television, but she's bossy and noisy and given to little fits of temper; pass. Tweed and Mabel Black Label, my Araucana hens, are somewhat antisocial. When I pick either of them up, they eye me with such deep suspicion that I feel like they can smell omelets on my breath. They're probably not the right chickens for television. My little bantam, Tina Louise, is so fast and frantic that I'm not even sure I'd be able to catch her to put her in the car. Helen Reddy, my Rhode Island Red, is lovely, but she's the lowest chicken in the social order of my coop, and I'm afraid if I took her away from the flock for a day, she'd lose her position altogether.

My rooster, Laura, is gorgeous and I'd love to show him off, so for a moment I thought of making him the television star. This is a bit of vanity on my part. Most rational people are a little afraid of roosters. Even though they're not that big, they can pack quite a punch. I have to handle Laura frequently (for instance, I spent a few evenings this winter massaging Vaseline into his comb, to ward off frostbite) and I've started fancying myself a bit of a chicken whisperer since he usually lets me pick him up and hold him without incident. The other day, I held him in my arms and started talking to him about the trip, and he was as relaxed as a lapdog. I went back to the house to do something and returned to the coop a few minutes later. This time Laura chased me into the corner, slapped me with his wings, and tried to kill me. Chastened, I scratched him as my TV entry. I've finally decided to bring my sweet hen Tookie, the oldest of my chickens, the only one of my original four who is still around. She'll get a bag of corn for her efforts—and residuals, of course.

Broadcast Chicken

I'm happy to report that my trip to Manhattan to appear on *The Martha Stewart Show* with Tookie went off without incident. I worried every step of the way. I worried whether Tookie would like the car ride, and whether she'd be happy being in the television studio, and whether she'd act out in some wild chicken-y way on camera. I even worried whether, when she was back home with her flock, the other chickens would sense some fundamental change in her (exposure to the bright lights of New York City and the sizzle of television fame might do that) and, full of doubt and suspicion, turn on her—a sort of chicken version of *The Return of Martin Guerre*.

It turns out that Tookie is a trouper. She sat quietly in her crate on the ride down and in the nicely appointed Martha Stewart dining room, noshing happily on frozen corn kernels and flicking her head side to side each time a production assistant rushed in, waving microphones and headsets and show breakdown sheets.

The one moment that really unnerved me was when I walked out on the set and realized that there were several dozen chickens there, running around or sitting on audience members' laps. Chickens, as a rule, are as cliquey as high-school girls, and are quite happy to tear to pieces an unfamiliar bird. The first time I introduced a new chicken into my flock, Tookie was actually the meanest of the mean girls, clucking angrily, making threats, and showing a lot of pointy beak. During my segment on the show, I sat with Tookie on my lap. There were a bunch of chickens scratching and chatting and making a fuss very near us. There was also, within striking distance, a huge feathery Araucana that was lolling in Stewart's lap. I could hardly breathe, wondering if Tookie would puff up and start pecking at the Araucana, or, worse, at Martha Stewart. But miraculously, she sat regally and calmly through the segment. And better still, now that she's home again, she has settled right back in with her fellow hens, and they with her, as if she had never been on network television at all.

Wet Feathers

The word "bedraggled" was invented, I'm sure, for chickens and turkeys and guinea fowl in a tropical storm. It's not just the soggy feathers. It's that certain look of consummate, abject wetness only poultry can convey. I had worried about how my birds would handle the hurricane that was going to be passing over our area the other day, so I checked on them this morning as the rain started. Most of the chickens were inside their coop, snuggled up. To my surprise, the ducks were inside, too. (I thought ducks like water! What's up with that?) My female duck was so nonchalant about the whole thing that she even laid an egg while the storm moved in.

The guinea fowl were outside, drenched and pathetic but apparently fine. They were running around in their usual state of hysteria, which I took as a sign of their well-being. My bigger concern was for my turkeys. They're too big to fit in the chicken coop, so last year, I bartered with a neighbor for her huge castoff doghouse. (My side of the barter was agreeing to take care of her ducks over the winter, but they settled in so nicely that my neighbor decided to leave them with me, so I ended up with both the doghouse and the ducks.) I went to a great deal of trouble to flatten a spot, put down drainage gravel, and set up the house, only to discover that the turkeys had no interest in it. As far as I know, they have never set foot inside. Even on the bitterest nights this winter, they slept out on their roost, huddled and defiant. I kept telling myself that turkeys wouldn't have survived as a species for billions of years if they didn't know how to take care of themselves, but still . . . what if they thought the house was actually for a dog and not for them? I've heard the story—rural legend, in my opinion—that turkeys will die in a rainstorm because they stand outside, looking up at the rain, and end up drowning. I would hate that. I never expected to have any feelings about turkeys, but I love them. They follow me around like puppies. If I say "gobble" to them, they all start gobbling, in unison. Sometimes they show up outside my office and tap on the windows until I look up at them, and then they wait there, with endless patience, until I come outside and greet them.

At last check, the turkeys were still there, not looking up into the rain like idiots, but simply waiting out the storm with a Patton-like stoicism, their usual somber dignity a little soaked and muddy, but intact. I'm in awe.

Summerscape

July sightings on the farm:

- A porcupine, quills bristling, shuffling down a path with its legs spread wide, as if it were wearing a pair of too-tight pants.

- Last season's fawns, now plumped out and grown up, their baby spots faded to a copper sheen.
- Snapping turtles, as big as hubcaps.
- Spring tadpoles, now July's bullfrogs, as wide as a man's hand, happy to stay up late, burping and thrumming.
- Swallows, diving and careening like drunks.
- Squirrels, so fat they have the beginnings of double chins, yet still capable of a front flip in the pike position—and a stuck landing!—at the bird feeder, where they can enjoy lunch and laugh at the squirrel proofing.

Crow

The rooster problem isn't going to go away anytime soon. The hen-to-rooster ratio (at birth) is probably one to one (if my math serves me), but the desirability ratio of hen to rooster is about twenty million to one. Most people who keep chickens want hens so they can get eggs. As a result, the world is filled with redundant roosters.

You don't need a rooster to get eggs from your hens. For some reason, even people who did well in high school biology ask me whether you need a rooster to have eggs, which is like asking whether a woman needs a boyfriend in order to ovulate. You do need a rooster if you want baby chickens, but you knew that. If you do have a rooster in your flock, he will serve as the chairman of the board, and he will romance the hens indefatigably, and he will perhaps do a little work as the hens' protector and savior, if so called upon. He will also crow, which some people (me among them) find charming, and others (perhaps a majority) find not so charming. The people who find it not so charming have made roosters illegal in many municipalities that have otherwise permitted chicken-keeping. New York City and Los Angeles, for instance, permit hens but not roosters within city limits. A rooster will also go crazy if he thinks something other than a hen has invaded his personal space—another rooster, for instance, or, problematically, a human being. A mad rooster is nothing to sneeze at. They have nasty spurs on their ankles and a knife-edged beak and nerves of steel.

Unfortunately, you often end up with roosters unexpectedly, because it's very hard to tell the sex of a chicken until it's fairly mature. I never wanted a rooster. The first chickens I bought came from a big hatchery with the guarantee that they were girls. Then I started buying chickens here and there, from people who were not certified chicken sexers. For instance, I got four young hens from a guy I met in one of my online chicken groups. Last year, one of the young hens—the demure and delicate Laura—had an impressive growth spurt and then sprouted wattles, spurs, and a bad attitude, and soon made himself known to be a rooster. He was spectacularly beautiful, with blue and black feathers and the face of a killer. We renamed him Lawrence but couldn't help but persist in calling him Laura—Laura just stuck, the way names do. I'm sure it would have entertained anyone watching to see me quaking in the corner of the coop, yelling, "No, Laura! No, Laura!" as he spurred me angrily. Laura got more and more aggressive, and we couldn't figure out what to do with him. I thought about offering him for adoption to my online chicken group, but there were surplus roosters being offered there almost every single day, so my hope of finding a home for him was dim. A few friends suggested we eat Laura, but I just couldn't do it. Anyway, he was so nasty that I assumed he'd be tough.

Laura's beauty turned out to be his redeeming feature. One day, a neighbor of mine who also has chickens came over for a visit. When he complimented Laura's luxuriant feathering and rosy wattle, I seized my chance. I said that Laura would be happy to come home with him and be beautiful and luxuriantly feathered at his house. I didn't really expect to close the deal, but my neighbor was really smitten with Laura. He proposed we do a rooster swap—a convention of country life I had not yet been introduced to, in which roosters are traded, usually because someone wants a different breed or color than the rooster they've got. I had hoped that once I offloaded Laura, I would be out of the rooster game altogether, but my neighbor didn't want two roosters. He also promised that his rooster—that is, *my* soon-to-be new rooster—was mellow and retiring. This rooster wasn't as studly and gorgeous as Laura, and my neighbor was willing to take on the disadvantages of a bad bird for the sake of beauty and the generations of beautiful babies he would father. That is how I ended up parting company with Laura and acquiring my Rhode Island Red rooster, whom my son named Statue of Liberty. Statue of Liberty has turned out to be just as low-key as my neighbor claimed. He loves to be cuddled and stroked. Laura is living large with his new harem. My neighbor, who seems to enjoy the challenge of Laura's belligerence, thinks he got the better end of the trade.

No Trespassing

Deer-hunting season approaches. My husband and I are not hunters, not at all, but we have a lot of land that a deer hunter would find bountiful, so every year we've had to figure out what to do. We could easily forbid anyone to hunt on our property, or we could give someone permission. My first impulse had been to tack up the "No Trespassing" signs and leave it at that, but then we came around, and for the last few years we've given permission to a neighbor. One thing that changed was realizing that we have a ton of deer on our land, more than are probably well-accommodated, and if the winter is harsh and the pickings are slim, there are definitely too many of them. It seemed more humane to reduce the herd by hunting—that is, by a good hunter who can hit his or her mark, rather than a Dick Cheney sort of hunter—instead of leaving them to struggle through the winter mad with hunger.

What convinced us, though, was more an issue of community. Hunting or not hunting is one of those indelible dividing lines between locals upstate and those of us who meandered up here from Manhattan. Letting our land be used for hunting, even if we don't do it ourselves, seemed a rare opportunity to straddle that line. The neighbor who hunts on our property shoots only one or two deer a season, and butchers them for meat. His hunting has a purpose and point that I appreciate, even if the appeal of hunting is entirely foreign to me. The closest I've ever gotten to imagining the thrill of hunting was finding an antler in the snow a few years ago. I was so excited that I shrieked for five minutes straight.

I still think big-game hunting is terrible. Those game preserves, where guides push animals into view for lazy thrill seekers to shoot, are a true sign of the end times. Even worse are those hunting setups I recently learned of in which the hunter, miles or continents away, sits in front of a computer watching a livestream of the hunting area. When an animal strolls into view, the hunter fires a gun by pressing a button on a remote control. It's like a video game or a sort of beastly snuff film, with a mounted trophy as the reward for leveling up. I think what I've learned by living in the country is that there's hunting, and then there's hunting, and that it's worth trying to appreciate the variations in the game.

Gobbled

Being a turkey owner at this time of year—that is, Thanksgiving—means answering a lot of questions that are preceded by looks of alarm and mild horror. "You . . . have . . . turkeys?" the standard setup goes. "Are . . . you . . . going . . . to . . . you know . . . eat them?"

I'm not going to eat them. My turkeys were an impulse buy. If I had still been living in the city, an impulse buy might have amounted to a pair of impractical dress shoes, but here in the country it means something like acquiring a plant I don't have room for or superfluous fowl. I actually never wanted turkeys. Unlike chickens—which I thought of as useful and amusing even before I had some—turkeys had no appeal for me. Like most people, I was under the impression that they were fantastically, mind-blowingly stupid. Their eggs have never had good press. Even though their feathers are pretty and their posture so upright and serious that they look like barnyard barristers, turkey faces—fleshy and red with carbuncles and wattles—are almost vulgar-looking. It's hard to think of them as attractive.

But then I visited a friend who had Royal Palm turkeys. They're a heritage variety that are too small to be raised commercially and are almost extinct. They're striking, their white feathers trimmed in black. Commercial turkeys have been engineered to have breasts so disproportionately huge that the birds can't stand up when they're full-grown. By contrast, Royal Palms are athletic and sprightly and curious. When I visited my friend, her Royal Palms followed us around like store detectives, and whenever they thought they were being addressed, they would chatter back. They do really say "gobble gobble," by the way. It was hilarious and irresistible.

When my friend hatched some of her flocks' eggs, I took four of the babies, tossed them in with my chickens, and watched them grow and grow. Along the way, I've become a turkey apologist. I am always defending them when I'm asked about things like whether they're so dumb they drown in the rain (apocryphal, as far as I know). No one believes me when I say they're a delight.

I am having turkey for Thanksgiving, but not *my* turkeys. My four toms (yes, all four of the poults I got from my friend turned out to be male) are not exactly pets, but I can't think of another term that quite suits them. My husband calls them "landscape animals," which is close, but still not right. Outdoor friends? Wards? Poultry associates? Or perhaps, at least at this time of year, Not Dinner.

Cattle Rustle

People who live in the countryside discuss agricultural tax deductions with the kind of zeal and wonder with which Manhattanites discuss rent-controlled apartments. That is, everyone wants one, but no one can quite figure out how to get one. An ag deduction is a discount on property tax for anyone using their land for an agricultural business. You need to gross $50,000 to qualify, so selling a bouquet harvested from your bed of petunias won't do it.

Since we decided to stay up here in Farmville full-time, for now, I have been casting around for a scheme. My chickens are productive, as chickens go, and if I charged $5,000 per egg we'd have it made, but I have a feeling the good folks at the IRS would disapprove of my math. Puppies are fetching several thousand bucks a head these days, so I investigated whether a puppy could be classified as livestock. I figured if you had five litters of approximately five puppies each, and sold them for two grand a puppy, you would make $50,000, plus it would be fun. Alas, when I mentioned this to my accountant, he nearly suffered a myocardial infarction.

The other day, our neighbor mentioned that he had just gotten six Angus steers. They're what are called "feeder cattle." They will live on his land, stuffing themselves on grass until the fall, when they will be sold to a farm that will feed them grain to fatten them up. We could have feeder cattle, too. All we need is a source of water and fencing (not a minor consideration, since cattle can walk right through most fences, and you'd hardly want to see your agricultural deduction strolling down the road). Cattle! For a suburban girl who also spent twenty years in Manhattan, this prospect is almost too exciting. In the next few days, I'll find out whether the fence guy and the cattle guy can coordinate—oh, and the accountant. Always the accountant.

So: The fence guy visited and gave us a price on securing the perimeter for our prospective mini herd of Black Angus. I now have a new appreciation of the various ways you can judge wealth in rural areas. It's not just by the size of someone's house or the make of cars in their driveway or the wheels of cheese in their cellar; it's the extent and type of fence around the property. All fences are about the price of gold—the roughest split-rail, the most unadorned three-strand electric, the might-as-well-be-made-of-diamond double rail crossbuck with six-by-six French

Gothic posts of fresh-sawn oak. By my calculation, the price of steak is about 30 percent fence.

Dog Memory

What I notice the most is the sound, or rather the absence of sounds: I miss the click of Cooper's nails on the wooden floor, the jingling of his tags (so exasperating at times that we considered buying those rubber jingle-stoppers), and, because he was an itchy dog, the drum-major's thump-thump-thump as he worked his back leg up and down to scratch behind his ear. I know I will experience phantom dog noises for a while.

Cooper, my nine-year-old Welsh springer spaniel, died unexpectedly last weekend, when we were away from home, so it felt very abstract until we got back last night. This morning I thought I heard him stirring in his bed, but it was just the window shade shifting in a bit of breeze.

If therapists didn't charge you and were willing to chase sticks, they would be dogs. The kindly and receptive silence, the respect for secrets, the inexhaustible supply of attention—these are a dog's, and a therapist's, finest qualities. Dogs, though, are more fun than therapists, more tender, more dear, and certainly more admiring.

Over the last nine years, I've written a lot of stories, and even a book, about animals. Given the endless number of interesting stories there are in the world, I've sometimes wondered how I ended up on this particular path. Certainly, I've always loved animals and they're very interesting, and are also an ideal foil for examining the human condition. It all started, though, when I got Cooper, nine years ago, after a dogless decade. I had gotten my first dog when I was in college, and her death, thirteen years later, was drawn-out and deeply sad, and I didn't think I had the stomach to go through having—and losing—a dog ever again. But of course I wanted one, and when I finally got Cooper, a lovely freckle-faced creature, the subject of animals—living with them, loving them, hoarding them, using them, and how our relationship to animals says something about who and what we are—was stirred up for me again and again. I'm glad of that. I will certainly not go another decade without a dog, because I know now that even though dogs break your heart, they fill it up, even when they're gone.

We decided to get right back on the horse—or, rather, on the dog: after finding a week with such a sad, quiet house almost too much to bear, we got a new puppy this weekend. Her story is a harsh illustration of what it means to be riding out the long wake of the Great Recession. The puppy—we named her Ivy—is a highfalutin purebred, purchased as an eight-week-old by a family that obviously had enough disposable income at the time to buy an expensive dog. Then the working parent in the family lost his job, and in short order they lost their house in a foreclosure and had to sell or give away what they could no longer afford—among other things, their pretty puppy. They also gave away their fancy cat. I was told that they don't know where they'll end up living, and they can't afford the expenses of pet ownership, so keeping the animals wasn't an option. Last year, when I was writing about mules in the military, I went to a mule auction in Tennessee, and many of the owners told me they were selling their animals because they just couldn't afford to feed them anymore. If you look on PetFinder.com, you'll see the usual array of cockeyed mutts and alley cats, but you'll also see a startling number of purebreds. I assume that like our new puppy, many of them are being given away by people who had gotten them when the world was a much brighter place.

Having to give a pet away is obviously not as dire and dangerous as losing your pension or health care or house, but it is a real and symbolic loss of comfort and companionship, and especially the happiness and sense of normalcy—a chicken in every pot, a puppy in every home—that seems like it's, well, what life is supposed to be about. I'm glad we have the puppy, and glad we could help someone out, but I'm also sobered by what it means about the times we're living in.

Seasonal

Every corny thing that's said about living with nature—being in harmony with the earth, feeling the cycle of the seasons—happens to be true. Noticing the approach of winter is inescapable here. The chickens stopped laying eggs a week ago; the garden has browned and crinkled; the cattle, which had fuzzed up like teddy bears in the last few weeks, have been hauled away to their cold-weather quarters. Even my cats have gotten into the spirit of the season, stuffing themselves with as much cat food as I can absentmindedly give them. The other day I realized I hadn't seen their rib cages in weeks. A nation of mice has dispatched advance troops to my garden shed and seem to have decided that the chicken feed stored there is the mouse provisions they ordered in the spring. Ladybugs have appeared out of nowhere in the space between my windows and screens. I don't know whether they want to come in or go out, but whichever it is, they are dying trying. The deer, usually happy to fill up on the grass and bushes far from the house, have begun to tiptoe closer, sampling, for appetizers, the hostas I planted this spring. Notices for firewood and snowplowing services are in the mailbox every day or are tucked under my windshield wipers like seasonal love notes whenever I park my car. I was never any good at remembering dates, but now I hardly have to. When the first bulb catalogues get delivered and the hens start laying again, that's all the notice I'll need to know that winter has passed.

Cat Fight

I've spent the past six months trying to broker a unilateral peace agreement between my cat Gary and a handsome stray who showed up on our property over the summer and, inch by inch, using charm and wheedling, has ended up living in our house. We have another cat, too, a big taffy-colored boy named Leo. He has taken the introduction of a new cat in stride, with the studied detachment and drowsy indifference cats have made their stock in trade, but Gary is another matter. She is obsessed with the new cat, staring at her across the room like she's some amazing kinetic sculpture or, worse, like she is an evil trespassing spy. The stray— we named her Mittens—seems to have sleeping as her number one hobby in life, which she attempts to practice even while Gary focuses on her with her hate-filled gaze. At first, nothing happens, which means the air is uncomfortably charged with imminence. Then comes that sound of cats screeching at each other—could you describe it as an electronic blast filtered through a broken amplifier? Ignition being cranked while the engine is already running, making that horrible, explosive, grinding *yawk*?—and the fight is on.

This is interesting to me because they have no real reason to fight. There is plenty of room in the house for them to keep a wide distance, and endless amounts of room outside for the same, and more than enough food, and from what I can tell, there is no romance being upended. Hierarchy in the house seems well established. Mittens has graciously deferred to Gary; Leo couldn't care less about power; and the dog just finds the whole thing, and, in fact, everything in life, exciting. So what are these two creatures fighting about? I trust in the fact that animals are pure in their hearts, efficient in their emotions. I admire that they don't seem to waste time hating each other if there isn't a specific purpose to it. Food, shelter, dominance, and love affairs seem to be the things that matter, and once those are sorted out, what else is there to say? Could it just be a personality conflict? Does Gary find Mittens unlikable? What a disappointment that would be. It would mean that animals are just as flawed as we are, susceptible to petty grievances and pointless conflict and capable of making awful sounds at each other when we really have nothing to say.

The Wanderer

At the risk of sliding into the deep, deep hole that is cat obsession, I have to tell you the next chapter in the continuing story of Mittens, the stray who showed up at our house a few months ago. For some time, we ignored the cat, who popped up one day, and then lurked around the backyard, skulking like a car thief, except when she was engaged in a yowling standoff with Gary, our bossy alpha cat. After a few weeks of this, Mittens—as my son christened her—inched her way to the back door. Even though I got the usual warnings of how this would mean we would never be rid of her, I started feeding her and made a comfortable spot on the back step for her to snooze. When winter came and Mittens was still hanging around, I let her in. I found it impossible to look at her through a veil of snowflakes without a surge of guilt and concern. As I expected, Mittens upset the finely calibrated animal dynamics in my household, but I felt it was the right thing to do.

All the while, I looked for Lost Cat posters featuring Mittens's piercing stare and fluffy black face. Nothing.

Mittens settled in the way an unemployed cousin who visits without a fixed departure date settles in—there but not quite there, until the day you notice Cousin has hung his clothes in the closet and started receiving mail. Mittens had become a sort of resident alien, whether we wanted it or not. I finally decided that if she was going to be settling in I ought to take her to the vet, to check her out. I also had a private worry that she might be a pregnant adolescent. Her belly was so round, and she slept all the time, which seemed like it might hint at some future baby Mittenses. While at the vet, I would have her scanned to see if she had an identification microchip. I thought it very unlikely, since she had been pretty moth-eaten when she showed up, which made me think she was a barn cat, half-wild, and not the sort of indulged pet who someone worried over enough to go to that sort of trouble.

The vet was full of surprises.

"Your cat is a boy," she said.

"Not pregnant, I guess," I replied brightly.

"No."

"How old is, um, he? A year? Maybe two?" I asked.

"Ten," the vet said. "At least."

Mittens—*Is that name too emasculating?* I suddenly wondered—was whisked away to be weighed and scanned for the microchip.

"He has a chip," the vet said, dropping my overweight elderly male cat on the exam table. The address on the chip was fifty miles from us. Mittens, the sleepiest, laziest cat on the planet, had hiked fifty miles to my doorstep? It was baffling. I didn't think I could bear any further surprises, so we headed home.

That evening, I called the number listed on the microchip. In my agitated state, I first misdialed and reached a woman in western New York who said she was very sorry that Mittens wasn't her cat and added that she would drive the two hundred miles to get him if he needed a new home. "My husband is allergic," she added, "but maybe he could learn to live with it."

I thanked her and dialed again, this time correctly. The woman, whose name was Linda, answered and listened as I explained how I'd gotten her phone number off the cat's subcutaneous chip. "Wow," Linda said, "you have Gomez? My god! How is Gomey?"

"He's fine," I said. "He's at my house. I can't believe he walked all this way." It turned out that he hadn't. Linda said that she had adopted the cat from a shelter three or four years earlier and had kept him for a short while, but he peed everywhere and didn't get along with her other cats, so she ended up taking him back to the shelter. A friend of Linda's was mad at her for giving the cat back, so she went to the shelter and fished Gomez out. For some reason, though, the friend wasn't able to keep him, either, so she gave him to a woman who lived not far from me.

I worried that I was losing the thread. "Who does he belong to?" I asked. Hard to say, Linda explained. She said she would call the friend who had pulled him from the shelter.

The next morning my phone rang before breakfast.

"*What* are you doing to Gomez?" a raspy-voiced woman shouted at me as soon as I said hello. "Why are you *dumping* him?"

"What are you talking about?" I shouted back. "I'm not *dumping* him! I've been taking good care of this cat for months! I'm just trying to figure out if he has another home!"

For a moment, she was quiet, and then she said, "Well, I was so ticked off at Linda for dumping him back at the shelter that I had to go back and get him. I can't have any more cats! I have dozens of cats!"

"I see," I said, even though I wasn't sure I did.

"So, I got Gomez," she continued, "and I found a gal who's sort of . . . sort of a cat person, she has a million of them, and dogs, and maybe even pigs, and I gave her a nice amount of money and took Gomez to her, but I think she stuck him in her basement and just threw food down there once in a while."

"Maybe that's why he ran away," I said.

"I wouldn't call her if I were you. She got a nice amount of money to take care of Gomez, but she threw him in the basement." She took a cigarette break, and then resumed the excoriation of Linda. Finally, she asked, "Are you going to keep him?"

I told her that I had grown to really love the cat. He was the most affectionate of all my many animals, perhaps because he was the most grateful, and his advanced age made me feel especially tender toward him. He had been bounced around so much that I hated the thought of bouncing him again—and we hadn't even explored the six years of his life that had led up to his being in the shelter where Linda found him.

When I had spoken to Linda, I had given her my address, because she said she had the cat's vet records. They arrived a few days after our call. Even though she had taken him in and then put him back out, she had been a conscientious owner. She had gotten him microchipped and had spent over $200 having him examined and wormed and vaccinated. According to the vet records, the day Linda's letter arrived was his eleventh birthday.

Spring Chickens

It's been a hard winter. Even though it's still chilly out and the sun is pale and weak, the chickens and turkeys and guinea fowl and ducks are already in a festive mood. Egg-laying has resumed. Mud is everywhere. There was so much snow around the coop this winter that the feeder, perched atop concrete blocks, got buried. During the worst of the weather, the chickens actually refused to come out of the coop. "You need some fresh air!" I'd say, poking them gently and feeling like a kindergarten teacher. If they had lips, they would have stuck out their lower ones and sulked. In any case, they did not come outside.

On the other hand, my turkeys must be pumping antifreeze through their veins. Because I spent a huge amount of time researching appropriate turkey housing, and even more time arranging to get a gigantic, somewhat unsightly turkey house for their comfort and pleasure, and because I then spent significant money having the gigantic, unsightly, much-researched turkey house set up and installed with a proper foundation, my four crazy Royal Palm toms revealed themselves to be entirely weather-tolerant and housing-intolerant, and chose to spend even the blackest, bitterest nights sleeping outside on a log. Thank you, turkeys. The guinea fowl—sensing my exasperation, maybe—decided to colonize the turkey house. Whatever. One cannot reason with either turkeys or guinea fowl. I really worried about my two ducks, Donald and Donald, because they don't belong to me—they're loaners from my neighbor— and I figured that if they didn't have a pond they'd go out of their minds. I set out a kiddie pool for them, but the water in it froze so solid that I couldn't even hammer it out. The ducks, even without a pond, seemed fine, although their resting state seems to me one of a busy restless anxiety, like slightly underpaid event organizers.

I lost two chickens this winter: Tookie and Statue of Liberty, my wonderful rooster. As I've mentioned, about a year ago, I gave my sociopathic rooster Laura to a brave neighbor, who gave me Liberty in return. Both

Tookie and Liberty were elderly (Tookie was nearly four, and Liberty might have been six), so the harsh winter might have simply been too much for them. All my other chicken losses in the past have been to predators, except for Chicken Orlean, who had some undiagnosable viral disease and had to be put to sleep. The ground was so hard from the cold that I couldn't even bury the birds. Sorry, Tookie and Statue of Liberty. I'm glad it's finally spring.

Ticks

The horror of spring is upon us. Yes, the early buds are lovely, as are the first touch of sun, the warm smell of soil, the darling baby animals wet with creation, blah blah blah. But, more to the point, spring carries tucked in its gentle bosom a ton of ticks, those miserable, godless, useless, deathless parasites that make the rural spring as gory and terrifying as a slasher film. My pleasure in spring is undone the minute my dog comes in after a nice romp outside with twenty ticks riding piggyback. (I am not exaggerating; in fact, for the sake of not grossing out my readers, I'm using a smaller number than we often find.)

My lowest moment occurred last week, when I was giving my son a bath and found a tick embedded in his scalp. That was the final straw. Creature lover that I am, I turned into a Valkyrie and killed the tick with mad vengeance, not just squashing it but stepping on it, cutting it in half, and flushing it down the toilet while screaming. I defy anyone to tell me what redeeming quality ticks have and what purpose they serve in the great circle of life other than to be disgusting. They have none. Everything that eats ticks could eat something else instead. They look ugly. They suck blood, which on a primal level is just wrong.

There's not much to do about the horrible ticks except mow your meadow down (which we did) and do a monkey-style preening of other family members every night (kind of nice for the family dynamic, actually). As previously noted, the myth that keeping guinea fowl will rid you of ticks forever must have been a campaign started by the Guinea Fowl Industry Lobbying Group, because it's nonsense. We keep a closet full of doxycycline, wear high white socks, and hope for the best.

Last week, during that spell of warm weather, there must have been a fresh hatch of ticks, because the dog and the cats were festooned with them, and we found a dozen on the floor. I had to spend the night in the city, and, honestly, I was delighted; I was so creeped out by the ticks that the idea of being in an all-concrete environment for a night seemed like a treat. I was planning to sleep in my stepson's apartment. Just as I was preparing to leave, he called to tell me that I might want to consider staying somewhere else, because there had just been a confirmed case of bedbugs in his building.

I give up.

Animal Roll Call

Summer is here, and to borrow a phrase from the restaurant-reservation business, we are fully committed, animal-wise. Our summer visitors, twelve Black Angus cattle, arrived a few days ago, and probably fainted with pleasure at the sight of our pasture, which is hip-high in alfalfa. The cattle are young and small, so when they're grazing, they almost disappear in the grass; they become nothing more than dark shapes drifting through the greenery, like storm clouds through a sky. If they eat their dozen or so square meals a day, they'll be gaining two pounds every twenty-four hours, which means soon enough the grass will be chomped down and the cattle will be bulked up. We don't name them, but we call out their ear-tag numbers with great affection when we visit and give them snacks.

I have new hens, too. I have acquired four young Swedish Flower chickens, a rare breed with a name that cracks people up whenever I say it, for some reason. The chicks are crazily speckled and adorable. I'm told that the breed is highly prized in Sweden and that the Swedish chicken authorities frown on exporting them. The person who hooked me up with them would only say that "someone" wearing a commodious brassiere smuggled a breeding pair into the United States. I think the safest policy for me is to know nothing more than that intriguing tidbit, although I can't help but spend time imagining what it would be like to have two chickens in my bra on a transatlantic flight.

Chicken society abhors a vacuum, so immediately after Tookie and Statue of Liberty died this winter, their positions as dominant male and female were filled. Helen, a sturdy Rhode Island Red, is now my alpha hen; Frowny, a fat white fluff ball with a glowering expression, is, literally, the cock of the walk.

My husband told me he was getting me a donkey for my birthday, and I'd be donkey shopping right now except that there's a good chance we'll be in Los Angeles for a while, starting this September. So instead of adding to the menagerie, I've been assessing the animals, trying to figure out who to bring and who to leave (temporarily) behind. How practical is it to have turkeys in Studio City, I wonder?

The Moving Menagerie

In a matter of weeks, my husband and I will pack up everything but our winter clothes and park ourselves in Los Angeles until next spring. My husband has business there; I am merely a camp follower. It is a sign of some special and strange quality of my life that the first question people ask when hearing this news isn't "How do you feel about moving to L.A.?" or "How will your son like living there?" but "Oh my god, what about the chickens?" This is a problem of my own making, so I accept it. The fact is that the question of what will become of my various animals is probably the subject most on my mind these days.

Some of those questions are easily answered. The cattle, for instance, will stay in New York, with our house sitters. (But really, wouldn't it be totally awesome to have twelve Black Angus in a Los Angeles backyard?)

The ducks and turkeys and guinea fowl, who need more space than we have in California, will stay, although I sure would like to bring them. (What an icebreaker at neighborhood get-togethers!) The dog, of course, will come with us. Funny how moments like this draw the line between animals that are more connected to the landscape (cattle, for instance) than to the humans who own them, versus those animals (dogs) that are extended family members. You would no sooner leave a dog behind with a caretaker than you would leave one of your kids. The cats and the chickens, though, do sort of straddle that line.

Re: chickens. It is legal to have them in Los Angeles, as long as they're a polite distance from your neighbors, and there's a lively L.A. chicken scene already in place (I just got my Los Angeles Urban Chicken Enthusiasts T-shirt, courtesy of one of the members). But our backyard in California is small. Moreover, there are zillions of coyotes and bobcats hanging out in the neighborhood, and they are not the scrawny East Coast models: like everyone in Los Angeles, the coyotes I've seen there look like they work out a lot with personal trainers. The idea of putting a coyote magnet in the backyard, someplace where the coyotes can bench-press four hundred pounds, is terrifying. At least for the moment, the chickens will stay here.

And what about the cats? Even though I still don't understand cats—to me, they're like foreign-exchange students here for the semester—we now have three, and I'm very attached to them. There's Gary, a little female barn cat; Leo, a brooding male who we got from a local shelter; and Mittens, the stray, who is now fully vested as a family member. The three of them are used to coming in and out as they please, which in Los Angeles means they would be a snack-size serving for a coyote in no time. (Isn't it weird that moving from rural upstate New York to the center of the nation's second-largest city means having *more* predator issues rather than fewer?) Cats in Los Angeles, in other words, are indoor cats or they're goners. Can we convince these cats that being outside these past few years was a big mistake? How will they react to that? Late at night, I picture us in our small house in Los Angeles with the three cats hurling themselves against the windows, yowling. This is when I take a sleep aid.

We have talked about bringing just one of the cats—maybe whichever seems the most adaptable to indoor life. That would be Mittens, because he's old and lazy. On the other hand, Leo has a heart problem, so maybe we should take him instead, to be sure he's being doted on. But that would leave Gary and Mittens here in New York together, and they hate each other. We could take—oh, never mind. This is the sort of thing that I suspect we will decide at the very last minute, because if you love animals and have to leave them, even for a little while, there's no simple way to figure it out.

Caution: Goats at Work

The other day, the *New York Times* reported that the city of Los Angeles is using a herd of South African Boer goats to mow down the weeds on some hard-to-access city property. Because of my impending move to Los Angeles, I was very excited to hear about this. I like the idea of living in a city that uses goats as municipal workers. Apparently, I'm not the only one delighted by this. It seems that the lawn-mowing goats have become quite an attraction, and crowds of people have gathered to watch them work their way through the weeds. Animals just have that effect on people, making even mundane things seem enchanting. When was the last time you heard of lawn-mowing drawing a crowd? I'm not absolutely sure of the scope of a goat's aptitudes, but it's nice to think they might be promoted to other jobs, too. If they could somehow be trained to write parking tickets or be process servers or repo men, they might manage to make those professions less despised.

I'm all for putting animals to work, although my own experience with hiring them has been mixed. My guinea fowl were purchased to eat the ticks on our property, but their effectiveness has been subpar. The cats were acquired to deal with the mice in the basement, but they don't like being in the basement because, well, I don't know why. Maybe because there are mice down there. We have acres of poison ivy, which goats apparently love to eat, and I was on the very brink of buying a little brown buck named Pepper and assigning him to poison ivy duty when I was warned that he was big on biting people on the rear end. Analyzing the cost-benefit ratio—eradication of poisonous plants versus integrity of my rear end—I went with the rear end. Even my slacker animals, though, do perform some yeoman labor. They are either pretty or funny or engaging, more than earning their keep by being interesting to be around.

Goodbye for Now

So: we did it. In 2011, we pulled up our stakes and headed west, accompanied by a limited representation of our menagerie—one dog, two cats. Those who couldn't come along with us were left in the good hands of neighbors and friends, who promised to provide regular reports on everyone's well-being. Because our move to Los Angeles was intended to be temporary, the animal arrangements were temporary, too. I fully expected to reclaim my creatures when we headed back to New York in the spring.

As soon as we settled in L.A., I discovered that we were contending with a whole new animal experience. Our house was well within the urban envelope, and yet animals abounded. Hawks and owls eyeballed us during the day. In the evening, gangs of lean, sullen coyotes huddled around our mailbox, looking for puppies and kittens to snack on. One day, at dusk, I took a walk down our block and spied the unmistakable hunched silhouette of a bobcat. There were mountain lions afoot. That first winter, the lion known as P-22 took time off from managing his busy social media accounts and set up camp in the crawl space under a house not far from us. A *mountain lion*, for heaven's sake. We were in the second-largest city in America, and yet it felt like we'd moved into a natural history diorama.

When spring 2012 rolled around, we prepared to head back to the Hudson Valley. A night or so before we left L.A., our house sitters in New York called with grim news. A raccoon had broken into the chicken coop and a massacre had ensued. All of the poultry—the chickens and ducks and guinea fowl—had been killed. I was knocked sideways. Over my years as a chicken keeper, I'd learned to live with the fact that chickens are, at best, provisional holdings, because pretty much every single thing in the universe conspires to eat them. The first time I lost a chicken to a predator, I cried for hours; the fifth time, I sighed deeply and went out and bought a new chicken. But this was on a different scale, an annihilation, and I began to feel like maybe I couldn't handle having chickens anymore.

I spent that summer without them. I rid myself of every reminder of my loss. I tore down the raccoon-breached poultry pen and sold my cute little coop to a neighbor who declared, with delight, that it looked like a spaceship for chickens. This purging was a bit of overkill maybe, but it made sense, because we had decided that we would return to L.A. for another eight months, so restocking on poultry didn't make sense.

Eventually, we fell into a rhythm: eight months in L.A. and then back to the Hudson Valley for the summer. Years passed. I spent summers in the verdant bosom of our farm, but because I was a short-timer I couldn't justify chickens. And yet. *And yet.* It drove me crazy to be there, knowing how delightful it would be to have a burbling flock following me around as I weeded the garden; how delicious my breakfasts would be made with eggs so warm they could have almost cooked themselves.

Then, wouldn't you know it, kismet. An old friend from high school sent me a message one June day asking if I might be interested in three hens and an affable rooster. They belonged to her daughter, who was moving to the city for a job. How could I say no? I pushed all misgivings out of my mind and bought another Eglu. The new chickens were a lively, lovely bunch, and they made themselves at home immediately. The rooster was a cheerful little bantam, about as big as your hand, busy all day long attending to his three red hens. Oh, I was so happy! I fell back into chicken husbandry easily, all the while knowing I was going to have to figure something out in August, when we headed back to L.A. once again. I floated the idea of bringing them to L.A.—just floated it, for the hell of it, even though I knew it was a cracked idea. Those coyotes that held their club meetings at our mailbox would have rejoiced had we brought the chickens to L.A., and not in a good way.

I noticed that I didn't let myself bond as intensely with this flock, probably because I knew their tenure was limited. I had always taken great delight in naming my chickens, and even if they came to me already named, I put my stamp on them by renaming them. Hello, Helen, and Beauty, and Tookie, and Tweed, and Mabel! This new flock came prenamed, but I just let them be, giving myself a little more emotional runway for when the inevitable farewell took place.

One day, the young woman who cleaned our house mentioned that she was about to have a baby. I was astonished—she was as slight as a twig. I asked her the particulars. Any day now, she explained, the eggs would crack. Aha. I didn't know she had chickens, thus the confusion. She wanted more babies, she added, but her rooster was getting very old.

"I have a rooster," I said, pointing out to the coop, "and he's going to need a home."

And thus, the deal was struck. Maria would welcome my three hens and my fertile rooster to her home at the end of the summer, relieving me of all the worry about where I would dispatch them when we headed west. I made some noise about maybe borrowing them back the next summer, but I didn't want to complicate things too much. As it turned out, that was a good thing. We loved our house in the Hudson Valley more than anything. But getting there from Los Angeles was starting to feel exhausting, especially because we didn't like to put our pets on a plane, so every summer my husband had to drive across country to ferry the dog and the cat to New York. Then we added a puppy, so John had to drive a dog, a puppy, and a cat. This wasn't a driving issue as much as a hotel issue; managing three animals (including one, the cat, who was violently opposed to the whole thing) in and out of a car and in and out of hotel rooms was a nightmare. COVID was the final straw. We listed the Hudson Valley house and sold it to the first people who saw it. Our chapter there was done.

We went to the farm one last time to clear it out for the new owners. It was a hard goodbye. I'd always dreamed that someday I would have animals all around me, in the house, in the yard, watching me in the garden, dotting the landscape, crowing in the morning, lowing in the moonlight, barking at the wind, and I had had that there. I had reveled in the animals' friendship and their strangeness; the way they are so obvious and still so mysterious; their colors and textures, their fur and feathers; the sounds and smells of their presence. I liked the way their needs set the rhythm of every day, and how caring for them felt elemental and essential. Living among them, as I had on the farm, was just as satisfying as I imagined it would be.

When the house was emptied, I took one last walk around. As I made my way through the trees and across the fields and down to where the coop had been, I collected a few things that could remind me of the farm forever and perhaps betoken some place in my future that would feel the way it had: a piece of quartz, a pine cone, a knob of moss, and one perfect chicken feather.

ACKNOWLEDGMENTS

My eternal thanks to the publications where these stories first appeared, for believing me when I insisted there was a great story to be told about Keiko, or taxidermy, or tiger ladies, or . . . you name it. My greatest appreciation is for *The New Yorker*, my home since 1987, and to my editors there, including Virginia Cannon, Chip McGrath, Tina Brown, and, most of all, David Remnick. Thanks, as well, to the crew at the *Smithsonian* (especially Arik Gabbai), the *Atlantic*, and Amazon. I am most indebted to the wonderful people at Avid Reader Press and Simon & Schuster, with my hugest thanks to Jofie Ferrari-Adler and Jon Karp, and to Jordan Rodman, Tamara Arellano, Carolyn Kelly, Alison Forner, and also to the unsung heroes who operate the printing presses and bind the books and make this all possible. Giant thanks to Kimberly Burns, the best of the best! Richard Pine, as always, a huge thank-you. To my family (Debra, Dave, David, Steffie, Jay, Gabbie) and my home team, Austin and John, you're the greatest. To my animals past, present, and future, stop chewing the book cover!

ESSAY CREDITS

"Animalish"—Amazon Kindle Originals, May 18, 2011.

"The It Bird"—*The New Yorker*, September 28, 2009.

"Show Dog"—*The New Yorker*, February 20, 1995.

"The Lady and the Tigers"—*The New Yorker*, February 10, 2002.

"Riding High"—*The New Yorker*, February 15, 2010.

"Little Wing"—*The New Yorker*, February 13, 2006.

"Animal Action"—*The New Yorker*, November 10, 2003.

"Where's Willy?"—*The New Yorker*, September 15, 2002.

"Carbonaro and Primavera"—*The Atlantic*, May 2003.

"Lifelike"—*The New Yorker*, June 9, 2003.

"Lion Whisperer"—*Smithsonian Magazine*, June 2015.

"The Rabbit Outbreak"—*The New Yorker*, June 28, 2020.

"The Perfect Beast"—*Smithsonian Magazine*, January 2014.

"Lost Dog"—*The New Yorker*, February 14, 2005.

"Where Donkeys Deliver"—*Smithsonian Magazine*, August 31, 2009.

"Farmville"—*The New Yorker*, 2010–2011, with an update in 2021 for this collection.

ILLUSTRATION CREDITS

ABOUT THE AUTHOR

Susan Orlean has been a staff writer at *The New Yorker* since 1992. She is the *New York Times* bestselling author of seven books, including *The Library Book*, *Rin Tin Tin*, *Saturday Night*, and *The Orchid Thief*, which was made into the Academy Award–winning film *Adaptation*. She lives with her family and her animals in Los Angeles and may be reached at SusanOrlean.com and on Twitter @SusanOrlean.